HISTORIC GARDENS
of GLOUCESTERSHIRE

For Olivia Endellion

HISTORIC GARDENS
of GLOUCESTERSHIRE

Timothy Mowl

TEMPUS

First published 2002

PUBLISHED IN THE UNITED KINGDOM BY:

Tempus Publishing Ltd
The Mill, Brimscombe Port
Stroud, Gloucestershire GL5 2QG
www.tempus-publishing.com

PUBLISHED IN THE UNITED STATES OF AMERICA BY:

Tempus Publishing Inc.
2 Cumberland Street
Charleston, SC 29401
1-888-313-2665
www.tempuspublishing.com

British Library Cataloguing in Publication Data.
A catalogue record for this book is available from the British Library.

ISBN 0 7524 1956 0

Typesetting and origination by Tempus Publishing.
PRINTED AND BOUND IN GREAT BRITAIN

Contents

List of illustrations

All illustrations are the copyright of the author unless otherwise stated.

Front cover: Sezincote. *By kind permission of Mr and Mrs David Peake*
Back cover: Detail of a 1741 painting of Hill Court by John Lewis.
                 By kind permission of Mrs Richard Jenner-Fust
Frontispiece: Wood engraving of Highgrove House. *Miriam Macgregor*

Text figures

Colour plates

Acknowledgements

At the start of these acknowledgements I should like to make a special mention of Nicholas Kingsley, the County Archivist, who has been a constant source of information and encouragement. His three volumes on the country houses of Gloucestershire have been an invaluable reference. Mike Hill, his co-author of volume three, has also readily shared his knowledge of the county's architecture. In garden terms I had a head start as a member of the committee set up to restore the Painswick Rococo Garden back in the mid-1980s and I have to record my thanks to Lord and Lady Dickinson and Paul Moir for their courage in taking on such an enterprise, and to Roger White, Nigel Temple and Paul Edwards for their input to our scholarly debates. I recall affectionately two people who have since died, but who epitomised Gloucestershire hospitality and firm friendship: Caroline, Duchess of Beaufort, whose enthusiasm for the gardens of the county was infectious, and Bob Parsons, whose company was always stimulating and whose joint tenure of Newark Park with Michael Claydon has been one of the most significant influences on my academic career.

Other friends, scholars and owners who have been particularly helpful are: David Lambert, Stewart Harding, Susan Gordon John and Eileen Harris, Tom Williamson, William Bertram, Henriette Clifford, Mark Horton, Emma Whinton, Liz Gawith, Claire Alford, Paul Evans, Howard Walters, Luke Gasparo, David Eveleigh, Michael Richardson, Nick Lee, Mrs Richard Jenner-Fust, Susan Sloman, Tom Oliver, Johnny Phibbs, Mrs Basil Barlow, Guy Acloque, Lisa Kopper, Simon Bonvoisin, Sheena Stoddart, Dianne Barre, Kate Felus, Headley and Anita Smith, Michael Stone, Antony Young, Roger Head, Tom Fenton, Jean Manco, Noel Gibbs, Clive Hester, Martin Fox, Susie Kay, Peter Ellis, David and Fionna Cardale, Patricia van Diest, Peter Mitchell, Neil Hewertson, Lord & Lady Vestey, Lady Ashcombe, Iain Billot, Stephanie McDonald, Anne & Johnny Chambers, Lord Neidpath, Mr and Mrs David Peake, Trevor Chinn, Jamie Ritblat, Lord & Lady Faringdon, Mr and Mrs David Abel Smith and Nicholas Barton.

Ann Pethers, Perry Robbins and Martyn Williams developed many of the photographs from my negatives and Stephen Morris undertook the archival photography. The staff at the Prince of Wales' office were most helpful in organising pictures of Highgrove, taken by Andrew Lawson, and Judy Dod was responsible for their speedy dispatch at a late stage in the editing. Peter Kemmis Betty was a most enthusiastic publisher, Tim Clarke a quietly efficient editor, Douglas Matthews has prepared a thorough index, and my agent, Sara Menguc, has been as encouraging as ever throughout the research and writing of the book.

For financial help with the illustrations I was a recipient of an Arts Faculty Research Fund grant from Bristol University and would like to thank Professor Baz Kershaw and his committee members for their generosity. The writing of this book has been conducted alongside my teaching on the University's MA in Garden History and I must thank my co-director, Michael Liversidge, for his advice on matters art historical and my current students for their lively debate on matters purely garden centred. My friend and co-author on architectural studies, Brian Earnshaw, has been a cheerful companion on site visits, undertaken several areas of the research and edited the text sensitively at manuscript stage. My father, my wife Sarah and daughter Olivia, to whom this book is dedicated, joined me on many of the garden visits, making memorable picnics out of scholarly expeditions.

Timothy Mowl
Bristol, Winter 2002

Introduction

This book began, as books on Gloucestershire should, with the county historian, Sir Robert Atkyns. My last garden book, *Gentlemen & Players: Gardeners of the English Landscape* (2000), had left me with doubts about broad-brush garden histories that treat England as one horticultural unit, with generalisations over stylistic sequences flowing from the assumption that the regions and the proud, individualistic counties all marched forward at roughly the same pace, following the same influences.

There is a framed engraving hanging in my study of the John Kip illustration of Sapperton Manor (**1**) from Sir Robert's *The ancient and present state of Glostershire* (1712). Sapperton was the historian's principal, though by no means his only, residence and I had a mental image of every path, lawn, flight of steps and summerhouse of that engraving from long familiarity. Allen Bathurst had bought the house and demolished it in 1730, but Sir Robert's tomb was in Sapperton church and one autumn day, when I happened to be passing, I looked in to pay

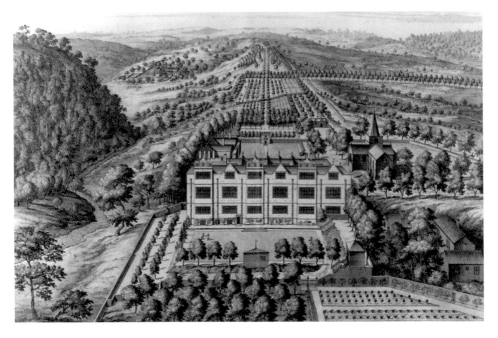

1 *Sapperton Manor in 1712, drawn by John Kip before its demolition in 1730. Its bowling green with terraces left and right can still be traced on the site. Upper Dorvel has been built on a line with the forecourt gatehouse*

2   *Arches and stonework from Sapperton were used to construct mock ruins around Alfred's Hall, Lord Bathurst's 1720-32 Gothick pleasure house in Cirencester Park. Only the two towers on the left survive, smothered in a thicket*

my respects. His swaggering monument presented no surprises, it was overweight and heavily architectural. What was surprising was to find in the rough field behind the church the ranked terraces, former bowling green and earthworks of the garden shown in the Kip illustration perfectly preserved in the meadow grass and brambles. That was not all. Next to the churchyard, and standing where Kip had hidden two labourers' cottages tactfully behind trees, was Upper Dorvel, the house which Ernest Barnsley built for himself in 1901 when he and his brother Sidney moved down the valley from their brief stay at magically remote Pinbury Park. The two Barnsleys and Ernest Gimson lie buried in the churchyard, under huge stone slabs with copper inscription plates, but Ernest Barnsley's long garden of topiary was intact. It was planted consciously in response to the sixteenth-century or earlier 'Nun's Walk' of dark yews which he had admired at Pinbury. One garden had led to another to begin that Arts and Crafts process of restoration, inspiration and innovation which produced a whole sequence of revived medieval Edens up and down the Cotswold valleys, climaxing in the great gardens of Rodmarton, Snowshill, Hidcote and Kiftsgate.

It had been a phenomenon peculiar to Gloucestershire and was only one of the Sapperton interactions. The Kip engraving showed tree avenues slicing off in three directions. The Bishop's Walk running north-east to south-west is still there, but when he bought up Sapperton after Sir Robert Atykns's death, Allen Bathurst determined to outdo the Atkyns' avenues and planted the Broad Walk, Roman in its scale and in its indifference to natural contours, striding six miles to link his Cirencester House with Sapperton. It was and remains a vast forest park rivalling those of the Isle de France and, though he brought arched windows and stones from demolished Sapperton Manor to create Alfred's Hall, the first Gothick park ruin in England (2), Bathurst never managed to link his distances satisfactorily with garden buildings of sufficient stature to contrive a unified Arcadia. Keeping up with the Bathursts resulted in the Beauforts indulging competitively in the same windy spaces, with an enchanting building like William Kent's Worcester Lodge set at the end of an over-ambitious perspective three miles distant from Badminton House. It was a very Gloucestershire mistake, an error of the Cotswold uplands, not an English error.

Standing there at Sapperton renewed all my earlier reservations. What was needed was a whole series of county by county individual garden histories, for counties such as Kent and Yorkshire are, in the best sense of the word, provincial, each a stylistic garden world of its own making, responsive to its own distinct topography. So I began this book about my own county and it has been an indulgence and a delight. In the course of it I seriously advance the claim that Gloucestershire is the richest county for gardens in England. Readers will make their own judgements, but oolitic limestone gives Gloucestershire a head start and although Northamptonshire shares that advantage it lacks the heights and drama of the Cotswold edge. Much as I enjoy the untouristed clay country of the Severn Vale and that stolen piece of Worcestershire around Newent, neither they, nor the Forest of Dean, have produced gardens to rival those of the limestone belt, Westbury Court garden excepted. The garden at Beverston Castle does not feature in these chapters because it has only a lawn, a dry moat, a seventeenth-century loo masquerading as a summerhouse and a few flower beds around the terrace. But try to visit it on one of its rare open days. Its unkempt towers and delicate decay make the limestone point convincingly. There is nothing in central France to beat it for casual garden charm.

While chasing up the scholarly references and inspired hints that my friend Nicholas Kingsley drops on gardens in the three volumes of his *Country Houses of Gloucestershire*, I gave up on any attempt to equal for the county's gardens his encyclopaedic coverage of the county's houses. The 'Historic' of my title has been my excuse. If a garden was neither innovative nor influential, whatever its period, then it is not deemed to be particularly historic or important and so is not included. Readers will soon detect prejudices: an indifference to arboreta and an actual dislike of Wellingtonias. Flowers, with the frightening exception of the Kiftsgate rose, are ephemeral. Next year an owner, or even a responsible custodian like the National Trust, may call for a reshaping; the essential bones of a garden are its hedges, its walls, its ornamental buildings and its water features.

A last word on access. Most of the important gardens of the county are regularly open to the public, or occasionally open either by written appointment or as part of the National Gardens Scheme. I have found very few owners who will not respond generously to enthusiasm and a courteous letter. With one exception, which will be apparent from the text, these Gloucestershire gardens and their happy owners have left me optimistic about human nature.

1 An uncertain spring in the gardens of south Gloucestershire

In a mildly pastoral way the countryside between the Cotswolds and Severn to the north of Bristol is pleasant enough, though unlikely to be voted anyone's favourite English or even Gloucestershire landscape. The commuter suburbs are edging up this way and the villages of a small worked-out coalfield beyond them have, with their abandoned collieries, brickworks and overgrown tramways, little rustic charm. Unexpectedly it is in these dim fields and traffic-ridden lanes that one of the most interesting sequences of gardens in England, spanning the cusp from medieval to Renaissance design, has managed, more by neglect than anything else, to cling on in fascinating ruin.

Creations around the cusp of any important stylistic movement tend to a lively character because, on the one side, conservative patrons are trying angrily to reassert past form, in this case the enclosed walled gardens of feudalism, while on the other the mould-breakers, the aesthetic revolutionaries, are making appealingly uncertain gestures towards a new ideal, in this case the garden forms and furnishings of Italy. It is this tension over their stylistic identity and direction that makes the gardens at Thornbury Castle, Acton Court and Horton Court so interesting and nationally important. Even one Henrician garden is a rarity, so three close together in this nondescript corner of the county present an opportunity for study and questions that garden enthusiasts will not want to miss.

The decision of Edward Stafford, third Duke of Buckingham, Lord High Constable and the richest peer in England, to begin building, around 1511, a castle-palace on an unstrategic, indefensible site in this backwater, could charitably be explained by the unhandy shapelessness of the Stafford estates. Despite his Home Counties title, the Duke was the last of the semi-independent Welsh Marcher lords. He was actually born in Brecon and drew much of his huge annual income from legal taxes in Welsh law courts. One of his many castles, Newport, had a water-gate and stood not far down across the Severn from Thornbury, so he was only a short boat trip away from his Welsh power base.

He has left a beautiful and evocative wreck of a very ambitious house and garden, but it is impossible to find one contemporary with a good word to say for the third Duke. Historically speaking he was a dinosaur who thought that the recent peaceful reign of Henry VII had been just an interval in the Wars of the Roses, and that the Crown was still a prize to be played for in a selfish game by great nobles like himself. He had, however, no gift for inspiring loyalty in either his servants or his relations by marriage, being given to 'fumes and displeasure' and prone to 'rail and misuse himself in words'.[1] He was not even good at tennis; he lost £64 in bets when playing with King Henry VIII, and he once told Cardinal Wolsey, who would have immediately reported it back to the King, that 'he would rather go to Rome than joust Henry', who loved jousting.[2] Even his enthusiasm for parks and gardens contributed to his ultimate execution in 1521 as he had thrown his peasantry off good farm land around Thornbury to create deer parks: Estewood, seven miles round, Marlewood, three miles round and New Park, also three miles round, 'not without', Leland recorded, 'many Curses of the poor Tenaunts'.[3]

On one occasion when the Duke saw Wolsey washing his hands in the same water that the King had just used he picked up the basin and threw it at the Cardinal. Then, when Wolsey angrily threatened to 'sit upon his skirts', Buckingham came to Court the next day defiantly wearing a very short coat.[4] In keeping, however, with his conservative cast of mind, he was notably pious, contributing lavish alms to the shrine of the Holy Blood at Hailes Abbey in the north of the county, and keeping his own private hermit, John Glade, at Thornbury. To keep a hermit and to play a bad game of tennis indicates the cultural balancing act that a great lord of his times might try to perform and that Buckingham notably bungled. It does also explain the symbolic character of his 'Privie' and 'Goodly' gardens at Thornbury. They were exclusively private yet at the same time they were contained within architectural structures that linked his superb domestic apartments with a neighbouring church that was open freely to public devotions.

Buckingham might have survived his tactless project of building a more splendid home than the King's favourite palace at Greenwich if he could have kept a guard on his tongue; but at various times he was heard to declare that 'he was a noble man and wolde be a ryall ruler', and 'If ought but good comes to the King the duke of Buckingham should be the next in blood to succeed to the crown'.[5] Henry lured him to London and put him on trial for treason. The Duke's chancellor, chaplain and ex-surveyor all scrambled to testify against him and in May 1521 off went his head.

What makes Thornbury such a rewarding and rare experience today is that it is still possible, for the price of a good lunch, to enjoy at least a third part of Buckingham's gardens in all their atmospheric decay.[6] The castle was neglected after the forfeiture of the Duke's possessions. Henry and Anne Boleyn stayed briefly in its unfinished rooms in 1535, but then the castle languished roofless until a cadet branch of the Howard family in the nineteenth century saw Thornbury's romantic potential and employed Anthony Salvin to effect a tactful restoration. It is now the kind of hotel, elite, well manicured, filled with heraldry and old portraits, that the Duke would, in a later age, have patronised. The drive sweeps in past the coronetted battlements of St Mary's church, which just before his downfall the Duke was beginning to convert into a colle-giate foundation to rival St George's Chapel at Windsor.[7] Next comes an enormous base court of roofless ranges, generously fenestrated on their elevations to the court but convincingly military on their outside walls, with gun ports and arrow slits.[8] The hotel has sensitively allowed these to mature into a wild ruined garden of ferns, ivy, broken Gothic tracery and whole suites of hollow rooms. On the right is the one massive donjon tower built before the axe fell on Tower Hill. There were to have been three more in a tremendous display of largely spurious fortifications. A gatehouse leads in to an inner court with a kitchen court behind it to the left and lastly, through a towering range of ducal apartments, comes the 'Privie' garden itself.

This is an enclosure to savour (**colour plate 1**). The high stone walls around it with their bay windows and battlements are the authentic outer boundaries of the medieval garden. It was a two-storey cloister, the upper galleries of which led out by two doors, still visible in the walls of the ducal apartments, to a lost gallery bridge across the churchyard and into a ducal pew in the north aisle.[9] Freakish good fortune has not only preserved the handsome bones of this 'Privie' garden and its 'Goodly' extension to the north (**3**), but also the careful description of it in all its brief prime, made by the surveyors Thomas Magnus and William Walweyn whom Henry sent, as soon as Buckingham was dead, so that he could gloat over his acquisition.

Without their description it would not be easy to understand the complex features surrounding this 'Privie' garden at first-floor level. They recorded that:

> On the South Side of the said ynner warde is a proper gardeyn, and about
> the same a goodly galery conveying above and beneth from the principall
> loggings booth to the chapel [at the far end of the range] and p'ishe
> churche, the utter part of the said gallery being of stoon imbattled, [which
> survives] and the ynner part of tymbre covered wt slate.[10]

3   *A reconstruction of the 'Goodly' Garden at Thornbury Castle in its 1520s prime from H. Avray Tipping's 1925* English Gardens. *The 'Privie' Garden lay beyond the cloister range connecting the ducal apartments with the church and its ducal pew*

What have been lost are the inner walls of the double-decker cloister, of timber and plaster covered by Devon slates, heraldically patterned like those the King would lay over the walls of his Nonsuch Palace in 1541-5. From the windows of the presence and dining chambers with their astonishing tracery, concave above, convex below, 'perhaps the most perfect in existence' as an awed David Verey described them, the Duke would have looked across at the church tower and down into the garth.[11] In 1520 he had paid 3s 4d to 'John Wynde, gardener, for diligence in making knotts', most likely Stafford knots, his heraldic device, of lavender and rosemary.[12] If their interstices were filled with herbs like savory, oregano, sage and elecampane, the scent on sunny days in that enclosed, almost windless, space would have been over-whelming, combining piety and perfume as Buckingham walked to his devotions. Or would he have preferred the colour of stocks, periwinkles, sweet rocket, iris, cowslip and daffodil, with tall foxgloves and hollyhocks at the corners? Whichever he chose he enjoyed them for only one spring and summer.

Next to the 'Privie' garden and still within the high walled enclosure was, the surveyors reported, a 'goodly gardeyn to walke ynne cloosed wt high walles imbattled. The conveyance thither is by the galery, above and beneth, and by other privie waies'.[13] So these high stone walls enclosed two gardens, the 'Privie' in its two storey cloister for all-weather exercise, and the 'Goodly', almost certainly separated from it by a painted palisade, for fair weather walking. Here the Howards in the nine-teenth century speculated imaginatively. All the thick battlements of topiary work enclosing little secret arbours are theirs, though the sixteenth-century planting would, without the yews, have been lighter in profile, more floral and more scented. In 1907 there was still the Howards' prodigious 20-foot tower of clipped yew guarding the door, now blocked, through the north wall. This door led, in the Duke's day, into 'a large and goodly orcharde' (**4**) which was

> full of young grafftes, well laden with frute, many rooses, and other pleasures; and in the same orcharde ar many goodly alies to walke ynne openly; and round aboute the same orcharde is covered on a good height [a raised bank], other goodly alies wt roosting [resting] places coverde thoroughly wit white thorne and hasill.[14]

Outside this again was a wooden paling and 'wt oute that ditches and quick set heggs'; always there was this emphasis on enclosure within enclosure.[15] Whitethorn was preferred for quick-set hedges because it grew fastest (five to seven years), it was easily trimmed, of a delicate colour and put out its leaves earliest in spring. Crab-apple stock was usually planted in it at 20-foot intervals and roses twined over it. So the covered walk around this third garden was not a gloomy affair of dark yew, but raised up on a bank and alive in spring with the blossom of the whitethorn trained over it; in autumn it would become a coppice of sloes and hazelnuts. The 'roosting places' would have been raised turf banks for seats with views out into the surrounding countryside: privacy cleverly united with vantage points.

4   *The 'Goodly' Orchard and the inner fortified gardens from the north-east at Thornbury in Mr Kitchin's reconstruction. Whitethorn and hazels, not yews, shaded the covered alleyways*

That was not all. As long ago as 1305 Piero de'Crescenzi of Bologna, writing in his *Ruralium Commodorum Liber*, following and often quoting word for word from Albertus Magnus's *De vegetabilibus et plantis* (*c.*1260), identified three garden types. First was the small 'herber', less than an acre in extent, for flowers and herbs; then there was the orchard, anything up to four times larger and laid out in regular walks to provide shade, privacy and ripe fruit; thirdly, but only for the castles of kings and great noblemen, there was a park for animals.[16] Buckingham had three deer parks in the surrounding country and the King's surveyors noted that at Thornbury he had, adjoining his 'herber' and his 'orchard', Crescenzi's third garden type:

> From out of the said orcharde ar divers posterons in sundry places, at pleasur to goe and entre into a goodly parke newly made, called the New Parke, having in the same no great plenty of wood, but many heggsrowes of thorne and great Elmes. The same Parke conteynneth nigh upon iii miles about, and in the same be viiic [700] der [deer] or more . . . Nigh to the said Newe Parke there is another parke called Marlwood, noething being between them but the bredth of an high waie.[17]

This suggests that in his garden thinking Buckingham was more thirteenth- than sixteenth-century.

If only all three had been restored by the Howards we would have a uniquely complete, three-part garden sequence, authenticated by contemporary witnesses who had probably eaten its fruit, heard its birdsong and tramped its walks. It was the garden of a traditionally minded Catholic nobleman, part devout in direction, part secular, sounding with church bells as well as with singing birds. It worked intricately on two levels with the rooms of the castle, and was grey with stone, green with 'herbery', but with nothing of that darkness of yews that we have come to associate with later Tudor 'Italian' gardens.

Over the course of the next two centuries enclosed gardens and wider, but still enclosed, deer parks would gradually come together, finally to fuse around 1730-40 to form that uniquely English achievement, the Arcadian Garden. Here, in 1521, the two are already adjoining and interconnected. The Duke's over-ambitious deer parks survive now only in name; but before moving three miles to the south-east, to Acton Court, the next garden chronologically in the Henrician sequence, it would be worth the four mile detour due north (past Newpark Farm) to the living, miraculously surviving, deer park of Berkeley Castle.

Whitcliff Park is a perfect time capsule, a boat-shaped enclosure of walls enclosing a little hill. It lies a mile from Berkeley Castle and was created in 1329 by the third Lord Berkeley, the murderer of King Edward II, two years after that event. At no point do its walls touch any public road, but six barns or houses are built against it, a sign of how commercially important it must have been locally. At its centre is a lodge tower, occupied by the deerherd and his family who lived in rooms under a banquet room, and a flat roof terrace for viewing any sport (**colour plate 2**). The present tower is of early nineteenth century date, but it is the successor to that first 1329 lodge and a later, 1613, Berkeley dower house.[18]

Red deer and fallow deer were kept in separate parks for both meat and the pleasure of the hunt. They could be chased on horseback and pulled down by deer hounds or marshalled to run past a stand where ladies and older gentry could try their luck with bow and arrow. First, however, their dung, or 'fewmets', had to be inspected to judge whether the stags were big enough to be worth shooting. On the several occasions when Queen Elizabeth tried her luck with bow and arrow the steaming fewmets were presented to her experienced eye in a silver dish.[19] An alternative park pleasure was simply to watch the deer moving and being fed. In 1694 Celia Fiennes wrote that Lord Tracy at Toddington in the north of the county had 'a very good parke, which stands so high that by the Lodge I rode up the banke I could see all the parke about and the deer feeding and running'.[20] So deer parks functioned somewhere between modern zoos and shooting galleries in a fairground.

There is a public footpath across this faintly sinister little park at Whitcliff and the walk is well worthwhile. But it is hard to repress the suspicion that those two dates, the murder in 1327 and the building of the lodge tower in 1329, were connected. Was the coveted licence to empark granted by 'the she-wolf of France', Queen Isabella, as a reward and as hush money after the convenient termination of her husband's existence?

5   *The grounds of Acton Court, Iron Acton from the air. Between the round horse pond*
    (top right), and the Court (centre), are the square banks of the farmyard with the
    dovecote casting a dark shadow. To the bottom left woodland screens the larger fishpond

Acton Court at Iron Acton could also be described as sinister, but for its looks, not its history (**5**). The Court is a real House of Usher with an enormous lowering presence, a gaunt hulk of red ironstone, recently on the edge of ruin yet preserving on its first floor the three bare rooms – guard, presence and privy chambers – of the east wing that was rushed up by Sir Nicholas Poyntz in nine months for the reception of King Henry and Queen Anne on their royal progress during the summer of 1535.

No one should come to Iron Acton expecting a beautiful garden, but one as char-acterful and interesting as its parent house and also highly controversial, a place for garden antiquaries to come and test their analysis of its bacon-striped and battle-mented enclosures against the conclusions of the experts, who were digging here extensively and inconclusively during the 1980s.[21] Acton Court is the detective mystery among Gloucestershire gardens and should be enjoyed as such.

The Court broods in the centre of a long rectangle of land running north-south, bounded on the north and east by a road, on the west by the original boundary line of a long, wet ditch and a very old hedge. On the south it is defended by a fish pond which has deteriorated into a marshy coppice but retains its Tudor dam and traces of an island that could once have been a garden feature, a miniature gloriette. The present entrance court is short and runs from the central door of the east range to the road on the east side. It has a handsome gateway with a five-centred arch and oak leaves carved in the spandrels, but the excavators found traces of buildings along the road wall of this court and proposed that it was originally the service court of the main house. But would Sir Nicholas have allowed the windows of his new royal east wing to overlook a base service court; and is not this the obvious place for a state entrance from the road to the royal apartments? At some stage the red walls of this east court were given a broad, bacon stripe band of decorative white plaster. The plaster has worn away, but left a defining stripe of pale lichen.

Acton Court's most notable garden feature is undoubtedly its south court. Twice the size of the east court it is surrounded by battlemented walls and was linked by a bridge across a deep moat to the lost south ranges of the house. It has yet to be excavated and on the strength of one mature pear tree is usually described as the orchard. A main entrance could once have stood here, but there is no trace of a gatehouse. In the south-west corner is a viewing bastion which would have given prospects over the big fishpond (**6**). Nearer the house is what looks like a gunport, with a narrow window slit commanding the moat. These two disparate features do not add up. Possibly there was once a second twin bastion on the south-east corner to overlook three further fishponds across the road and a walled deer park. The tower lodge of this park still stands among the delightful early nineteenth-century Gothick buildings of Acton Lodge farm. If such a south-east bastion ever existed a range of eighteenth-century barns has replaced it, so the function of this important area remains unresolved. Was the wide, battlemented court like the 'goodly orcharde' at Thornbury, a garden for ladies of the house to walk in and enjoy the views?

Then there are the areas north and west of the house. During the excavations the north field yielded up a confused map of banks and trenches which baffled the research team. Their report concluded: 'They are most likely to be connected with an elaborate garden and park'.[22] But is it likely? A house as large as Acton Court would have had an extensive farmyard and stables. These were usually sited on the opposite side of a manor house to its main entrance and contained a dovecote, not as an ornamental feature, but as a resource for providing pigeon pies. There is the ugly ruin of a dovecote in the centre of this northern area and, if some of these linear features are ignored, a large square section of banks can be isolated which

6   *The Bastion Walk at Acton Court, viewed from the fishpond wood. The height of the wall demonstrates Sir Nicholas Poyntz's indifference to defence*

may have bounded the farmyard. A pond further north of this square was the farm's horse or duck pond,[23] and another linear feature that leads out to the road in a north-westerly direction could have been the farmyard's exit point, avoiding the formal gardens.

That leaves the western sector. Here the archaeologists suggest there was a canal; but going where, from what and to what purpose? No less than eight dumps of later material have made it difficult to come to any more precise conclusions. What added frustration to the work was the discovery in 1985, among foundations, of the battered wreck of the earliest sundial yet found in any English garden, carrying the date 1520 and the initials, NK, of Nicholas Kratzer, Court Horologist to Henry VIII.[24] Sir Nicholas Poyntz appears to have leap-frogged his father Sir Anthony and succeeded his grandfather, Sir Robert Poyntz, on his death in 1520. All these garden works could then be Sir Robert's and contemporary with the Duke's at Thornbury. Alternatively Sir Nicholas, an assiduous and well-rewarded courtier, could, in a flush of enthusiasm, have begun all the surviving garden works and commissioned Kratzer to make a sundial in imitation of his royal master.

If all this debate over unresolved and insoluble problems sounds tedious it should not put garden enthusiasts off a visit to Iron Acton. Its future custodian may well decide upon ambitious new planting and various visitor attractions but now, in its forlorn emptiness of rooms and courts, the place has a rare authenticity of textures and an intense feeling of a lost era when some building gestures might be richly rewarded and others might end with the sweep of an axe. Newark Park, which concludes this chapter, will reveal how Sir Nicholas Poyntz's gardening paid off.

Acton Court is a problematic and interesting garden, an archaeologist's delight, but no one would seriously claim that it set out to charm. Horton Court, on the other hand, house, church and garden, lies like the ideal and improbable creation of a female novelist in its Cotswold combe. For this little crook of hillside to contain not only a Romanesque hall house, 850 years old, but also the earliest approach to a Renaissance garden loggia in Britain seems too much architectural good fortune to be true, lightning striking twice in one very small village. Horton's garden can be seen too as a sad and significant place historically, for its loggia proves how quickly Italian design and Renaissance aesthetics could have come to our offshore island if Henry VIII had not broken with the Roman Catholic church and isolated England culturally from the purer classical forms of southern Europe.

The genius who created this small garden was Henry's trouble-shooting ambassador extraordinary, the Italophile priest, William Knight. London born, Knight went through the Establishment's educational mill of Winchester and New College, Oxford, but then soared much higher, studying Law at Ferrara and spending years in Italy, some of them in Rome where he made influential contacts. King Henry appreciated his rare qualities, sent him on embassies to Spain and Switzerland and rewarded him accordingly with numerous Church appointments, sinecures for the most part, but one of them, the prebend of Horton, must have particularly appealed to Knight. That in itself is remarkable. At a time when the average garden fancier indulged in herberies, painted palings and woven tunnels of whitethorn, William Knight appears to have had a sensitive appreciation for the actual lie of land in what we today consider an idyllic valley. Was he an Arcadian gardener long before his time? If not why should a man familiar with Rome, Paris, London, Florence and Bologna choose as his favourite retreat this miniature landscape under the Cotswold edge?

More to the point is what Knight did to improve the landscape. His Ambulatory is a six-arched loggia set at right-angles to the garden front of the house (**colour plate 3**). It commands a connoisseur's view across and down the combe over what were, in his day, three fishponds. Immediately below the Ambulatory a steep terrace has been scooped out, a six foot drop, creating a level area, the present lawn, as a setting for the arches. It is just large enough for a limited, prebendal game of bowls. Around the corner to the right, beside a small orchard, are two more terraces with the inevitable twentieth-century features of a swimming pool and a rose garden. What are missing are the enclosing stone or brick walls which, in an Elizabethan layout, would have cut each one of these pleasant little valley spaces off from one another. As for the loggia itself, if a cusp is 'a tooth-like meeting point of two branches of a curve', then these arches, which Knight, who would have been familiar with the Spedali degli Innocenti in Florence, persuaded Gloucestershire masons to create for him, are exactly that cusp point where ogival English and segmental Italian arches meet. Their columns are slender, almost fluted, their capitals are minimal and the points of their arches are as blunt as the masons could make them without abandoning their native Gothic. The whole building breathes a frustrated awareness of

7   *Hannibal, the 'good' pagan, stylized with the confidence of a Pisanello medal, on the wall of the Horton Court Ambulatory*

Italian models, of elegant sun-soaked loggias and sleepy afternoons in the Florentine sun. It is purely ornamental, nostalgic and symmetrical, yet raised up here to face east in a damp, green Gloucestershire valley.

Gardens of this age usually raise problems, and the Ambulatory's problems are the four Cotswold stone medallions, mortared into its back wall in symbolic order. The two central figures in a deliberate crucifix shape are the good pagan Hannibal and the good emperor Augustus. On either side are the bad pagan Attila, the destroyer of Roman order, and the bad emperor Nero. Alan Brooks dismisses them as 'recalling in a cruder way those at Hampton Court', which were imported by Cardinal Wolsey in 1521, exactly the date registered on a stone, which was originally in the garden, but now set into the chimneypiece in the hall at Horton.[25] But they are not necessarily cruder than Wolsey's conventional five roundels, merely conceived in a different artistic register, brilliantly stylized like Pisanello's medallions. The Hannibal and the Atilla are memorably intense caricatures of savage warriors, every jut of beard and slant of cheekbone sculpted in dramatic relief (**7**). Nero and Augustus are coin-like portraits, but still professionally executed. In the light of the Raphaelesque carving on the jambs of the entrance doorway to Horton Court, which is certainly work of Knight's occupancy, the likelihood is that the medallions in the Ambulatory were Knight's Italian souvenirs, carved from coins or prints which he had brought home, and added to the building in a gesture, perhaps of despair, that his masons could get no closer to Florentine models.

There is something lacking in the planting, or rather the total lack of planting, around that top terrace. Knight would have remembered Italian yew hedges and the near-architectural impact of their dark, straight lines. A yew hedge in an English garden would have been unlikely in 1521, but then so would a garden building like the Ambulatory. Planting of some kind, preferably a compact hedge of rosemary curved around the top of the terrace on each side of the steps, would improve the garden's punctuation immeasurably. This may have been the first Italian garden in England, and a little positive re-creation would be welcome, as would a restoration of all three fishponds in the combe. As for those other green terraces around the corner from the Ambulatory, the upkeep of plain turf is cheap, but grass is most unlikely to have been Knight's Italian solution. Such a sheltered spot is likely to have held a 'herber', of herbs medicinal and edible, but now it would have to co-exist with the swimming pool.

Were the Poyntz lords of Acton Court a little jealous of Horton's flattering topography and discontented with their own flat fields and tamely undulant deer parks? It is more than possible if their severely elegant lodge at Newark, which teeters even further than Horton over the cusp point towards classicism, is considered. Unlike Acton Court, Newark Park at Ozleworth in the high Cotswolds is situated, not like Horton under the edge, but on the very precipitous brink of it. It was a house built between 1544 and 1556 by Sir Nicholas on the proceeds of Kingswood Abbey, which had been Sir Nicholas's reward after the Dissolution of the Monasteries for all his entertaining of the King and his amoral indifference to the implications of royal statecraft.[26]

In the garden chronology Newark has no right to a place in this chapter. It was a sixteenth-century lodge in a walled deer park, perfectly sited for hawking from its own rooftop, but its sixteenth-century park walls were rebuilt in 1792, when the park was being landscaped, its top gate lodge is dated 1798, while the hillside terraces, lake with two islands and the vertiginous scenic drive up from Ozleworth Bottom all date from the late eighteenth century. It is the original house, not the garden, that is just, by one or two years, Henrician in date, and it is Sir Nicholas Poyntz's concept of the house that makes it significant in Gloucestershire garden history. Here, at one stroke of cool, simplistic architectural design, the English villa is being launched. Unlike its Venetian and Palladian contemporary villas it was not part-farm, part-house. Purely and directly it was a resort for leisure and pleasure, a rich family's bolt-hole in which to escape the cares of estate management, to entertain friends and to enjoy sport in wild countryside.

This represents the first, barely perceptible, edging together of garden and park, that process mentioned earlier which would lead eventually to the eighteenth-century Arcadian garden. Standing on the roof of Newark (**colour plate 4**) or on the narrow steps of its south entrance front, it is easy to believe that the Poyntz family were as aware of, and as pleased by, the landscape unfolding below them as William Knight must have been by the little hills, woods, orchards and ponds around his Ambulatory at Horton. And from its conception Newark (New Work) was not a mere lodge for picnics with a viewing stand, like Acton Lodge farm across the road

8   *Newark Park, built in the 1550s, interprets an Italian Renaissance villa in Tudor Gothic with just its entrance doorway gesturing towards correct Serlian forms*

from Acton Court. It was a house for full-time residence with a whole party of guests. The requirements of the house in planning terms appear to have constrained its unknown architect into a remarkably advanced design. Its east front (**8**), three bays wide, three storeys high, with a broad central canted bay, anticipates everything, except the sash windows, of the villas that Sir Robert Taylor would be designing, as a novelty, in the mid-eighteenth century: Harleyford, Asgill and Sharpham. As a final, confident touch the architect, Court trained, gave his client, who had been prepared a mere twenty years earlier at Acton Court to rush up a gauche heap of late Gothic provincialism, a chaste Doric doorcase for his garden entrance.

Earlier in the century, such was the feudal mind set, the Duke of Buckingham had laid out gardens at Thornbury that were in every detail akin to those described by King James I of Scotland in his poem 'The Kingis Quair', written between 1425 and 1435:

> Now was there maid fast by the touris wall
> A gardyn fair, and in the cornerer set
> Ane herbere grene, with wandis long and small
> Railit about; and so with treis set
> Was all the place, and hawthorn hegis knet.[27]

Less than 30 years later in Henry's reign a house was being built simply for the enjoyment of its grounds and prospects. The relationship of a house with its park was taking primacy over the medieval need for a fine house to act as the centre for a village economy or to assert political prestige; and Newark's garden door could have come straight out of the pages of Sebastiano Serlio's *L'Architettura* (1537-75). Now at Newark symmetry, order and classicism were in the wind.

2 Lost gardens of the Elizabethan-Jacobean continuum

Owlpen Manor exemplifies the problem with the Elizabethan gardens of Gloucestershire: not one of them really survives. The county may seem to abound in enchanting examples, multi-walled, multi-terraced, teeming with dark clipped yews, quaint sundials and staddle stones, but these are all either satisfying and ingenious fakes of the turn of the nineteenth century or else, like Owlpen, gardens of the late seventeenth and early eighteenth century which have mellowed into Elizabethan appearances to be hailed, by Arts and Crafts enthusiasts, as genuine Tudor creations.

The reason why no gardens survive from the Elizabethan period is that the building boom in Gloucestershire only started in the late sixteenth century, and the vast majority of the houses of this period are actually post-1600.[1] If houses like Stanway and Cirencester had elaborate gardens, they would have been swept away in later alterations. A 1615 estate map of Badminton suggests how little pleasure ground was attached to even the grandest houses at this time.[2] In addition, to survive, like the fortunate Henrician trio of the last chapter, a garden has to become unfashionable, neglected and finally abandoned so that only its hollow places and the bones of its walls remain untouched by later revisions. The wooded valleys and sudden viewpoints of the Cotswolds have always proved too attractive to permit that benign decay. Undoubtedly there are a few scraps of Elizabethan garden walls surviving unremarked in later gardens but, apart from Kempsford's riverside terrace and ruined garden house, there is nothing of any significance; certainly nothing to equal the Henrician three.[3]

As some compensation for these losses Gloucestershire's good fortune is that the county's gardens, as they were in 1712, have been richly recorded in Sir Robert Atkyns's *The ancient and present state of Glostershire*. Several other counties – Oxfordshire, Staffordshire, Hertfordshire and Kent – had their county histories published at around this time, but none of them as generously illustrated as Gloucestershire was by the bird's eye views of John Kip, the celebrated illustrator, with Leonard Knyff, of England's greater country estates in *Britannia Illustrata* (1707). By 1712 the prevailing garden fashion across the country had been, for some 50 years, that of Franco-Dutch formalism. Professional nurserymen working in highly organised capitalist enterprises had transformed the appearance of whole areas of parkland and their conventional formalities lie heavily on most of Kip's Gloucestershire plates. Nevertheless, it is possible, by cautious detective work, to piece out, underneath Kip's conventional garden symbols – his over-neat alternations of round and conical bushes in the borders of frets, his multiple cabbage patches,

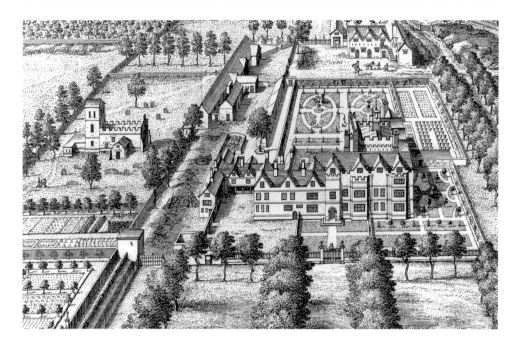

9 *Hatherop Castle drawn by Kip. The many small walled enclosures of the Tudor gardens were, by 1712, being taken over by formal parterres. Twin gate towers at the bottom left foreshadow the park gate lodges of the eighteenth century*

uniform orchards and improbably complex parterres – some elements and at least the general characteristics of the lost Elizabethan gardens of the county.

There appears to have been, working upon an inherited confusion of small walled or fenced garden areas, a tendency towards increasingly formal forecourt approaches, a fashion for twinned terraces and twinned garden pavilions and a positive craze for bowling greens. Kip's view of Hatherop Castle exemplifies this multiplicity of confined areas (**9**). Five of them appear to have developed functionally over the years around the disorderly façades and service buildings of this little castle-manor. There are three in the front, including a plain, grassed forecourt, and two at the rear. At one side of the front gardens there are twin pavilions or lodges guarding the route to the farm and stable areas at the back of the castle.

It is not possible, in a 1712 view, to decide upon the function of each one of the five enclosures, but a kitchen yard and a separate vegetable garden are obvious enough. What is intriguing about this homely clutter of interconnected spaces is that, centuries later, they would be exactly the kind of gardens – outdoor rooms leading from one distinct area of character and utility to another – that the great Arts and Crafts garden designers of the Edwardian period would be aiming to recreate. Utility and a humane domestic scale of gardening would have come full circle. Formalism and axial layouts, broad sweeps of open 'natural' parkland, would have been tried and found wanting, multiple enclosures would be back in fashion again.

The controlling influences working upon this happy tangle of gardens, the twin terraces, twin pavilions and complex forecourts, would climax in the county at Campden House in Chipping Campden, a Jacobean building on a grand scale, begun in 1613; but these disciplining fashions were building up much earlier. Kip's view of Kempsford Manor suggests that they were probably current before the Dissolution of the Monasteries released so many prize properties to be developed, along with their gardens, by the opportunistic gentry.

Kempsford was unusual in that it was not a monastic possession, but the manorial endowment of a collegiate foundation in Leicester, and ruled for the benefit of the college by a Provost. Consequently it was not suppressed until 1548 in Edward VI's reign when the Thynne family acquired it. The gaunt collegiate courtyard block which Kip illustrated is supposed to have been built by Sir Thomas Thynne between 1580, when his grandfather died and 1639 when Sir Thomas died (**10**). But it was called the 'Provost's Lodging' and the home farm in the immediate foreground was called the 'Porter's Lodge', while the walled garden, with its twin raised terraces and twin pavilions on the terrace overlooking the infant Thames, was known as the 'Provost's Garden'. This suggests that the Thynne additions were superficial and that the garden dated from before 1548. Kempsford's distinction is that it is the one garden in Gloucestershire where it is still possible, though on private land and in the otherwise modern garden of the Old Vicarage, to take an Elizabethan garden walk. The Manor itself was demolished long ago, but the riverside terrace, now called Lady Maud's Walk from its traditional association with a daughter of Henry, Duke of Lancaster, remains together with one of the twin pavilions. This is now in a ruined condition, but its mullioned and transomed window is Tudor rather than Jacobean in style.

Not all gardens had the twinned accommodation. Kip's view of Hardwicke, in the flat lands outside Gloucester, shows a single, entirely indefensible, gatehouse commanding the forecourt. At Shipton Moyne the Estcourts' banqueting house was again a gatehouse, twin towered and reached from the main house along a broad, raised terrace and up a flight of outside steps. This was the more logical arrangement. Siston Court, the largest Elizabethan house in the county, built at some time between 1572 and 1598 by the Denys family, had just one two-storey viewing tower at the end of a terrace walk alongside its large bowling green (**11**). But behind the tower Kip illustrates what could be a dower house or a lodge, another pleasure pavilion with its own separate walled garden.

The social significance of this twinning has still to be researched, but Kempsford's pavilions are not alone in Kip's plates. He illustrates twin pavilions in the gardens of Sneed, Hampton, Wotton (with two sets), Hill Court, Flaxley Abbey, Hatherop and the Great House, Henbury. This last is Commonwealth in date, and the neat classical pavilions at Flaxley are clearly creations of the Boevey family, who bought the Abbey in 1648. But there is a chain of influence here running from Tudor Kempsford to late seventeenth-century Flaxley. Taken together with the many bowling greens that feature prominently often, as at Siston, acting as the principal focus of the layout, these pavilions indicate a sturdy preference for the outdoor life, for garden pleasures as an escape from the smells and confinement of the great houses, and a distinct reluctance

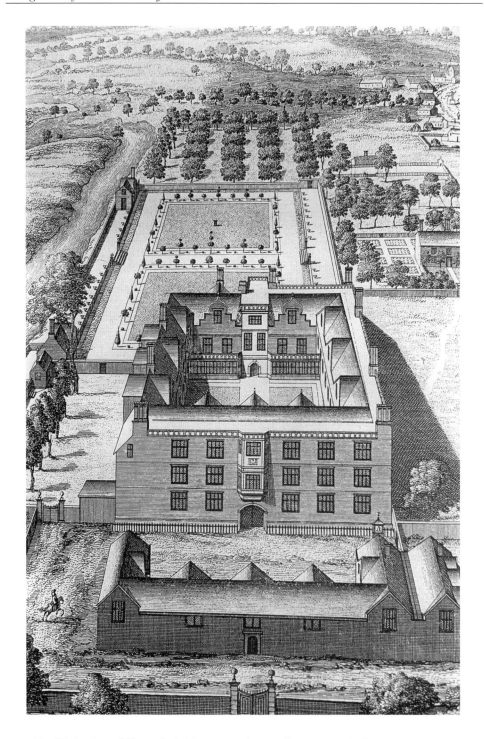

10 *Kip's view of Kempsford Manor reveals its collegiate, pre-Reformation origins.
One of the twin garden pavilions on 'Lady Maud's' riverside terrace walk along
the Thames survives in a modern garden*

to rely upon state rooms as the absolute focus for the entertainment of guests. Clower Wall (Clearwell), the seat of Francis Wyndham, has two bowling greens, both in use on the Kip engraving, and there is one each at Lypiatt, Barrington, Cassey Compton, Sapperton (**colour plate 6**), Siston and Badminton. Bowling alleys for skittles or a boule-type version of the game mentioned by Gervase Markham in his *Countrey Contentments, or the Husbandman's Recreation*[4] appear in Gloucestershire gardens at Stoke Bishop, Badminton and Sandywell, while one curious twinned feature in the grounds of Siston could even be a double alley.

When considering the forecourts of Elizabethan gardens any influence from the usage of carriages can be discounted. By Kip and Atkyns's time a carriage-and-six had become a status symbol of maximum consumption, and if a house owner possessed a carriage he usually persuaded Kip to feature it. Forecourts were, therefore, areas of ceremony and designed to be approached on foot and with respect. Even in Kip's time the coach-and-six at The Greenway, Shurdington, is shown parked with a fenced forecourt, a flight of steps and a broad terrace dividing it from the front door of the house.

At Siston and Toddington, the two major Elizabethan houses in Atkyns's book, the approach has been made as impressive as possible on paved ways across a forecourt set between the towering side wings of the main house and walled off on its open side. Toddington, built in the 1620s, has an ornate gatehouse with twin side pavilions under ogee domes (**12**). Their battered wreck survives in a marshy field across the

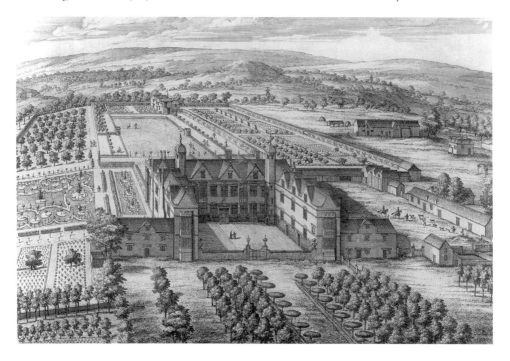

11   *At Siston Court Kip's view shows the farmyard, bowling green, vegetable gardens, orchards, bowling alleys and a formal parterre lying in organic confusion around the great Elizabethan house. Only the avenue approach is a sign of seventeenth-century planning*

park from the new Toddington, which was designed and built by Charles Hanbury-Tracy in 1820-35. Sir John Tracy, who built the old house featured in Atkyns, was not satisfied by this one porter's lodge, but added another walled forecourt with a smaller yet still ornate gateway. Over, Southam and Eastington have also doubled their forecourts by these extra and dysfunctional walled or fenced enclosures. Hardwicke was already protected by a wide moat with a bridge leading to the gatehouse (**13**). Even so the Tye family, resident since medieval times, felt it necessary to dignify their house by a large railed forecourt on the other side of the moat, with austere flanking stable and service wings. These, however, by their cross-mullioned fenestration, are likely to be post-Elizabethan. It would be after 1660 and the accession of Charles II that the many medieval moats around Gloucestershire country houses: Hardwicke, Flaxley, Dumbleton, Cassey Compton, to name a few, found a new function, reshaped into the precisely geometrical, stone banked canals and water features of Franco-Dutch style garden layouts.

The gardens of Campden House are the natural climax to all these lost twin terraces, twin garden houses, forecourts and stony compartments. They represent an extraordinary survival. In the usual course of topographical change the great house endures but its surrounding gardens alter past recognition. At Campden the great house of Sir Baptist Hicks, the rich London haberdasher and would-be viscount, lasted a mere 30 years, burnt down in 1645 by the Royalist hooligans who were supposed to be

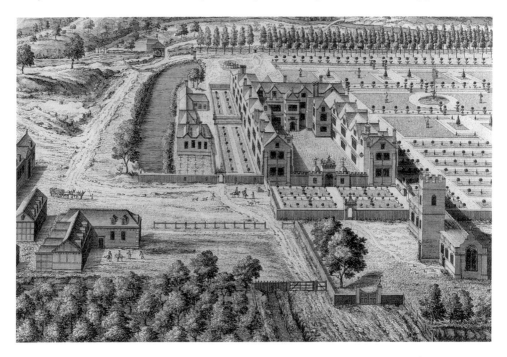

12   Toddington Manor's Jacobean system of forecourts and twin gatehouses would have made access to the house by carriage impossible. Formal gardens have been laid out to the left, but a drying green still stands next to the moat

13 *At Hardwicke Court the medieval moat and gatehouse have their place in a formal seventeenth-century Dutch-style garden like that surviving at Westbury Court. Twin stable ranges add a bucolic dignity to the forecourt; vegetable gardens lie to the left*

defending it. Yet its gardens still hang on in a romantic, ruined half-life. Sir Baptist's descendants retreated to the stable block, an ungainly apartment that still bulks loutishly along Calf Lane, and allowed the garden to remain, chiefly because its several ambitious garden pavilions could serve as a small housing estate for their retainers.

Today the evocative relics of Sir Baptist's confident Jacobean formalism and even the ditches, ponds and streams of his daughter, Lady Juliana Noel's, Caroline water garden, can be inspected and enjoyed from a number of viewpoints in the church-yard, side lanes and footpaths of this least changed and most satisfying of Cotswold wool towns. But before any retracing of the gardens it is rewarding to visit the tombs of their creators in a side chapel of Chipping Campden church. The carved images of Sir Baptist and his wife, staid and prostrate under a correct canopy of black and white marble, lie in dramatic and entirely appropriate contrast to those of Lady Juliana and her husband Edward Noel, second Viscount Campden. Between the two generations there is a gap in life style which is reflected at Campden in tomb style and garden style. Sir Baptist was a mainstream Elizabethan, born before Shakespeare, though he lived on for years after Shakespeare's death. His garden is rich but orderly. His daughter and her husband were of the Cavalier generation, contemporaries of John Donne and the Metaphysical poets, a wilder and more experimental generation, given to extravagant conceits and surprises. In *To his Coy Mistress* Andrew Marvell wrote:

> Thy Beauty shall no more be found;
> Nor, in thy marble Vault, shall sound
> My echoing Song: then Worms shall try
> That long preserv'd Virginity:
> And your quaint Honour turn to dust;
> And into ashes all my Lust.
> The Grave's a fine and private place,
> But none I think do there embrace.[5]

Yet Juliana and Edward on their monument assert the contrary. They are standing excitedly, having just burst out of the black marble doors of their tomb, holding hands lovingly, she plump in her fetching grave clothes, while Lord Campden's shroud is raised to expose his muscular thigh.

Campden's gardens, even in their ruin, still reflect this change from the formal to the informal. Beside the gate to the churchyard are the neat twin lodges to the lost house, each capped by an ogee dome and linked together by a pie-crust parapeted wall, to create what are probably the first true park gate lodges in the country, standing apart from and quite separate to the axis of the parent house. The best view of Sir Baptist's half of the gardens, the upper and architectural half, is from a corner of the churchyard. One of the twin pavilions, the hunting pavilion, with its exotic, almost oriental, silhouette, is very close. At the far, town-end of the grand 'Terrass Walk' is the second, the garden pavilion. In between them stands a gaunt fang of fire reddened masonry (**colour plate 5**). This is all that remains of Baptist Hicks' extrovert palace: eleven bays and three storeys of glittering windows topped by shaped gables and an onion dome lantern tower that recorded his presence by a light burning at night and a flag flying in the daytime.[6]

The inventive spirit of that building survives in the impudent invention of these two banqueting houses. Originally, as they faced each other along the 'Terrass', they had open Renaissance-style loggias with stairs into their upper rooms. Each was connected on its basement floor with the second terrace down the steep hill slope on which the gardens were laid. The east or hunting pavilion had an exit out onto the Coneygree, a deer park commanded by the windows of its upper room; the west or garden pavilion gave out from its lower room onto the nursery garden and walled vegetable plot. This would have been of prime importance for the substantial salads which were commonly served at the main meal of the day: cucumbers, Jerusalem artichokes, turnips, onions, carrots, beetroot and skirrets (a root vegetable) as well as greens: lettuce, cabbage and the whole range of herbs for flavouring.[7] Next to the site of the vegetable garden a little house still stands, almost as fanciful in its design as the twin pavilions. Variously described as The Almonry and The Laundry, it either housed Sir Baptist's steward or his head gardener. The west pavilion probably served as Sir Baptist's 'elaboratorie', for bulbs and specimens which he could show to his friends before leading them down to the Great Garden, then on to the Great Orchard, on two lower terraces, to sample his fruit.[8] It would have been the east, or hunting, pavilion which served as the true banqueting place, an exotic grandstand topped by spiral chimneystacks and a parapet where Gothic shapes have been contrived in Jacobean strapwork.

The Great Garden below these pavilions was not set out in the usual knot patterns, but in broad Union Jacks of herb hedges and banks (**14**), designed as a compliment to King James I for achieving peacefully the union of the two kingdoms, England and Scotland. It was a patriotic variant of gardens which Gervase Markham had described in his *The English Husbandman* of 1613: a single square subdivided into four quarters by cross paths. Markham had suggested that the squares, within their borders of southern wood, rosemary, box or lavender, should be planted with germander, hyssop, thrift, pink or 'gillyflowers', the modern carnations.[9] At this period gillyflowers, particularly those introduced from Poland with a strong clove perfume, were considered virtually the equal of roses in garden precedence. The row of almshouses which he built across the lane from The Almonry is designed in the shape of a capital I for Iacobus, yet another compliment to the King, who did eventually respond by making Sir Baptist the first Viscount Campden, though only a year before Sir Baptist's death.

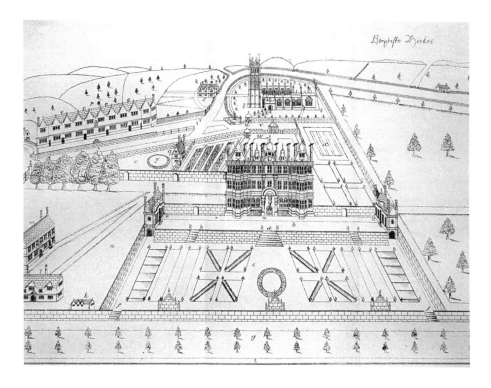

14 *Almost everything in this view survives except Campden House itself. From left to right: the stables, the almshouses, the west banqueting pavilion, the Almonry, twin gate lodges and the east or hunting pavilion. Two Union Jack parterres celebrate the achievement of King James I*

An ornamental wall divided the Great Garden from the Great Orchard on its alternate broad and narrow terraces; the Orchard ended with a long, narrow canal which today is usually dry. It was there, at the water, that Sir Baptist Hicks' symmetries came to an end. They must have been an impressive evocation of the Franco-Italian gardens seen on his business trips to Paris to buy the Italian silks, velvets and rich embroideries that had made his fortune.[10] Though French inspired, his garden was still recognisably English and even Gloucestershire in its details. Nowhere in the pages of Jacques Androuet du Cerceau's celebration of the glories of recent French chateaux building, *Les Plus Excellents Bastiments de France* (1576 & 1579), are there any direct precedents for this English obsession with twinned banqueting houses or for the wilful patterning of the Campden parapets. Campden's garden buildings were very English and classical mannerist in style.

To recapture the spirit of the lower gardens that Lady Juliana created after her father's death in 1629 but before the Civil War broke out in 1642, it is necessary to follow Calf Lane past the stables. As the lane winds downhill and the boundary wall sinks lower it is just possible to make out the wreck of an informal water garden where the Scuttlebrook emerges from an arch and follows a contrived lateral course before joining the larger Cam brook. All this area would have been out of sight of the house and reached by paths through the orchard, a region of little lakes with serpentine banks, a tentative reaching out towards an informal garden style in reaction against that rigid Union Jack of planting and the geometry of the terraces.

Some imagination is required to people the one broad, right-angled canal, 350m long and largely dry, the two asymmetrical lakelets it links and the pond, which still holds water and contains an island, with music and with ladies and gallants enjoying its paths. But it is at this place, more than anywhere else in England, where there are vestiges at least of the garden style which Sir Henry Wotton, one-time ambassador to the Venetian Republic and Provost of Eton, was trying to describe in his 1624 *The Elements of Architecture*: gardens 'irregular or at least cast into a very wild *Regularitie*'. Sir Henry hardly understood what he was trying to express, but he knew, probably from visiting a garden of the Countess of Bedford, that there was a new spirit of freedom and experiment abroad in English garden design during those last golden but fated days of King Charles I's personal rule. He urged that a visitor should be able to walk 'by several *mountings* and *valings*, to various entertainments in his *sent* and *sight*', to experience changes of mood 'as if he had been *Magically* transported into a new Garden'.[11] That must have been exactly what guests of the Noels experienced, coming down from the Union Jack parterre and the Great Orchard terraces, and entering this water world at the foot of the hill.

For a last reminder of Lady Juliana a visit to the Campden gardens should end by taking the field path on the left of Calf Lane to Haydon's Mill on the Cam. Across the field from here is Lady Juliana's Gateway. It is not a handsome structure, but low down on its jambs two vases have been carved and from each vase three delicate stone lilies sprout. Their fragile charm against the crude stonework of this arch could be taken as symbolic of the refined, aesthetic spirit in which she conceived the garden additions to her father's geometrical terraces: the only flowers remaining from what was once Gloucestershire's most innovative and dualistic garden.

3 Vegetable formalism – the reign of pretension and utility

A number of pretty garden pavilions – examples at Quenington, Beverston and Hannington Wick, just over the Wiltshire border from Kempsford, come to mind – are neither gazebos nor banquet houses, but handsome and virtually windowless outdoor privies. Their function comes as a salutary warning. Similarly, those resoundingly grandiose gardens in the Franco-Dutch style that John Kip recorded around so many Gloucestershire country houses are not always what they seem. Kip's layouts are carefully coded and need to be equally carefully read.

First there is the question of scale. A visit to Flaxley Abbey armed with a copy of Kip's view (**15**), which he dedicated to its owner, the cheerful widow-lady, Mrs Catarina Boevey, will ensure that all subsequent views by Kip are taken with caution. He could be a shameless flatterer. The canal he illustrates to the right of the house reaches away to the first wooded hills of the Forest of Dean and appears, to a casual estimate, anything up to a quarter of a mile long, a water feature worthy to stand alongside the royal canals at Hampton Court. That square formal garden beside it, each of its four quarters a simplified *parterre à l'Anglaise* divided into four further matching quarters, looks equally royal in scale. It comes, therefore, as something of an anticlimax to realise that the wooded hill is in fact very close to the house and the parterre area, now a plain lawn, is modest in size; there was never the room on the existing terrain for any statements of regal scale. The garden was formal but it was never grand; it offered only a pleasant, token formalism to dignify an amateurish conversion of one-time monastic premises. The twin pavilions of its forecourt, now lost, commanded another even smaller *parterre à l'Anglaise*, which is a lawn today. Only the little orangery, just visible in Kip's view behind the house, is still in place, though altered.

Kip and his co-artist, Leonard Knyff, who worked with him on the even more impressive formal layouts of their *Britannia Illustrata* (1707), both came from Holland. They had, naturally, continental expectations of a garden's scale and order. They were also creating illustrated books at almost the end of an exceptionally un-English period of garden design and after a faintly discreditable forty years of English history. These are often glossed over in history books because of the consti-tutional advances made when an opportunistic aristocracy took advantage of ill-advised kings. From 1660 to 1702 Britain was at first a client state to France, ruled by a king, Charles II, who had built up a notion of the ideal garden during his years of exile in Holland and France and who was now taking a substantial pension from Louis XIV. There followed, after the brief, disastrous 1685-88 episode of James II, an astonishing political reversal in which the Stadtholder of Holland, a state against

15 *Kip's flattering view of the gardens at Flaxley Abbey. The canal, now dry, is actually little more than a straight pond. The three forecourt gardens and the twin pavilions have all been swept away, but the orangery behind the house survives in an altered state*

which Britain had recently fought three fierce wars for commercial supremacy, was brought over to rescue a Protestant elite and middle class from Catholicism. Yet from a garden viewpoint there was no change, only more of the same as the Stadtholder William and his Stuart Queen, Mary II, were both devoted to a formal Dutch style of garden design which only differed from the French by its marginally greater emphasis on straight canals.[1]

All this political change and insecurity meant that landowners intent on advertising their loyalty to the reigning king had to produce modified provincial versions of Versailles, Het Loo, Marly or Heemstede. There were two books which gave confident, if sometimes contradictory, illustrated texts on true French garden design, but these both came out too late to have had much influence on the impressive Franco-Dutch layouts in either *Britannia Illustrata* or Atkyns's *Glostershire* (1712). They were George London and Henry Wise's *The Retir'd Gard'ner* (1706) and John James's *The Theory and Practice of Gardening* (1712), which was a translation of Dézallier d'Argenville's *La Théorie et la Pratique du Jardinage* (1709). These two were published to pontificate over a style that had long been popular and was just about to become unfashionable, so Gloucestershire's formal gardens must have evolved from other sources.

In the previous chapter it was evident that substantial remains – moats and walled enclosures – were still surviving in the midst of Franco-Dutch avenues, axial layouts, canals and parterres. Before the books of James and London and Wise came out the continental manner had been absorbed piecemeal, sometimes from prints, sometimes from continental travel, sometimes from professional gardeners and nurserymen like George London and John Rose, who had actually served apprenticeships in French gardens. As well as being tests of loyalty to uneasily reigning kings, these formal gardens were the result of the capitalist enterprise of various nurserymen selling their produce along with their advice. Elms, hornbeam and yew in various stages of growth, bulbs, bushes, flower pots, lead statues, seats and fountain apparatus all cost a small fortune and their sale made prosperous gentlemen of the nurserymen them-selves. It was always, however, a foreign imposition, basically dysfunctional in the average Gloucestershire estate and, with the exception of the gardens at Dyrham and, possibly but by no means certainly, those at Badminton, Kip's Gloucesteshire gardens were rather less noble than they appeared. Long before the technical jargon of *The Retir'd Gard'ner* and *The Theory and Practice* became available for the pretentious garden expert to use in order to baffle his or her neighbours, a Gloucestershire simplification of French practice had been evolved.

According to London and Wise who, it should be remembered, stood to profit by convincing their readers and customers that real gardens should be labour intensive and highly expensive, there were 11 different types of parterre which should replace old-fashioned walled enclosures, knots and frets. John James believed that there were only four; and as he was closer to Gloucestershire realities his four are worth listing.

Parterres de broderie were not true gardens in any modern sense as they were patterns culled from embroidery, far too complex to be achieved in plants or even in box hedging. They had to be executed in coloured earths and industrial waste and were liable, therefore, to be washed away by any cloudburst: typical examples of the French penchant for extreme mannerism in all artistic forms.

Parterres des compartiments were the same, but with the pattern repeated four times in four separate quarters of a square and, probably for reasons of labour, in somewhat simplified forms and edged with box. There was a true *parterre des compartiments* on relatively level ground immediately in front of the house at Dyrham, its repetitive fleur de lys designs sited to be admired from the terraces on the left, from the state rooms of the house and from William Talman's 1701 orangery. But Dyrham was not a normal provincial garden. Its creator, William Blathwayt, was, as Secretary of State and Clerk to the Council, very close to King William III. He had spent years in Holland and would have been one of those rare Englishmen who took the continental parterres seriously.

Parterres à l'Anglaise were, as the faintly contemptuous French name suggests, the standard English gesture towards formalism on the cheap: grass cut into curvaceous

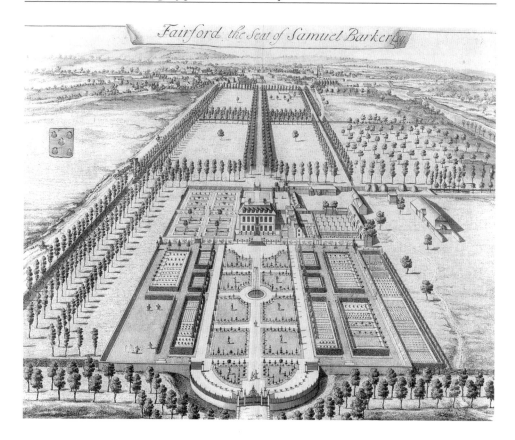

16 *Formal vegetable gardens, formal lawns and formal avenues would have made the
upkeep of the grounds at Fairford Park simple and economical*

patterns, bounded with box and then a path and a border. These borders could take
the form of either a carp back bed, raised in a central hump, for flowers, or the
standard English punctuation for lazy seventeenth-century gardeners: a conical bush
alternating with a lower round bush. To justify this easy way out most English
commentators of the time boasted of the superior quality of English turf.

Cut-work was James's confusing last category, which he defined as patterns of box
hedging entirely filled with flowers. To London and Wise 'cut-work' was closer to the
parterre à l'Anglaise: patterns of grass upon coloured gravel and sand, or (and they claimed
this as a separate category) patterns of coloured gravel or sand within areas of turf.

To see how the average Gloucestershire gentleman handled these formal alterna-
tives it is only necessary to look at two of Kip's most ambitious views: Fairford Park
(**16**) and Abbey House, Cirencester (**17**). Both gardens were laid out on level ground,
but Abbey House was virtually a town rather than a country residence, standing with
its next door neighbours in the shadow of the parish church.

Initially both gardens look, as they were intended, extremely impressive. They
have long axial layouts, Fairford's double avenue is aimed like a bow shot at the distant

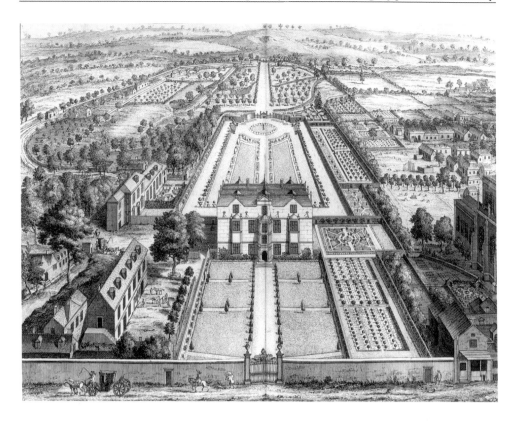

17   *Like Fairford Park the gardens at Abbey House, Cirencester, featured plain lawns with an exedral termination flanked by vegetable gardens and orchards. The tiny garden next door boasts twin garden arbours*

town; Abbey House's avenue, by the size of its trees only recently planted, fades through an orchard to a prominent hill. Each house has a short, grassed forecourt and a long, back garden of lawns with an exedral ending of wrought ironwork and a gate leading nowhere. It is characteristic of an age only recently coming to terms with the carriage that both houses were approached in practice not through their formal gates and avenues, but quite casually from stables at the side. In neither layout are parterres prominent, but both have twin raised terraces looking down on plain lawns bordered with alternate round and conical yews. Conifers border Fairford's terraces, the terrace at Abbey House is lined with flowers in pots or urns. All eight of Fairford's back lawns are centred by statues and their whole composition focuses on a fountain. A single statue in a round lawn acts as focus to the rear garden of Abbey House.

The upkeep of these lawns would have been light; the labour intensive areas were the vegetable gardens and orchards at the side of the showpiece lawns. At Abbey House they were hidden behind walls, at Fairford behind hedges. Fairford had ten vegetable gardens, one of them very extensive; Abbey House had five orchards. Kip indicates vegetables by a varied range of dots and larger blobs. He drew what could be a bean yard, vineyard or hopyard at Fairford, a house manifestly intended to become entirely self-supporting. Valentine Strong had designed its façades in 1660-1 in an austere Puritan minimalist classicism for a man, Andrew Barker, who had prospered under the Commonwealth. Barker will have intended the gardens to exemplify that Commonwealth pattern of scientific husbandry established by the Anglo-Prussian philanthropist, Samuel Hartlib. Abbey House, in contrast, belonged to the royalist Master family who had suffered sequestration during those same years and learnt no horticultural lessons. Yet both gardens conform closely to the same general layout. Fairford indeed is likely to have been the earliest formal garden in the county: the creation of a Puritan gentleman following French fashions prudently and, by the size of his vegetable plots, commercially.

It is impossible to leave Abbey House without mentioning Kip's delightful glimpse into a humble town garden set behind shops to the right of the main subject. Even this has twinned alcoves and a miniature, but quite elaborate, parterre. Over the wall from this the royalist grounds have a skittle alley and two 'cut-work' gardens, by James's definition of that term: flowers set within low box hedges. It could be significant that Fairford, while it has a full-sized bowling green, scorns any such floral complexities.

Once the eye becomes attuned to Kip's markers for vegetable plots examples of them proliferate, but in no clear pattern. Hill Court in the Severn Vale has, apart from its flowerpot-lined twin terraces and two square lawns, nothing but vegetable gardens and orchards, the former grown so intensively that they fill half the stable yard and reach out axially into the distance in paled enclosures.[2] The Greenway, Shurdington is much the same: it has only one severe reach of yew flanked lawns, while the remainder of the grounds is taken up by orchards, vegetable gardens growing next to the forecourt, avenues running axially and laterally, and a square fishpond with a pier and fishing temple. Yet this apparent utilitarian disarray had underlying metaphysical significance.[3] William Lawrence, who inherited the little estate in 1697, had lost his first wife and his only son, William, and intended these various plots and crossed avenues as a garden of mourning symbolizing the ages of man. Those forecourts represented infancy and youth; the lawn with its cypresses and yews 'signify'd our Manly State, and the more Large and Florid Enjoyments of Life'. Kip shows a tree in its centre, but William had put a statue of Time there, pointing to the cypresses, 'a tree always made use of in Funeral pyres, and . . . therefore by reason of its cold dark Shade and bitter Leafe, set here as an Emblem of Death'. The two orchards, old and new, represented old age and second childhood while another yew at the end of the orchard walk was meant to 'show the Boundes of Life'. The flower garden lay within that small walled enclosure beyond the pigeon house and this had a border of daisies around an escutcheon of his wife's arms, meant to represent 'a Crowd of Eyes come to gaze upon her Funeral'. Finally the fishing temple on its pier was a place to reflect upon all this. Lawrence was born in 1637: a throw-back to that Caroline age of Metaphysical poets who enjoyed death and gardens with an equal bizarre fervour. Shurdington is a welcome reminder of native religious feeling and the spirit of the earlier half of the century surviving into this time of alien formalism.

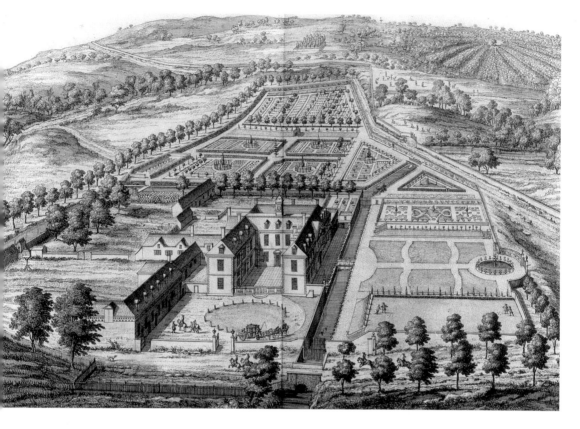

18   At Little (Cassey) Compton a carriage approach has been created; across the canalised
     moat are a parterre, an exedral lawn and a bowling green; beyond the house is a huge,
     strictly formal and ornamental vegetable garden

It is easy to be taken in by the garden designer's cunningly superficial manipula-
tion of formal order. The gardens of Sandywell Park, south-east of Cheltenham, and
Dumbleton Hall on the Warwickshire border, are at first glance entirely floral, ornamental and formal, but closer inspection reveals a ninety percent utility of vegetables
and orchards. The dazzling cut-work to the left foreground of Sandywell is not a
'cut-work' in John James's sense. The box hedges are packed full of vegetables not
flowers, but the design still revolves around an ornamental statue. Dumbleton's
garden front faces five plots, all contained within a geometrically exact canal, but its
raised terrace walks overlook four vegetable plots. There is only one *parterre à
l'Anglaise* of patterned lawn fronting a fountain basin and an exedra. Little Compton
(Cassey Compton), south of Sandywell Park, plays the same tricks with examples of
every permutation except the *parterre de broderie* (**18**). Its forecourt has adapted to the
carriage with a carriage sweep; its bowling green beyond the canal has long-short
yew borders, then comes a very sober *parterre à l'Anglaise* with a fountain basin and
the usual exedra. Next comes a *parterre des compartiments*, so complex as to be almost
'*de broderie*'. This is a walled, terrace-flanked ladies' garden. Just across the canal is a

little herb garden and then the vegetables take over, with four big box-surrounded compartments, each centred on a complex roundel of clipped yews. The greenhouses and forcing beds stand next to them and up the hill, away from the valley frosts, reach orchards and yet more vegetable plots.

Siston Court, due east of Bristol (**11**), has a similar balance of ornament and utility with an enormous walled vegetable and fruit garden away from the house, and a notably curvaceous *parterre à l'Anglaise*, pretending manfully to be a *parterre de broderie*, close under the windows of the house. Toddington Manor near Broadway, and Rendcomb Park near Cirencester are exceptions to the reign of the leguminous. At Toddington (**12**) the Tracy owner may have urged Kip to ignore any utilitarian aspects of the grounds, to confine the orchard to the bottom corner of his plate and concentrate on a curious pattern of lawns. Some of these are laid out in strips, at least seven others are centred by statues with a fountain spouting tall and two long walks set with flowers in urns. That mysterious area of posts which could be a bean garden, a hop garden or a drying green features here again, close to the service block.

At first Rendcomb Park (**19**) looks to be a replica of Fairford Park, with yet another of those elegantly dull, post-Coleshill, houses of the Restoration. Its gardens have been laid out formally, but in an entirely different spirit to those at Fairford. Sir John Guise, who planted them out in the early 1680s, was no follower of Samuel Hartlib. Everything in the Kip engraving is ornamental, but ornamental in that thin *parterre à l'Anglaise* manner of patterned lawns, exedral, or semicircular-shaped ironwork, and long-short yews. The two canal basins below the Wilderness look impressive on the plate, but a walk along the grounds today suggests that they could have been no more than 6ft wide. A long straight ride has been cut up the hill through the Wilderness and Sir John has had the lesser rides and walks on either side of it made asymmetrical. It was in 1685, while Rendcomb's grounds were being laid out, that Sir William Temple published his *Upon the Gardens of Epicurus* with its famous discourse on 'Sharawadgi', the supposed Chinese art of designing gardens by an elusive principle of the asymmetrical.[4] This, Temple speculated, may have been artistically superior to the geometrical symmetries of the gardens which Europe had been creating in its post-Renaissance phase. Whether Sir John Guise had Temple's book in his Rendcomb library is not known, but the asymmetries of those ways through his Wilderness are strikingly deliberate.

These Kip-recorded layouts have left little trace. What is valuable about them is their witness to the truth of Sir Reginald Blomfield's claim, made in his influential *The Formal Garden in England* (1892), that 'The kitchen garden is not to be a dreary wilderness of vegetables, but should have its broad, trim paths, its borders of lavender or roses, its well or fountain, and even its arbours or "turrets of lattice fashion", as in the garden of pleasure'.[5] How far Edwardian gardeners took Blomfield's advice and phased the ornamental in with the utilitarian, in the Sandywell, Dumbleton fashion, will be discussed in a later chapter. But there is a temptation in modern gardens to underplay self-sufficiency. In garden books of the seventeenth century at least twice as much printed advice is devoted to the cultivation of vegetables, herbs and trees as it is to flowers. More than half of the average Gloucestershire Franco-Dutch gardens of this period were vegetable gardens; *dulce* and *utile* attractively linked.

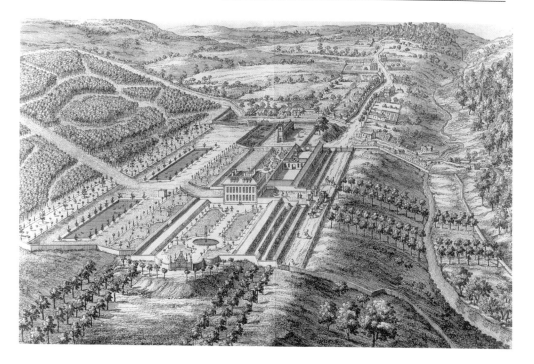

19   *The casual Wilderness walk on the hill above Rendcomb Manor may be an attempt at the quality of 'Sharawadgi' as described by Sir William Temple in 1685*

The grounds of Owlpen Manor (**colour plate 7**), north-east of Wotton-under-Edge, which were mentioned in the previous chapter as a late formal layout, were more *dulce* than *utile*. Thomas Daunt faced at Owlpen the same design problems of a steep hillside site that Sir John Guise had met at Rendcomb. Terracing was the solution and all his costs are recorded, showing how essentially local were the answers, not simply in the 'Acton stone for stepps', the peach, apricot and nectarine trees, but even in the formal hedging.[6] It was not for nothing that Gloucestershire had both a Box and a Boxwell. On 3 March 1721 Daunt wrote:

> Paid Thomas Jennings ye gardner 13 days work 19-6 – his journey to Bristol. Ditto paid him for 100 yds of box edging 16-8.
> Sept. 29 paid Tho. Jennings for work about making a lower platt.
> Ditto to Tho. Jennings for Box from Boxwell for edging . . . to labour about ye lower platt £1-5-6.

Box is three miles east of Owlpen over the hills and Boxwell is a village the same direction to the south. It sounds as if the box plants were being deliberately culti-vated and marketed, an industry which will have slumped badly in the next 20 years as a more relaxed garden style set in. Turfs, gravel and hill stone 'to lay under ye steps & pallasades' were all locally supplied to Owlpen, and the 'greens' that John Barnet had brought in on 3 March of the same year, 1721, could well have been those prodigious yews that would eventually make the garden both notorious and admired.

There remain the three formal gardens of the county which have left more than their images in Sir Robert Atkyns's book. Two of these, Badminton and Dyrham, were among the greatest gardens in England, but have retained only fragments from their seventeenth-century prime. The third, Westbury Court, was never more than a middling garden of the period; but it survived almost intact into the twentieth century to be restored after 1967 by the National Trust, not quite to its original state, but to something equally interesting: the condition which mid-twentieth-century garden experts believed a mid-twentieth-century paying public would expect a late seventeenth-century garden to look like.

There is no danger that seventeenth-century Badminton's grounds will ever be restored to the condition recorded in *Britannia Illustrata* and Atkyns's *Glostershire* (**20**). One of the honorific titles of an English duke is that of 'most high and puissant Prince', and the park at Badminton is more like a principality than anything else. Around that vast, generally ugly, but always fascinating house, an appropriate park has grown up. It is a level, ill-watered, curiously limestone-dusty landscape of trees that rarely grow to an impressive height. The first Duke of Beaufort and his wife Mary settled there almost by accident in the last years of the Commonwealth and simply stayed on. The Duke, who was only Lord Herbert at the time of their marriage, was the park creator, a man for ambitious boundaries and at one stage of his career Lord Lieutenant of four counties. His wife was the gardener, an intense, religious woman, the rich widow of Lord Beauchamp, given to melancholy, but able to work herself out of that condition by caring for plants. With her second husband she raised a family, founded a political dynasty and created at Badminton a garden legend, rivalling and often exceeding in range Queen Mary's collection of exotics at Hampton Court. After the first Duke's death she commissioned Leonard Knyff to make those topographical drawings of Badminton, later published in *Britannia Illustrata*, that record its amazing condition in 1701, explaining 'my chief aim is to show what a noble place my dear Lord has left'.[7]

By that time there were 60 avenues criss-crossing each other over the uneventful park. One set radiated out from the house, another from an arbitrary *rond-point* to the south-east. The curious complex has been interpreted as a representation of the Copernican universe, one point being the Earth, the other the Sun; which was which is a matter of opinion.[8] Most of the park's present features are of later eighteenth-century date, innovative, gently dilapidated and, like so much about Badminton, slightly eccentric. But a '*maison de plaisance*', Swangrove House, is of about 1703, the time of the first Duchess, and Walk Avenue, which runs some two and a half miles to the south-east, is still broken by that *rond-point* two-thirds of a mile from the house. Of the tight rectangle of garden compartments which Knyff drew to the east of the house nothing has survived.

The most remarkable feature of this was the Wilderness with its four quarters of geometrical mazes and hidden interior gardens. These had been shaped out of 'plashed' elms and ash, not yew. Plashing was when the trees, set usually 3ft apart and in rows 6ft across from each other, were 'shorn smooth to the top which is left as a tuff or a crown'.[9]

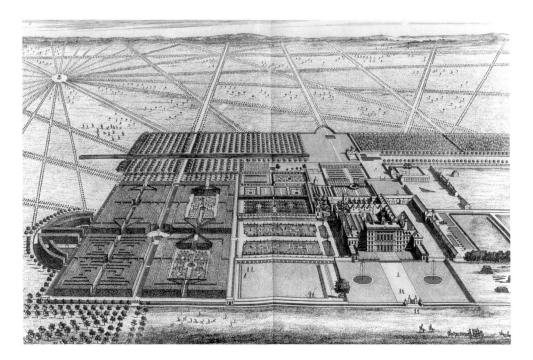

20 *Badminton House and the grounds as a statement of ducal territorial power. Two flower gardens have been carved out of the heart of the intensely geometrical Wilderness. Understandably William Kent failed to turn this ruthless layout into a humane Arcadia*

Cassandra Willoughby walked in the Badminton Wilderness, so it was no flattering invention of Knyff. She recorded it as being 'very fine, ye trees so large as to make it very shady: they are all Ash and Elm except the shrubs to thicken it in ye bottom . . . Ye earth is covered with a variety of plants and primroses, periwinkles, etc.'[10] How those shady trees and a ground cover of spring flowers can be accorded with the shaven tops and narrow alleyways of Knyff's plate is not clear. Perhaps the flowers grew in those two hidden interior gardens. Kip's version of the Wilderness in Atkyns's volume shows that since Knyff drew the mazes for *Britannia Illustrata* the two gardens had been hacked out of their cores, so there may have been some criticism of its neurotic excess.

The orchards at Badminton were simply fields planted with trees, there was no invention, and the two forecourt lawns were austere with a fountain in each lawn. It would be interesting to know if a hydraulics system on that dry plateau ever managed to make them spout to the height which Knyff and Kip both recorded. Behind the broad bowling green and skittle alley lay a sequence of seven or eight formal gardens, a very old-fashioned arrangement, surviving possibly from the earlier house, and there appear to be herb or even vegetable areas among the elaborate *parterres des compartiments*.

It was the orangery overlooking the third sequence back which was the real glory of the gardens and the Duchess' pride. She fought a fierce competitive war with Queen

Mary as to who should have the first collection of exotics from the Far East and the Caribbean. The 'orangeree', as she called it, was her 'stove' or greenhouse, 110ft long against a wall 18ft high. By copying a Dutch 'glass case', virtually a modern greenhouse, the Queen scored in the game as she did also with a cashew tree and her pineapples. But the Duchess was the first in England to grow the zonal *Pelargonium* and the North American sweet fern. Her 'stove', though not a 'glass case', still produced custard apples, bananas, aloes, cotton tree, Cape figs, guavas and cacti. Sir Hans Sloane, the Secretary of the Royal Society, reported: 'I never saw West India plants in such perfect condition out of their own climate as there'.[11] The Duchess 'had them brought to the Table fresh from the Tree and others ripened in Sugar'.[12] Not content with eating her exotics she paid the Dutch artist, Everard Kickius, to paint them and to train one of her underfootmen, Daniel Frankcom, to draw and record them.[13] She catalogued all her collection and personally pressed leaves and blooms in thick folders so that, as with her husband's avenues, there would be some permanent, semi-scientific, record of what she had achieved. 'I am busy with my dried plants', she wrote to Hans Sloane, 'if I had a good assistant I believe I could make a catalogue of 2000 plants, and very few common ones'.[14] But she was so naively undiscriminating that she pressed a leaf from an African honey tree on the same page as an ivy leaf that her son, the second Duke, had picked in the Badminton Wilderness. About the Duchess, as about the Badminton that the two Dutchmen recorded, there clings a distinct air of the first, or Caroline, half of the seventeenth century rather than of the second, Carolean, Franco-Dutch and scientific, half to which she really belonged.

Badminton was laid out with very little topographical help from Nature. Dyrham Park, on the other hand, was perhaps more topographically blessed than any other garden in England. Even today, when three-quarters of the landscape that William Blathwayt drove his head gardener, Thomas Hurnall, to create in that enchanted combe behind the twin-faced house, has gone, the dramatic lie of the land still carries those parts that remain with a rare magic. If the whole inspired complex of terraces, fountains, cascades, wilderness and basins had been preserved, Gloucestershire would have had a garden to set against Tivoli (**21**). For all Blathwayt's Dutch ties and his travels in the Netherlands with Edward Southwell in 1697, the garden he projected and achieved was more Italian than Franco-Dutch. The gardens of seventeenth-century France had their origins in Italy and, by transposing their features to the steep irregu-larities of the Cotswolds, Blathwayt inadvertently recaptured their Italian identity.

Dyrham House is a Janus with two distinct faces: a west front of 1692-6 by Samuel Hauduroy, with a *cour d'honneur* in very subdued Baroque style, and an east front by William Talman of 1698-1704, which stands uneasily tall. Nevertheless it still walls in the combe like a stage set by some competent designer with a good library of architectural books from which to draw for directions and details. This remarkable sandwich of a house (the two wings are almost completely separated by a long interior courtyard) is an indi-cation of Blathwayt's taste and character. John Evelyn considered him 'a very proper, handsome person, very dextrous in business', but from the tone of his letters to Hurnall, hugely impatient.[15] He swept up his heiress, Mary Wynter, married her in 1686, buried his father-in-law in 1689 and Mary in 1691, at which point he began impetuously

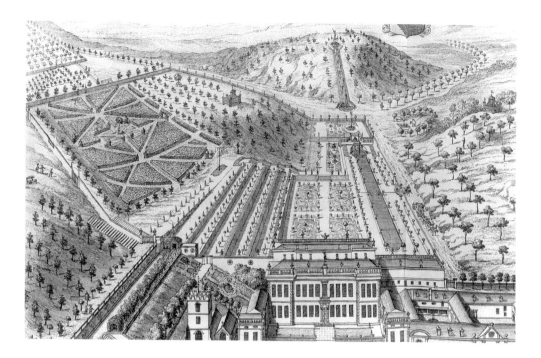

21   *Dyrham Park and England's lost Tivoli gardens as captured by Kip. Neptune on top of the hill is all that remains on the east side of the house of William Blathwayt's hyperactive Dutch-style garden imposed upon a steep English hillside*

rebuilding the old Tudor house to the designs of Hauduroy, a cheap architect. Then, and this is the extraordinary thing, after a mere two years interval to allow Hauduroy's building to settle, he chose another architect, Talman, and paid him to build a second house no more distinguished than the first and stylistically quite unrelated to it.

The gardens which Blathwayt then went on to create, fore and aft, east and west, of his house reflect something of this impetuosity and absence of informed taste. In their 1704–50 heyday Dyrham's grounds had everything: six terraces, a wilderness, cabinets by the dozen, two pavilions, a cascade of 224 steps, two cataracts, three canals, *parterres des compartiments* with *broderies*, Neptune inappropriately poised on a hill top, assorted statues, four or five fountains, one of them a riot of stone carving, four long beds of flowers in the west garden and even, alongside them, a lively looking vegetable patch.

Two factors rescued this collection of parts: Dyrham's topography of three steep hills with two deep valleys, and Dyrham's unfailing springs of water pouring out from the limestone above the house through even the dryest summers. George London advised Blathwayt on the design of the grounds, but Dyrham Park is not a typical George London garden. The terrain rather than the nurseryman was in control and it is significant that when Hurnall was buying seeds he went for them to James Fuller, 'att ye Orange Tree in ye Strand', not to London and Wise's Brompton Park nurseries in Kensington.[16] He bought Norway, Silver and Scotch fir cones, 'Phillirea or Allaturnus,

Piracantha and Yew berries, Juniper, Althea ffrutex, Spanish Broome, Dutch Savory, Pott Mariorum, ffrench Sorrell, Clary, English Thyme, Hysop, Chervill, Matted Pink, Sweet William and Red and White Valerian seeds', a notably conventional selection and not one which would have impressed the Duchess of Beaufort. Hurnall planted some trees that were mildly exotic, though not by Badminton standards: Virginia pine, sassafras, Virginia flowering oaks and tulip trees. But the pleached limes along the churchyard terrace are probably the only survivors of the original Blathwayt planting.

Today so much has been altered that a visitor is best advised to go along with the National Trust's flow of direction but with a copy of Kip's prodigious illustration in hand. In Blathwayt's time the approach to the house is supposed to have been from the west, which was sensational enough with the great Dutch fountain (lost now) splashing away on the right, niched walls and terraces rising dramatically on the left. That would have left the real stars of the garden to be viewed first from the windows of the principal rooms of Talman's east front, and then explored at leisure. Now, with inspired firmness, the National Trust has banished cars from the park and gardens, forbidden an approach from the west and made all visitors come down by bus from the east. This makes sense as a follower of Capability Brown, aided by neglect and decayed stonework, swept away everything from the eastern garden except Neptune, a statue by Claude David (**colour plate 8**) from whose feet the profuse springs originally poured, to tumble down the 224 steps and through three fountains before plunging under the orangery and feeding two cataracts in the east garden.

The bus trundles down the drive which Charles Harcourt Masters, a Bath surveyor, laid out in 1798-9 following the line of a Blathwayt avenue. Its sweeping curves are a perfect introduction to the breathtaking surprise view of Talman's façade rising across an idyllic green valley. It is, however, always open to visitors to walk the drive and that is the advised course for anyone reasonably energetic, as Dyrham's eastern landscape, even minus the waterworks, is one of the most satisfying in England. Kip does actually show a coach approaching by this route.

Down by the house it is possible, looking back to the east, to recreate Blathwayt's vision. The *parterres des compartiments* and the canal would have reached only the length of level ground. Up to the right there was woodland crowned by one of two curious matching arbours, both domed and turreted. Its north-east twin stood on the hill opposite. Blathwayt created these as rural studies where he could read quietly while enjoying the prospect and the sound of the cascade. He wrote on 8 July 1704:

> If Mr Oliver can shew how the Stand for Books in ye Arbors are to be made as at My Lord Fauconberg's I would have one made forthwith for that Seat Arbor which stands in ye corner of ye Wilderness to ye N.E. looking towards Bristoll.[17]

It was naturally on this south-facing slope that his garden features were concentrated. The Wilderness, unlike that at Rendcomb, was cut by straight walks in Union Jack patterns, not by wandering paths in casual asymmetry. This is a little surprising as Blathwayt had served Sir William Temple when he was ambassador at The Hague and he owned copies of Temple's *Gardens of Epicurus* and his 1704 *Oeuvres Posthumes.*

Apparently Sharawadgi was not a concept that appealed to his impatient nature. What was charming about his Dyrham Wilderness, however, was the scatter of 14 little cabinets, probably of wicker-work, placed on its walks to offer a seat to anyone tired by the steep climb. Was Blathwayt fat and breathless in old age, one wonders? Stephen Switzer, normally the advocate in his *Ichnographia* of more informal garden manners, was very taken by Blathwayt's Wilderness: 'I never in my whole Life did see so agreeable a Place for the Sublimest Studies, as this in the Summer, and there are small Desks erected in Seats for that Purpose'.[18] Was he referring to the two 'Arbors' or the 14 cabinets?

At the five terraces below the Wilderness invention flagged and the conventional punctuation of conical and round bushes set in, though the second terrace down did lead into a long shady arbour above the church. It is only when Westbury gardens are enjoyed, as the climax to this formal chapter, that a true appreciation of the detailed charm and variety actually poured out on such terraces and walls can be made. Kip offers detail but not scent or colour or the sound of falling water which, along with birdsong, must have filled this favoured valley.

One of the more unusual attractions of Dyrham is still this mysterious plash of water falling. It can be heard underground in the court that divides the two halves of the house, and at the extreme western wall of the garden there is a thick bush of rosemary covering an iron grating. There, if the branches are pushed aside, it is possible to look down a deep well and hear an unseen waterfall sounding away in the darkness. Apart from this unexpected garden pleasure the west grounds are only a shadow of what they were. The geometry of the lower basin or 'mill pond' has been softened, but the outline of a later fountain can be glimpsed deep down in the upper basin. One cataract splashes down its steps (**22**) while the Baroque retaining walls of the Hauduroy building period still support the impending slopes. It is all handsome but, unlike the east garden, it does not reach out to touch the Arcadian sublime.

Initially, after Dyrham, the garden at Westbury may come as an anticlimax. It lies low on the west side of the Severn in that river's sinister tidal phase. Westbury Court, the parent house, has been demolished, rebuilt and then demolished again to be replaced by an old people's home. The garden has survived it all, not so much mirac- ulously but because people have always recognised its quality, enjoying it through two *claire voies* from the main road (**colour plate 9**). Today, lovingly restored and gently distorted by the National Trust, it offers a truer insight into how a Franco-Dutch formal layout really worked than any other garden in England, the Privy Garden at Hampton Court included. A leisurely tour of its limited acreage, preferably in autumn when the original focus of its planting becomes most apparent, will make sense of all those other lost gardens in Kip's plates. In September its flowers are fading and its fruits are coming into their own as the Trust holds its Apple Days and sells the flavours and rough textures of the past.

Westbury's canals were built and its garden laid out by Maynard Colchester I and his nephew, Maynard Colchester II, between 1697 and 1715. Unusually there was a direct Dutch influence upon the design as the first Maynard Colchester was a friend of Catarina Boevey, the widowed owner of neighbouring Flaxley Abbey. She was Dutch born and had presided over the digging of that small canal in her own garden. Most of the work at Westbury was done and the shrubs in place by 1707. A Kip of

22   *Blathwayt's stepped cascade in the west garden at Dyrham ends in a once formal pool which Humphry Repton characteristically tried to make more natural*

that date shows one long straight canal and another with two arms. Between them they created a rectangular peninsula joined narrowly at two points to the 'mainland'. Later, around 1715, the nephew extended the second canal to create a T-shape, pulled down his uncle's twin pavilions at the end of the first canal, and built a classical gazebo overlooking on one side the road and on the other a walled garden for flowers, to counterbalance the previous emphasis upon fruit and vegetables.

Maynard Colchester II also pulled down the picturesque Tudor Court that Kip illustrates, replacing it with a Palladian house that lasted until 1805. For many years thereafter the garden was kept, like that at Owlpen, as a pleasure park for occasional visits. It was not until 1895 that the grounds came into their own once more when yew hedges and outdoor rooms had become the fashion again. A new house was built enclosing the Tall Pavilion. This too was demolished after 1960; the Trust coming to the rescue in 1967 in the proverbial 'nick of time'.

It is the Tall Pavilion which has always been the key to Westbury (**23**). From its upper room everything is visible; only that arm of the second canal which once lapped almost up to its walls has been lost. So this was not a garden for surprises, but for order, husbandry and produce. Modern visitors demand flowers, and they have them in abundance at the walled garden. The original accounts, kept in the County Record Office, and quoted extensively in the National Trust guidebook, tell an accurate story of the planting. On 20 April 1702:

> Pd. Coz. Colchester for 4 perimyd [pyramidal] hollys, 1 perimead yew, 6 lawrestinus headed, 6 headed phillereys, 3 perimyd phillereys, 2 headed honysuckles, 30 plain phillereys, 5 mizerian treas [Daphne], 12 tuberoses.[19]

23 *The Tall Pavilion, not Westbury Court, was the key and the focus to Westbury's gardens. From its upper room all the watery geometry of 1697-1715 makes visual sense*

The first emphasis is upon shape, that regiment of conical and round alternate bushes that people most of Kip's gardens. Then in October were planted

> 60 Cherries, 6 apricocks, 3 plumbs, 2 nectarines. [Next year in November:] 24 standard cheries, 30 Scotch firs, 4 sweet briars, 4 woodbines, 6 wall cherys, 4 plumbs, 4 apricocks, 2 wt. & 1 red sweet water grape, 6 peaches.[20]

Trees not flowers predominate; there had been '500 hollys & ews' bought in March 1698 to mark the bones of the garden, costing a mere 10 shillings. In November 1702 there was some floral leaven to this with: 'Pd. Coz. Colchester in full 1000 iris's, 100 crocas 50 jonquills, 50 hyacynths double, 50 double narcissus's, 50 anenomys, 50 ranunculus's, 150 tulips', but then, after this entirely spring directed list, came '1000 ews. £3:17:0'.[21]

These lists indicate, and Kip confirms, that the central near–island was a big vegetable garden surrounded by fruit trees and the usual ranked alternate round hollies and conical yews. When the National Trust has done so much at Westbury, a restoration to earn the gratitude of all garden lovers, it seems churlish to complain, but they have left the near-island a green lawn, walled by yew hedges. That was not how the Maynard Colchesters intended it. The great charm of the long walk down the main canal is its authentic planting with herbs, lad's love predominating, with espalliered Jacobean, Carolean and

24 *Where the Maynard Colchesters had their vegetable garden at Westbury, the National
Trust has left a plain expanse of lawn and planted alongside it, to satisfy twentieth-
century expectations, a prettified* parterre à l'Anglaise

Georgian fruit trees ranged against the warm brick, a festival of almost-lost tastes and
textures, vast Jargonelle pears and juicy Calville Rouge d'Hiver apples of about 1600. It
is a living fruit museum and a national treasure. So why not replant those plums and
cherries on the near-island, with rows upon rows of equally authentic onions, cabbages,
carrots and asparagus? To transfer, as the Trust has done, the lost *parterre à l'Anglaise* that
Kip records near the old house, to this north side of the garden was a mistake (**24**). The
design is not even accurate; Kip shows beds of sand in the lawn of a bowling alley with
conical yews in the centre of the sand.

The nephew's walled garden is an admirable show ground for period flowers, the
roses in particular offering a second museum or time trip, this one of scent. A
shapeless yellow rose, Céline Forestier Noisette, is most recommended. It is,
however, the conclusion which Westbury and the Trust's work offers to this chapter
that is most important. Sir Reginald Blomfield may have gone over the top in his
assault upon the garden pundits of the eighteenth century. He calls Horace Walpole's
quote on William Kent: 'Kent leapt the fence and saw that all nature was a garden'
a 'masterpiece in claptrap', Addison's arguments 'a fallacy', Pope 'the most artificial
of writers', Capability Brown and Humphry Repton the men 'who between them
irrevocably destroyed some of the finest gardens in England'.[22] But Blomfield had a
point and Westbury reinforces that point. It works, it excludes Nature and imposes
order, it is most enjoyable, productive, creative and, in its dark geometry and
reflecting waters, achieves one kind of beauty. That needs to be born in mind before
the supposed 'improvements' of subsequent chapters are considered.

4 Formal gardening in Arcadian decline

For anyone who loves gardens there has to be a heightened interest in and curiosity about a period of complete aesthetic change in the design of the grounds about a country house. At some point in the first 30 years of the eighteenth century there was such a shift, when formal lines of geometrical order phased out into an artful imitation, not of nature but of those Arcadian landscapes painted by Claude Lorrain and Nicholas Poussin. Either the garden dwindled and the park expanded, or the garden absorbed the park. It depends upon the point of view; and garden historians, fascinated by the implications of the change, will always be debating who initiated it, when, and around which influential houses. But there certainly was a new way of looking at how man could manipulate Nature and, most unusually in the history of European art, England was leading it, a clear 30 years ahead of the other nations of Western Europe.

It is, therefore, a reasonable matter of local pride that Gloucestershire, which throughout the seventeenth century had trailed dutifully behind court and national fashions, moved suddenly into the ranks of garden front runners with three parks on this intriguing cusp between the formal and the informal. All three can still be explored and argued over today: one only with difficulty and an eye for imaginative reconstruction, another with the help of its garden buildings and the hindrance of later planting, but the third miraculously surviving in the entirety of its great six mile axis, thanks to primogeniture and the estate passing down from one informed and caring father and son to another in succession.

The three, in no significant order, for this was a time when innovative ideas in garden and park design were treading on each others heels, were Charles Bridgeman's Lodge Park, at Sherborne in remote country on the Oxfordshire border, Sir John Vanbrugh's Kingsweston, in the Bristol suburbs, and Cirencester Park, which Allen Bathurst created to the west of that Cotswold capital with a little help and advice from the poet, Alexander Pope. Kingsweston will be taken first as it was, from any style-breaking perspective, more a failure than a success.

For those 12 years, 1710-22, when Vanbrugh was designing first the house and then the grounds at Kingsweston, he was personally in control and making the decisions, not confined, as at Castle Howard, by the interference of his patron Lord Carlisle, an experienced gardener, or Nicholas Hawksmoor, his assistant architect who actually built, after Vanbrugh's death, most of the grand garden buildings that Vanbrugh had proposed. From 1716 onwards Vanbrugh was designing garden temples for Lord Cobham at Stowe in Buckinghamshire; but there again the siting and the

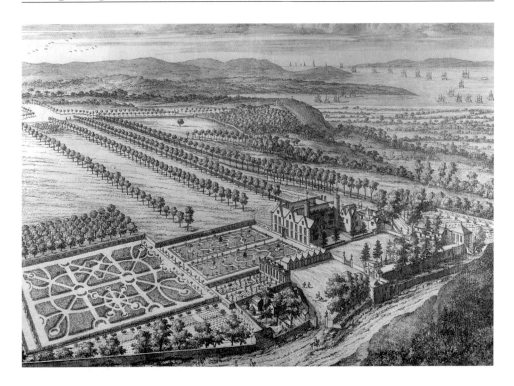

25   Kip's view of Kingsweston House illustrates the magnificent natural potential of the site and the formal layout which John Vanbrugh signally failed to revitalise. Penpole Point is just visible overlooking the river Avon and its shipping

planning of the grounds were to the direction of Lord Cobham and Charles Bridgeman. Vanbrugh was not in control, he simply designed temples as park markers at the end of Bridgeman's straight avenues. A convincingly Arcadian Stowe would not be groomed into existence until William Kent's planting and felling in the 1730s.

Vanbrugh had shown a fondness for odd, quite un-Arcadian structures: pyramids, a length of pseudo-medieval walls and, of course, that Grand Bridge at Blenheim, a Roman-style viaduct which Capability Brown would have to rescue from absurdity by creating a lake for it to span instead of a trivial brook. So, until he came to rebuild Kingsweston for Sir Edward Southwell, beginning perhaps as early as 1710, several years before his employment at Stowe, there is no evidence that Vanbrugh had any concept of informal gardening or any Claudeian visions of Arcadia. Lord Carlisle, had, however, created an informal woodland garden of wandering paths, statues and a temple in Wray Wood, next to the house at Castle Howard, which could well have impressed him.

Thanks, as usual, to John Kip, we know exactly what the house and grounds at Kingsweston looked like immediately before Vanbrugh got to work (**25**), and, thanks to an estate plan of 1720, what had happened to the grounds during the next ten Vanbrughian years. The Kip engraving is brilliantly clear: a large U-shaped Tudor house, bought by Sir Edward's father Sir Robert for its tremendous views out over hills,

26 An estate plan of
    Kingsweston drawn in
    1720 demonstrates the
    unimaginative conservatism
    of Vanbrugh's alterations to
    the gardens. Avenues have
    proliferated, but a
    wilderness after the style of
    Wray Wood at Castle
    Howard has been planted
    at Penpole

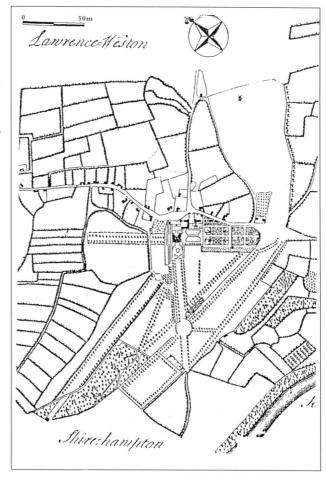

water, shipping and distant mountains, has a double avenue leading out south to an
exedra of trees at a junction of further avenues. Away to the south-west, beyond a wood
at Penpole Point, a gazebo looks out over estuaries and ships. To the east are two formal
parterres à l'Anglaise, a vegetable garden and an orangery with its own enclosure; to the
north is the real entrance court as opposed to the grand southern approach route up
the double avenue, which was obviously never used. At this northern entrance are
clustered a bowling or skittle alley with a viewing pavilion at one end and a banqueting
house at the other, stables and service ranges. To the west there is nothing but another
vegetable garden sloping downhill to that eye-catching view.

By 1720 the new house is in place and changes have been made in the grounds
for which Vanbrugh will have been responsible and on which it is reasonable to base
a judgement of his garden sophistication (**26**). From the west front a short new
avenue points down towards the great view. To the south-west a long avenue directs
the eye to the Penpole gazebo which Vanbrugh has either placed or is preparing to
replace with a handsome new gate lodge with a first-floor viewing room. A prelim-
inary sketch for this lodge has robust rustication on the ground floor and austere

Serlian windows to the upper room.[1] As built the lodge was given much plainer rectangular windows to light the prospect room, and on the 1720 estate map the little wood beside it has been turned into a wilderness feature, with paths and small clearings reminiscent of Lord Carlisle's Wray Wood at Castle Howard. It seems fair to label Penpole Lodge and the Wilderness as a move towards a more relaxed and templed Arcadia. Unfortunately in 1950 the lodge was demolished as unsafe by Bristol Municipal Charities.

There had been no change in 1720 to the double south avenue. Sketches, not actually in Vanbrugh's hand but copies made by a contemporary, survive and these prove that the architect was planning in February 1718 a heavy 'Great Court' to the south front, walled and guarded by a deep moat or 'fosse', and entered by a pyramid-crowned arch similar to his 1719 Pyramid Gate at Castle Howard.[2] Sir Edward replaced that scheme, building the retaining walls, but omitting the gateway and opting for a much simpler oval carriage sweep around a statue on a tall plinth. This south forecourt was recorded on a careful drawing of 1746 by James Stewart.[3] On the 1720 map the formal gardens before the east front have been little altered, but they have been extended by a further double parterre and an exedra of trees is being planted extending that axis to the park boundary where Vanbrugh's Echo will soon stand. A new double avenue connects this half planted exedra with a rond-point at the end of the south avenue. This multiplying of avenues is thoroughly old-fashioned and formal, unlike the planting at Penpole. The map is unclear at the north front where a courtyard of sorts seems to exist with a new building on the central axis from the north front; the loose boxes and orangery of the Tudor house have been retained.

It is here on the more chaotic north front of Kingsweston that so much of Vanbrugh's garden intentions have survived, presenting more problems than answers. Potential visitors should be both warned and encouraged that, at the time of writing, the house and its grounds are in an ideal state of benign neglect. The structures are in no danger, but weeds are running shoulder high around the Loggia, the paths are rough and most of the woodland is mature but densely undergrown and romantically picturesque. Visitors can wander at will but, though almost half a million Bristolians live within an eight mile radius and housing estates lap up to the park walls, the place is wonderfully deserted, atmospheric and enjoyable. A pleasant tea house exists in a vaulted Vanbrughian basement. In a word, Kingsweston is in its prime. Relish it before the heritage industry moves in as it has done at Dyrham, restoring, replanting, explaining, bussing and assiduously servicing.

On the way in from Shirehampton the rocks and the dark, brooding trees take over and the suburbs miraculously recede. A cottage range along the steep lane bears the marks of having been run up to Vanbrugh's casual sketches. Their massive keystones help to get the eye attuned to his architectural overkill of weighty lintels, blown-up eaves and general exaggeration of detail. Then a very short drive pitches the visitor into the stony drama, overgrown shrubs and problems of the north forecourt. Immediately on the right is Vanbrugh's Brewhouse, a little further on, half-seen amidst weeds, buddleia and elder bushes, is his Loggia. Lowering up on the left, like a workhouse in Gormenghast, is the north front, all stained stonework, planes and recessions. It is usual

27 *Vanbrugh in a mood of correct Palladianism – the Loggia at Kingsweston*

to complain that Robert Mylne, working here in 1763-8, wrecked Vanbrugh's first concept by bringing the central wall forward; but it would take an earthquake really to damage a Vanbrughian façade so powerfully over-expressed.

The problem here is that Vanbrugh failed to rethink his garden buildings radically enough. This was the old Tudor formal entrance court. He kept the courtyard but turned it into the servants' entrance to the house, a tradesmen's route to the kitchens with its architectural façades made grimly purposeful to convey their function. Yet he retained the old pleasure structures in what had now become the back yard of Kingsweston. A handsome Palladian front, avant-garde for 1718, was added to what had been the side elevation of the old brick banqueting pavilion (**27**).[4] Lastly, in a weird clash of styles, Vanbrugh built the Brewhouse in his own machicolated, round-arched version of a medievalism that existed only in his imagination.[5] The Brewhouse has, admittedly, a sullen charm, but why site a functional eclectic 'folly' in the back yard of a big house? And was it wise to make the Loggia face south along the side of the house into the level park, when one of the most dramatic views in the West Country lay out at right-angles to the west?[6]

From this problem area of garden opportunities missed, a walk around the house will reveal the potential of the grounds. That great Claudeian view to the west has in the twentieth century been defiled outrageously by the oil refineries, factories, docks, warehouses and railway sidings of Avonmouth, but it still has a perverse beauty. At Kingsweston the birdsong has always to compete with the muffled roar of a motorway, and a new drama lies in the park's strange isolation in the midst of over population; dog owners have the grounds largely to themselves.

On the south front Vanbrugh's magisterial parody of a Palladian façade remains intact, but all the avenues have gone. Instead there is a vast, empty meadow of rough grass fringed by an apparently impenetrable shelter belt of dark, mature trees. There remains the east or garden front. Far from lightening the mood on this side of the house, Vanbrugh devised another façade in that ogre's castle classicism which the English have come to accept as a kind of native Baroque. Both the south and the east fronts have a tremendous presence and would be star turns in Clementine Rome, but they could hardly have presided over a casual Arcadia of scattered trees and classical temples. They demand ordered vistas and Vanbrugh saw to it that they got them.

He extended this eastern arm, retaining and adding to the formal gardens and building the Echo, a serious three-arched garden house of deeply rusticated stone, its parapet topped by urns with grotesque masks.[7] This is the most hauntingly beautiful area of the gardens, largely because it is so decayed. The formal beds have gone to weeds and rubble. The easternmost extension of the original formal gardens is marked by giant spheres of gadrooned stone, half buried in the earth (**28**), and alongside are fluted stone pilasters clamped onto the wrecks of mid-twentieth century brick structures straggled over with brambles. The ball finials are identical to those shown as carriage drive markers on the Stewart drawing of the south entrance front, and the pilasters could well be survivors from the classical orangery which once commanded its own small formal garden.[8] As the ground rises the trees close in to form a high, green cathedral vault and at the top of the slope is the Echo, roofless and containing a broken altar to some unspecified god.[9] In July the foliage is so mature and dense that from the Echo the ogre's east front of the house is not visible. It is a perfect demonstration of the aesthetic paradox that nothing, not a ruined church or a ruined castle, is a romantic as a classical ruin. Greece and Rome in their decay are essentially romantic because order and perfection have been broken and that profoundly disturbs expectations. All this, however, is an accident of time, not an intention of Vanbrugh's. His siting of the Echo was sturdily reactionary and formal. He placed the building for order to face order, and for visitors to look back admiringly at his house of power. If he had sited it just a few yards further up the hill it would have commanded an inland vista to the east of the Avon as satisfying as that from Penpole Gate, but apparently he was not interested.[10]

28   *The East Walk at Kingsweston, unkempt and romantic. Gadrooned ball finials from Vanbrugh's layout can be seen in the foreground*

A postscript must be added to the 1720s landscape improvements at Kingsweston, one for which Vanbrugh may have been the inspiration, though the principal design for it is dated 1724, two years after his supposed departure. This is a site plan for a 'Project for Conger Hill' in the *Kings Weston Book of Drawings*.[11] There are four other related drawings for this mount, one a 'Plan for Longcombe Lodge on Congerhill', and three designs for garden pavilions.[12] The site plan is the most revealing in terms of sight lines and planting. Judging from the views commanded from the mount of the Avon, Cote, Leigh and 'Snead Park', it is apparent that the view-point was proposed for the eastern end of Penpole Wood where the 1720 map shows a circular clearing. At the bottom of the slope tall elms were to be planted, one between each of the seven sight lines. A walk, 12ft wide, spiralled up the mount to reach a 'Cabinet of Yew', 16ft in diameter, imitating the pattern of a nautilus shell and enclosed by a yew hedge 3ft high.

No trace of this spiral path remains, but contemporary plans, notably Rocque's 1736 survey of Burlington's grounds at Chiswick, suggest that such narrow footpaths, meandering through woodland between straight formal avenues, were common features. Batty Langley illustrates a selection in his 1728 *New Principles of Gardening* (**29**). On the wooded slope behind Hill Court, near Thornbury, one such corkscrew trail, known to the Jenner-Fust family as 'the Curly Wurly', still survives, winding interminably up to a lost viewing pavilion which commanded the Severn (**colour plate 10**). This very rare feature was, on the evidence of a plan drawn in 1728 by Thomas Warburton for Sir Francis Fust, laid out in the 1720s.[13]

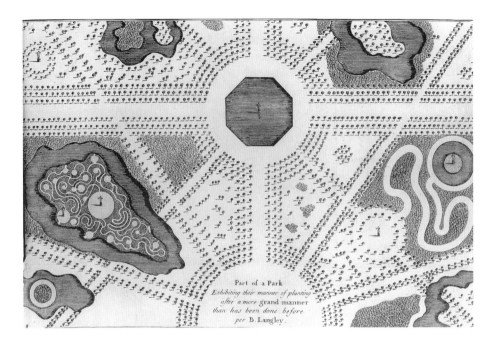

Part of a Park
Exhibiting their manner of planting
after a more grand manner
than has been done before
per B. Langley.

29   *A plate from Batty Langley's 1728* New Principles of Gardening *captures the indecision of that period between straight avenues of the old formalism and the frenetic wriggling paths of a new relaxed garden style*

Hill Court, illustrated on the back cover of this book, preserves this relic of undemanding garden walks for ladies, while Kingsweston still presents a richly enjoyable urban experience. But the park of the Sherborne Stand offers a seventeenth-century grandstand for greyhound racing and very little else. It has to be included here rather than in the previous chapter because, until 1725, there was no park, only the Stand and the race-track walls. However, John Dutton incomprehensibly decided that he needed a second park across the Cheltenham-Oxford road from Sherborne, his house down in the valley of the Windrush, so in 1729 he called in Charles Bridgeman, a prestigious name in park design.[14] Trained by George London, inspired by Lord Cobham and soon to be Royal Gardener, Bridgeman prepared a map of the New Park for Sherborne, which has recently been identified in the Bodleian Library and which represents an important advance in Bridgeman's garden planning (**30**).[15] The master of straight lines and regimented avenues has been more than half converted to the sinuous lines of the Rococo. Tree planting and dam building went on until 1743 when Dutton died. In that year everything stopped and the usual country pursuits resumed on the undramatic landscapes of the Cotswolds' gradual eastern slopes. Today it is just possible, with the eye of faith and a pair of wellingtons, to trace some outlines of the only 'untouched' Bridgeman park in the country. All his others have been altered or completely transformed, often by William Kent, so there is some academic interest in the dry bones of Bridgeman's Gloucestershire venture, laid out on that cusp

64

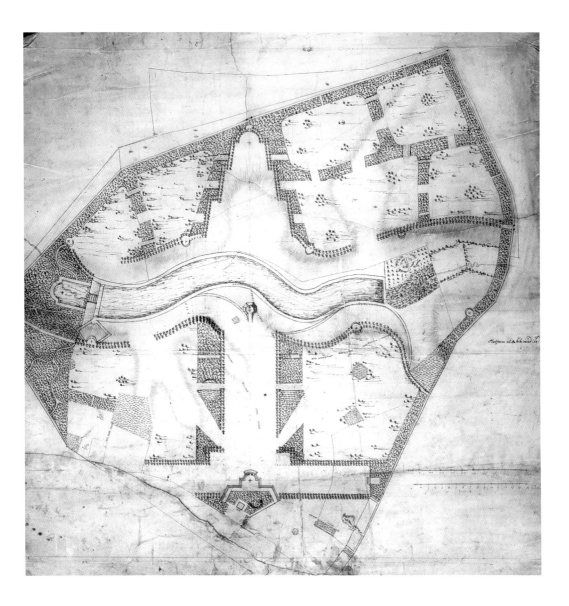

30 *Charles Bridgeman's plan for the New Park at Sherborne shows that a master of straight avenues was experimenting in 1729 with the serpentine lakes and paths of the Rococo. The Sherborne Stand at the bottom of the plan faces away from this new planting*

time of the late 1720s when informality was in the air. For that reason it is included here, but to be honest half an hour's study of that faded Bodleian map will be more rewarding than several hours tramping around a shallow, marshy valley with scattered woodlands that the National Trust may eventually turn into a revived Bridgeman park.

The Sherborne Stand itself is, on the other hand, worth quite a long car ride. It was for many years credited to Inigo Jones by authorities as informed and as close in time to Jones's client as Lord Burlington and Colen Campbell. Later experts have closed in and pointed out decorative details too naively vernacular to be by Jones, who was a London Welshman trained in Denmark, Italy and France. It remains an exceptionally confident, beautiful classical structure and one that can reasonably be described as a park building. Once seen it is a presence easily retained in the mind's eye: an almost royal building set in featureless countryside and reached down a dull, straight, mile-long side road.[16] Jones or some other top Court architect must have sent Sir John 'Crump' Dutton, John Dutton's father, a design somewhere around 1636, and local Cotswold masons would have realised it, adding their own bucolic, decorative touches.

Deer coursing was the seventeenth-century's version of modern greyhound racing with an electric hare. A deer functioned as an electric hare does today. Terriers set a frightened animal tearing away from a pen near the present main road. At a stated interval keepers would release the two greyhounds to chase the deer on a measured one mile course down the steadily narrowing funnel of the walled enclosure. The race would end by the Stand, which would be full of cheering spectators, who had been betting on the dogs, and there would be judges to decide which dog had been first to jump the winning ditch. In such meetings the aim was not usually for the deer to be caught and killed, but for it to pace the dogs. There would be several runs at any one meeting and the day would end with dinner and drinks in the splendidly appointed banqueting chamber on the first floor of the Stand.

Crump Dutton had been a congenial old soul who contrived to be on both sides in the Civil War and ended up on good terms with Oliver Cromwell. His sincere aim in building the Stand was to create a friendly, and no doubt practical, solidarity among the county gentry and to feast with them as often as possible. It was, in fact, a country sports club conducted in a very grand manner. His son's aim is more obscure. Could he have wanted to outpoint his popular father by creating an eighteenth-century version of a theme park? Deer coursing was becoming less fashionable in the eighteenth century so Bridgeman could have been called in to update a flagging institution, in which case it was a vision that failed.

Because this new park had no house, the Stand was the focus of Bridgeman's layout. A broad avenue led down behind it between square coppices. These were cut through to left and right by angled rides pointing down to the sites of statues on the ridge above a broad serpentine lake, which had been created in the shallow valley bottom by damming the little River Leach. On the opposite ridge a wide clearing, flanked by symmetrically receding woods, rose uphill to close the vista. All this was commanded, not by the Stand, but by a viewing bastion to its rear with a second smaller, raised platform on the bank of the serpentine. Further open spaces in the woods on this opposite side of the valley were set with clumps of trees planted at random.

This means that, at the end of a career of formal planting, Bridgeman was making two advances towards a more natural planting style. He had realised that the S-curves of the French Rococo could become the basis of a lighter, more feminine order and he has emphasised his serpentine's sinuousity by flanking it on each bank with serpentine double avenues of trees that open to occasional round clearings. Was Sherborne's serpentine the inspiration for the 1731 Serpentine in London's Hyde Park?[17] The dates suggest it could have been. His second modish innovation was one which is more usually attributed to William Kent: that of clumping trees to break up the harsh edge of a plantation line. At the south end of the lake he planted a small Wilderness around a formal building. So Bridgeman, who in 1725 had been laying out Spring Wood conventionally in rigidly straight lines at Hackwood, Hampshire for the third Duke of Bolton, in 1729 was being given a free experimental rein here in Gloucestershire by the second John Dutton.[18]

To move from this frail ghost of a landscape in the north-east of the county to Cirencester Park down in the south is a lesson in the importance of luck, longevity and primogeniture in a garden's life. Allen Bathurst was in his ninety-second year when he died.[19] He inherited wealth and the Oakley estate on the death in 1704 of his father, Sir Benjamin, a politician, faithful Tory and one-time Governor of the East India Company. In 1705 Allen was elected MP for Cirencester and in 1712 he was made a baron in order to create a Tory majority in the House of Lords to pass the Treaty of Utrecht. The death of Queen Anne in 1714 meant that his party would be out of office for 50 years; his political career was over so he could devote the rest of his life to his estates. Between 1715 and 1718 Cirencester House, on the western edge of Cirencester, was rebuilt to a notably bad design and from that time onwards has always been eclipsed by its park. In 1716 Lord Bathurst bought the Sapperton estate six miles away to the west and began to indulge in his real enthusiasm for silviculture with the extension of Oakley Grove, a wood halfway across his new, enlarged estate, and on the other side of the old Cirencester-Hampton road.

In 1718 he invited Alexander Pope, a fellow Tory and the most distinguished poet of the day, to stay with him. Bathurst was a generous, cheerful charmer, fond of dancing, hunting, wenching, wine and snuff, unpunctual and changeable but with a shrewd head for finance and investments. Pope was a dwarfish cripple, a Roman Catholic, a lifelong bachelor, emotional, witty, hugely learned, spiteful and over sensitive. He became Bathurst's devoted friend and advisor on park and garden visuals and to that task brought two innovatory perceptions. The first, implicit in much of his poetry but precisely formulated in a *Guardian* essay of 1713, was that 'the amiable Simplicity of unadorned Nature' could be superior to 'the nicer Scenes of Art'.[20] This suggested that formal geometrical garden design was in bad taste. Pope's second aesthetic leap was that,

> . . . twilight groves and dusky caves,
> Long-sounding aisles, and intermingled graves,[21]

– all the accompaniments, in fact, of Gothic melancholy – could be intellectually enjoyable.

It is not easy to understand how two men of such different natures were able to relate so well to each other and to form such an enduring relationship. Bathurst, to the end of his long and happy life, would persist in shaping his vast park by means of straight avenues – Pope's despised 'Nicer Scenes of art' – and Bathurst was anything but melancholy in his own personal disposition. Yet from their letters it is apparent that they were very close. After a time apart in 1735 Pope wrote to his friend:

> I dream of you still, & you are the object of all my Dotings; like an old Woman who loves the man that had her Maidenhead: You animated my Youth, my Lord, Comfort my age![22]

While Bathurst, following another period of separation, wrote threatening humorously,

> to send one of my wood-Carts & bring away your whole house & Gardens, & stick it in the midst of Oakly-wood where it will never be heard off any more, unless some of the Children find it out in Nutting-season & take possession of it thinking I have made it for them.[23]

It appears from their letters that when Pope made his visits, often several months in length, they did not stay, as might be expected, in the newly completed house with Lady Bathurst and the children, but with a house party bent on sports and gambling in a variously named 'bower', 'cottage' or 'Wood House' in the middle of Oakley Wood, a hunting lodge in all but name. As this was where Alfred's Hall, the earliest recorded Gothick garden building in the country, would go up between 1722 and 1732, Pope's letter of 8 October 1718 to the Blount sisters is worth quoting as it makes clear how such a lodge worked socially. It is sent from 'Oakley-Bower':

> I am with my Lord Bathurst, at my Bower, in whose Groves we had yesterday a dry walk of three hours. It is the place that of all others I fancy, & I am not yet out of humour with it, tho' I have had it some months . . . I write an hour or two every morning, then ride out a hunting upon the Downes, eat heartily, talk tender sentiments with Lord B. or draw Plans for Houses and Gardens, open Avenues, cut Glades, plant Firrs, contrive water-works, all very fine & beautiful in our own imagination. At nights we play Commerce, & play pretty high: I do more, I bett too, for I am really rich.[24]

Writing to Martha Blount, his lady friend, he could hardly mention the presence of whores, but Lord Bathurst was famously lecherous. When trying to persuade him out to his Twickenham villa in 1735 Pope shamelessly promised Bathurst he would find one or more of Pope's maidservants sexually available.

From the start the poet was bowled over by 'the finest wood in England'. In his first thank-you letter he declared 'To say a word in praise either of your Wood or You, would be alike impertinent, each being, in its kind, the finest thing that I know, & the most agreeable'.[25] He wrote to Robert Digby in July 1720 that he was lodged in 'one blissful Bower' in 'the Elysian Groves of *Cirencester*'.[26] To Lady Mary Wortley Montagu he enthused in 1721 about 'the noble Scenes, Openings, & Avenues of this immense Design at Cicester. No words, nor painting, nor poetry, (not even your own) can give the least Image proportionable to it.'[27]

These comments suggest that Bathurst's woods were already mature and his schemes to link Sapperton to Cirencester by six miles of avenues were well advanced. But in reality the two estates would not be properly united even when Bathurst died in 1775. At that date the road from Cirencester to Hampton still cut the Sapperton half, with Oakley Wood, off from the Cirencester half, with the Home Park. So Pope, arriving on the scene in 1718, would still have had time to influence the course of Bathurst's avenue planting. He had, by then, two much-praised poems to his credit, *Windsor Forest* (1713), which celebrates the beauty of mixed tree planting at the various seasons, and *Eloisa to Abelard* (1717), a true Gothic horror story of a brilliant scholar who was castrated by an enraged father for seducing his daughter, a nun. It was the fame of this last that may have persuaded Bathurst to write on 21 October 1723: 'I am resolved to begin the alteration of my wood house, and some little baubling works about it, which you shall direct as you will.'[28] He obviously considered Pope to be an authority on the Gothic ages. What happened next is infuriatingly unclear, but in July 1732, nine years later, he wrote to Pope: 'I long to see you excessively for I have almost finished my hermitage in the wood, and it is better than you can imagine.'[29] This hardly sounds as if Pope had had much of a hand in the design. Mrs Delany wrote in 1733 to Jonathan Swift, who had supposedly stayed in the earlier 'wood house' the night before it fell down: 'Lord Bathurst has greatly improved the house in the wood, which you may remember but as a cottage. It is now a venerable castle and has been taken by an antiquarian for one of King Arthur's.'[30]

Mrs Delany had got the story wrong. Bathurst had called it King Arthur's Castle as a joke. The 'antiquary' thought it was Saxon. Pope dreamed up the notion that this was where King Alfred, disguised as a minstrel, had spied on the Danish camp, hence the final name, Alfred's Hall. But why do no comments on it survive in Pope's letters? He absorbed fame and flattery like blotting paper yet on this important building there is silence. Bathurst may have devised it as a surprise for him, keeping the original 'cottage' or 'bower', which obviously had not fallen down, adding a round tower to either end, with some crude Gothick fenestration, then scattering ruined walls with random fragments of Tudor Sapperton Manor, Sir Robert Atkyns's family seat, which Bathurst had recently demolished (**2**).

Pope's role in launching Gothic garden buildings must remain in doubt, but a letter of 14 August 1736 proves that Bathurst really did consult him seriously about architectural detail.[31] He enclosed two plans for a pavilion, probably the Hexagon, to 'be backed with wood' and urged a visit from his friend for advice on the project ending, 'I have a most manifest want of you at this present juncture'. Cirencester House is such a lamentable building that critics tend to dismiss Bathurst as an architectural incompetent. They should walk up the great chestnut avenue from Cecily Hill in Cirencester and stand for a few minutes taking in the simple perfection of the Hexagon and its absolute rightness of proportion in relation to the mature arc of beech, yew, oak and chestnut behind it (**colour plate 11**). Bathurst designed this commenting: 'I think that rough stone [the rustication] exceedingly pretty', and the Hexagon represents garden architecture and garden design of the highest quality.[32]

Lord Bathurst's fortune was not only that he had, from 1716 to 1775, almost 60 years to follow through his first ambitious project for one vast park on a six mile axis, but that he had an open mind. He was able to see the relevance of his poet friend's 'amiable simplicity of unadorned nature' to his own old-fashioned fondness for disciplined lines of trees. He lived through three garden styles — the Franco-Dutch, the Arcadian and the Rococo — reacting wisely to each one. But behind his adaptations was the one vital commercial priority which has preserved Cirencester, not absolutely to Bathurst's exact form, but basically to his grand allocations of space. He always aimed to make a fat profit from the sale of timber and its processing, and that is what his descendants, in their admirable conservative common sense, have continued to do to the present day. Forest gardens, shrewdly run, can make money; Arcadias and Rococo layouts just lose it. Today 15 men work the park in teams with 12 motor saws, two loading tractors, two trucks and a transporter tractor. The 600 acres are thinned and tended and a proportion of the timber goes to a sawmill to make fencing. That explains the apparently miraculous survival of a great early eighteenth-century park into the twenty-first century under an eighth Earl Bathurst.

The clearest demonstration of how Pope's ideas eventually modified, but did not destroy, the strong avenue bones of Bathurst's park is afforded by the two maps, 'Home Park' (**31**) and 'Oakley Great Park' (**32**) in Samuel Rudder's *New History of Gloucestershire*, published in Cirencester in 1779, four years after their creator's death. Such is the conservatism of the estate's administration that the Rudder maps will serve, at least partially, for modern explorations. The one great change has been the sweeping away of the 'Rococo' belt of trees and paths in the bottom right of the Home Park map and their replacement by an awesome avenue of tall chestnuts centred upon Cirencester parish church, rather than on the inept façade of the house.

This map makes it clear that three straight avenues, meeting at a *rond-point* around the 1741 Queen Anne's Monument, have been destroyed by clumping, though their courses are still plain. Another avenue, which must have linked the Hexagon to Hartley's Temple (now lost), has received the same treatment, and a number of winding paths thread the woods around Pope's Seat (top right) and the Seven Rides. Near the house an entire Rococo layout of twining paths, a lake with natural shores, an ice house in a grove and the Horse Temple, has been laid over the earlier straight avenue. This was done around 1735 in Pope's lifetime; the Hexagon was one of its corner markers. On the other map, 'Oakley Great Park', the imprint of Pope's advice is seen in the way that natural valleys, Three Mile Bottom, Haines Ash Bottom and Lady Georgina's Drive together with a sinuous Rococo path threading through Alfred's Hall garden from Rough Hills meadow (lower left), to Park Pale near Park Corner (top right), have all been given paths to soften the ten straight rides that meet at Ten Rides. Today the two parks fuse reasonably convincingly together at the polo ground, near the Round Tower at the foot of the Oakley map. That is where the public road once ran, and even now the link-up is not perfect.

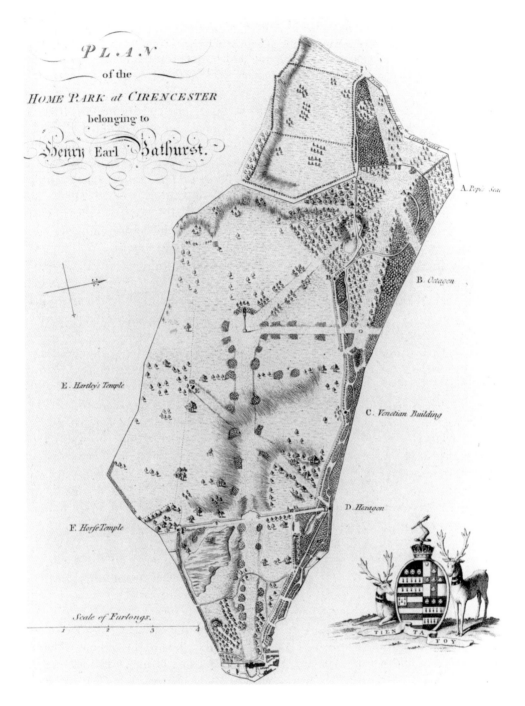

31   *Samuel Rudder's 1779 plan of the eastern half of Cirencester Park. Four avenues have been clumped in the Brownian spirit and a miniature Rococo garden created next to the house, but the Broad Walk has yet to link up with Oakley Great Park*

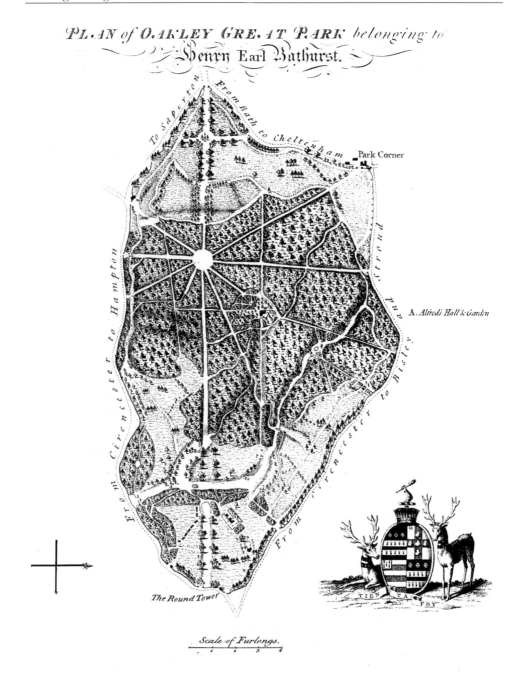

32 *Oakley Great Park from Rudder's 1779* New History of Gloucestershire. *The Cirencester-Hampton road still divides it from the Home Park. Numerous winding paths soften the grid of straight avenues and Alfred's Hall sits in a park within a park*

While there can be few pleasures in Gloucestershire to equal walking a park so evocative of Broceliande, that enchanted Breton forest of Arthurian legend, visitors should be warned that Cirencester is not a park to be absorbed and dismissed in a one or two hour visit; it deserves a full day. That six-mile length can easily expand into a 16 mile round tramp, with a very good chance of getting lost in the tangle of inviting alternative routes through Oakley Wood. Many visitors setting out to see Alfred's Hall have ended up elsewhere, tired and frustrated. There is a visitor's centre near the Ewe Pens and Earl Bathurst, with rare courtesy, invites visitors to walk the park free of charge from any of its normal entry points. The happiest six-mile solution, one that avoids the repetition of a round tour, would be to arrange to be dropped off or picked up at either Cecily Hill gate in the town or by the lodge where the Bath Ride meets the A419 near the point where the side road from Coates comes in.

Starting from this last point has the advantage of climaxing later in the day at Cecily Hill, a street of remarkable architectural richness and handy for Cirencester's tea shops. The Bath Ride climbs quite steeply to Ten Rides where the axial Broad Ride sweeps through eight lesser ways. Expect no distant views of house, or of Sapperton churchyard – the terrain is far too broken – but Cirencester church tower is just visible. It is rewarding, even in these times of political correctness, to sense Oakley as Pope and Bathurst experienced it: a hunting forest. On a recent visit I surprised two deer, one dappled, one smoothly fawn. For a moment the two surprisingly large and elegantly beautiful creatures looked at me, then made a show of not very frightened flight, bounding away down the sunny ride. They were eminently roastable and would have been a delight to chase on horseback with dogs, whether successfully or in vain. A fox is a mere excuse for a hunt, but because venison is delicious a deer hunt must have been far more satisfying and enjoyable as well as being, by modern standards, morally reprehensible.

Three rides enter Ten Rides from the north; the ride furthest to the right, but not the unmistakable Broad Ride, leads through lovely, half open, mixed woodland to what remains of Alfred's Hall. Originally this ride led into a rectangular formal garden enclosed within yew hedges. Now all its planting – yews, hollies and laurels – has grossly overgrown and entirely lost its geometry. The shrubs darken the light and frame, across another ride, the sad wreck of Alfred's Hall, its crumbling walls propped up by scaffolding and half smothered in bushes. A little coloured glass survives in the large traceried Gothic window, one high battlemented fragment still rears up above the tree line and over its Gothic entrance door the Bathurst crest and bold Gothic lettering of a later date still proclaims its name. Across an open glade the Wood House, older than the Hall and the scene of Bathurst's gambling and drinking parties which Pope enjoyed so much, still stands intact and inhabited, one of the loneliest houses in Gloucestershire.

Watercolours by Thomas Robins record how different it all was when Alfred's Hall was first built (**2**).[33] The Hall itself, an artless jumble of towers and castellations around a central dining room, stood within a pretty mock medieval enclosure entered through a gatehouse. Outside this was the formal garden and the forest trees stood respectfully back. There were no shadows or darkness; it was a place for picnics and games with just the excitement of exotic architecture.

After absorbing the present 'gloomth' and Bathurst's 'little baubling works' there is a choice of ways. A winding path south-east could, with luck, lead to the Horse Guards, one of Bathurst's jokes: two Ionic sentry boxes guarding the Broad Ride with naïve charm. Another route to the east ends in Rough Hills, a beautiful meadow in the woods one belt of trees away from Ivy Lodge, the polo ground and the more orderly half of the park. But this is the point where it is easy to get lost, a rare pleasure in urbanised Britain and one to be enjoyed.

When eventually Ivy Lodge is reached the spaces around the polo ground are not completely aesthetically satisfying. Bathurst, somewhere around 1736, when he appears to have been in funds, built Ivy Lodge, Square Tower and Round Tower as interesting events at the place where the two parks met. Individually each building has an attractive profile and a strong eclectic character, but they are too far apart and not large enough in scale to pull visually together across the broad green plain. Perhaps it was then, in 1736, that Bathurst appreciated the more miniature scale of architecture and planting of the Rococo and retreated to make his Rococo garden close up against the house. Rudder's map shows a clumped avenue running on the line of the Broad Walk, across the present polo ground, and that would have connected wood with wood as Pope's gratuitously sexual poem required:

> Here waving groves a chequer'd scene display,
> And part admit, and part exclude the day;
> As some coy nymph her lover's warm address
> Not quite indulges, nor can quite repress.
> There, interspersed in lawns and opening glades,
> Thin trees arise that shun each other's shades.[34]

Pope's Seat is easily missed because the *rond-point* of the Seven Rides which it was built to command has been destroyed by the polo ground. But it is still worth searching out, on the edge of the trees, a little pavilion with much of that vermiculated masonry that Bathurst enjoyed, and it has two seats rather than one. From the Round Tower onwards the way tends to be tiringly straight unless a side trip is made to Queen Anne's Monument, a 50ft Doric column in the middle of the old axis to the house. It was Bathurst's sincere tribute to the Stuarts who ennobled him as a baron; he would be 88 before the Hanoverians decided that he had worked his passage back to respectability and raised him to an English earldom. Back in 1715 he had, as a Jacobite, contributed £1,000 to the Old Pretender's war chest, but then few potent lords expected the Hanoverian dynasty to survive. When Bathurst died his son is said to have had a busy day burning incriminating documents.

Back on that glorious but interminable chestnut avenue there will be time to reflect that the Jacobite association explains why lords as affluent, influential and respected as the Bathursts were never raised, as were several lesser peers, to a dukedom. Certainly their park is ducal and the 'Duke of Cirencester' would have had a fine ring. The last pleasure of their park is the entrance to it from Cecily Hill. This has always been Cirencester's Mayfair and Park Lane, where the best families of the town have built their fine period houses to cluster respectfully close to the Bathursts. Here they could feel just one step down the social ladder, see Bathurst trees and if, as is likely, the family has always kept an open park, take exercise in its avenues and play tennis on its courts. Close to the gates like some defensive castle stands the North Gloucester Militia's Armoury and not one gate lodge but three, or is it four? Then the inevitable return to the twenty-first century.

5 Thomas Robins and Thomas Wright – Rococo rivals

There is only a very fine line, one more often drawn subjectively than objectively, between an Arcadian and a Rococo garden. Both terms are used to describe a distribution of ornamental buildings designed in eclectic, exotic styles across an area of grass, trees and, usually, water. The period of their joint popularity stretched roughly from 1720 to 1750 with extensive overlaps before and after. Arcadias feature classical or, as they were known at the time, 'Grecian' temples and pavilions. Rococo gardens featured the same but added a wider eclectic mix of Gothick, Chinese and Turkish imitation buildings, all intended to delight and surprise visitors while serving as places for their rest and refreshment during a tour of the grounds.[1] Most garden historians tend also to associate Rococo gardens with sinuous lines in the layout of their paths, streams and woodlands. The garden which Thomas Wright designed for the Duke of Beaufort at Badminton in 1750 is a prime example of this. It never advanced, however, any further than a plan on paper.

One authentically Rococo pleasure ground entirely shaped on sinuosities was laid out by Samuel Driver between 1759 and 1763 at Adlestrop Park, where James Leigh was extending his house in the Gothick style and must have thought that a garden with a Chinese bridge and a classical temple on a viewing mound would make an appropriately eclectic setting for the Gothick bows of his new façades. Unfortunately that obsessively curvaceous garden within its undulant ha-ha was swept away in 1799 by Humphry Repton. Driver's plan survives with its serpentine canal, irregular lake and wriggling paths, but what the plan does not convey is the intensity of James Leigh's flower and flowering shrub planting (**33**).[2] If the lists of his seed and plant purchases of 1762-3 are studied, Leigh's pleasure ground must have been an anticipation of the nineteenth-century Gardenesque style. Every one of those winding paths and curved shrubberies was bordered by colourful flower beds, and the shrubberies themselves were planted with exotics like 'Candle-Berried Myrtle', 'Catalpa', 'Carolina Guilder Rose' and 'Carolina Cluster Cherry', 'Maple Leav'd Tulip Tree', 'perfum'd Cherry' and 'Hydrange'.[3] As will be seen later in this chapter with Lord Botetourt's planting at Stoke Park, it was those introductions from the south-eastern seaboard of America and the Appalachians that were exciting mid-eighteenth-century English gardeners.

The flower beds at Adlestrop featured 22 different species of rose in addition to the usual 'cottage garden' faithfuls: 'Affricans marygolds, Hollyhocks various sorts, Double Larkspur, Sweet sented pease, Nasturtion, Love lies ableeding, blue Lupins major, Convolvulus minor, Candy Tuff, Stript Columbine'.[4] Trees tend to survive while flowers soon perish and are forgotten; but Adlestrop's flower lists, all ordered

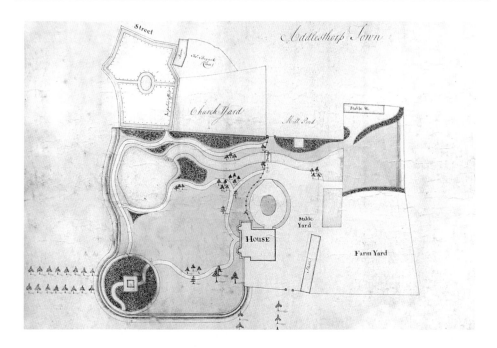

33   A Rococo garden layout prepared by Samuel Driver for Adlestrop Park in 1759 consists entirely of serpentine sinuosities. In the bottom left is a wooded mound with a garden temple. Only the Gothick front of the house survives

by James Leigh from Samuel Driver, are a reminder of how colourful and close to Victorian and twentieth-century suburban gardens some of these Rococo Arcadias must have been. The upkeep of this teeming floral pleasure ground, together with the regular production of 'all sorts of Kitchin Garden Stuff and Family phisical Herbs and also plenty of Melons & Cucumbers of the best sorts in their seasons', was entrusted by contract to William Bricknell. He was paid 'the sum of Thirty Eight pounds a year by quarterly payments' with 'Diet & Lodging', provided he 'demeen himself both within doors and without as a servant ought to do'.[5]

Fortunately a pleasure ground similar in style and acreage to that at Adlestrop, Benjamin Hyett's garden of 1744-8 in the little valley behind his house, Buenos Aires at Painswick, was realised and survives today, restored as a great garden pleasure. Painswick garden is always described as Rococo, yet has only one sinuously lined path in its whole circuit. Another defining feature of a Rococo garden has, therefore, to be suggested: that of a miniaturisation of features and the concentration of their composition within a smaller area than in an Arcadia.

The problem facing the second, third and fourth Dukes of Beaufort when they considered bringing their park at Badminton into a fashionable new landscape design was very much the same difficulty that was facing Allen Bathurst at Cirencester over the same period. Both their parks were so enormous that they responded uneasily to any treatment, sinuous Rococo miniaturisation or Arcadian cosmetics of trees,

34 *Dramatised by its transparencies, William Kent's 1745-50 Worcester Lodge at Badminton is a triumph of composite styles – Palladian set above Vanbrughian Baroque*

temples and lakes. Only long straight avenues gave much coherence to their vast acreage of the under-watered, high and dry Cotswolds.

Until her death in 1715 the dowager Duchess of the first Duke kept her husband's avenues intact as an act of dutiful piety, but she died just as the national mood in landscape was beginning to change radically. The naturalising of the vast park began under the third Duke who called in Charles Bridgeman, probably between 1729 and 1730, assisted by architects, including James Gibbs, to prepare a new landscape with garden buildings. A painting of the north front labelled Bridgeman's Design for Badminton shows the park before the house cleared of avenues, and the landscape enlivened with pairs of obelisks and domed temples in a symmetrical layout.[6] This may well have been a plan on canvas only, for after 1745, when the third Duke died, his brother brought in William Kent to rescue Badminton's dull terrain, probably not in person, but by supplying designs for garden buildings.[7] Most of these had been realised by 1750 and the fourth Duke proudly, but unwisely, commissioned Canaletto to record on canvas Kent's understandable failure.[8] For failure is what it undoubtedly was, despite the fact that Kent had produced for the Beauforts the finest garden building of his distinguished career to dramatise that plateau of thin limestone soil. This was the Worcester Lodge, a dining pavilion for the Duke poised nobly above a gate lodge with attendant pavilions under stubby pyramids, one of which housed the lodge keeper (34).[9] It can be seen, just, the merest silhouette, on the horizon of

Canaletto's painting, three miles distant from the parent house across a desolation of grass, undersized trees and a scatter of other Kentian classical buildings.[10] These last lie about a mile away in the middle distance, but are still rendered Lilliputian by the ridiculous scale of the park.

Did Canaletto ever get out to the Worcester Lodge, was he loaned a telescope to take in its amazing profile, or was he merely working from drawings of a building that was yet to be completed? He seems to have expressed his own despairing contempt for these English landscape values by including three coaches in the middle distance; the implication being that 18 horses and a major expedition would be needed before their Graces could eat in that remote, though gloriously elevated, dining room, on Kentian chairs and under a rich Kentian ceiling of the four seasons.

While Kent's drawings survive in the Badminton archives, all his buildings except Worcester Lodge have disappeared: the domed temple, a nine-arched bridge over an unconvincing lakelet and a second temple bridge of three arches. In addition to the classical structures which Kent proposed there is a charming sketch of a Gothick, ogival-arched seat in a copse.[11] So at least an element of the Rococo was intended for the otherwise Palladian Arcadia. The relative absence of trees is another puzzle, though a visitor today will still find Badminton under-planted and under-grown. As Horace Walpole wrote in another context, at Euston Hall, Suffolk, 'Clumps have their beauty, but in a great extent of country how trifling to scatter arbours, where you should spread forests.'[12] Allen Bathurst would have agreed. There has to be some question as to whether Kent ever visited the park. If he had surveyed the terrain he would surely have opted for larger buildings on the Worcester Lodge scale set among more loosely clumped plantations. As it is the formal avenues were retained with blocks of trees planted between them. A Kent sketch of the main lawn shows how he was designing to keep the arrangement, probably forced upon him by the fourth Duke, of the existing hunting avenues.[13]

The lesson of the Canaletto painting is that a lively topography of valleys and hills and a thoughtful disposition of temples is required for a successful Arcadian park; but at least Badminton can reward the casual traveller on the A433 to Didmarton with one of the most memorable park glimpses, not in England only, but in Europe. The Worcester Lodge is still absurdly underrated and underpraised. Considered simply as theatre it ranks with Gloucester cathedral tower and Tewkesbury Abbey nave among the highlights of the county. A bend in the road opens up a sudden wide arc of beech trees and there, recessed in the centre of it, is Kent's daring projection of normally horizontal classical units into verticality. Trained for nine years in Rome where the Baroque was reluctant to give way to the Rococo, he has ignored the Rococo completely, piling a tall Palladian pavilion upon a rusticated Baroque arch flanked by squat Vanbrughian pyramids. He then calmed the vertical surge of it all by a pediment, a low octagon and a shallow dome. It stands like some arrogant icon of the English class system. The lodge keeper and his family inhabit the pyramidal side pavilion on the left, with their cabbage patch and dahlia garden, while the Duke's dining chamber and viewing galleries rise unashamedly superior above them. The blind windows and niches of this upper stage throw the daring transparency of its central fenestration into paradoxical contrast, while internally those huge French windows leading out onto narrow balconies give the room a disturbingly vertiginous quality. It is interesting that Kent had to break away from his patron-friend Burlington to achieve his finest and surely least 'antique' classical building. He has virtually projected the conventional classical language, as understood in the eighteenth century into Post-Modernism, as that term was understood in the 1980s.

A striking example of the contemporary stylistic indecision between Palladian and Rococo was being built not a dozen miles away from Kent's Worcester Lodge. Down in the Severn Vale, at Frampton-on-Severn, Richard Clutterbuck, a lifelong bachelor and rich Bristol customs official of Frampton Court, was indulging himself in a garden orangery as impudently poetic as Kent's lodge was commandingly elegant (**35**). Both buildings have a fair claim to be considered as great architecture and, though neither can be precisely dated, there are indications that they were more or less contemporary, of the late 1740s.

In 1743 William Halfpenny had begun to transform Stouts Hill at Uley into a small but engagingly cheerful country house for the raffish bachelor, Timothy Gyde, with two delightful octagonal rooms set either side of an entrance hall lit by large ogee-headed Gothick windows of hexagonal glazing. Gyde went on to build a 'dancing hall' in nearby Lampern Wood and to construct a Gothick front for the Lye Farmhouse, visible from his drawing room windows, to turn it into an eye-catcher.[14] The Gydes and the Clutterbucks were both Cotswold clothier families, related by marriage. Frampton is only six miles away from Stouts Hill and it is likely that Richard Clutterbuck was impressed by the daring novelty of Rococo-Gothick Stouts Hill and employed Halfpenny to work the same magic for the long straight arm of a T-shaped canal in his Frampton garden, a Rococo-Gothick building in a strictly formal Baroque park layout.[15] Unencumbered by the claims of any existing building, Halfpenny, like Kent at Badminton, achieved his masterpiece. The Frampton Orangery sits, a vision of carefree symmetry, at the head of its reflecting canal. Two octagons face the water with a flight of steps for Clutterbuck to step down and bathe, or for Neptune and his nymphs to climb out and dine. Behind the first two octagons a smaller third one, containing the staircase, rises to pull the composition together. This essentially classical geometry is overwhelmed by the curvaceous ogees of the window heads, their Gothick shapes being England's tentative, insular approach to the true French Rococo. It is a stage set for Mozartian plotting, a perfect garden place for idle pleasure.

Halfpenny was originally a North Country joiner by trade, devoted to mathematics and the publisher of a number of light-hearted pattern books for fellow tradesmen. But here he has entirely ignored the harmonic proportions of window to wall space that made Palladian elevations so predictable. Instead he has taken plate 38 from Batty Langley's *Ancient Architecture, Restored and Improved* of 1741-2, and lavished the motif generously, its hexagonal glazing countering the graceful ogee curves, to produce a beautiful building that still trembles on the edge of the absurd. Despite his northern origins, Halfpenny was Bristol based and Bristol, an essentially brash, mercantile and industrial city, favoured the Rococo rather than the Palladian for its merchants' houses and Assembly Rooms. So there are signs that the Rococo was

35   *Roughly contemporary with the Worcester Lodge, William Halfpenny's Orangery at Frampton Court is an enchantingly poetic composition of the Rococo and the Gothick based upon classical octagons interlocked. Its canal is entirely formal*

emerging as the preferred style of the West Country middle classes while the aristocracy clung conservatively to the Palladian for their garden buildings. It is a matter of regret that when the fourth Duke of Beaufort was robbed of Kent's services by his death in 1748, he did not turn to employ Halfpenny, a far more positive architect than Thomas Wright, 'the Wizard of Durham'. But Wright had inveigled his way into the ducal service by 1748 and was to become, by the patronage first of the Duke and later of his widowed Duchess, the most influential figure in Gloucestershire garden design for the next 20 years.

Though he designed many buildings in his lifetime, Wright was never a mainstream architect in either the Palladian or the Rococo. He was primarily an astronomer and writer of popular science, a favourite of aristocrats who engaged him to lecture to their wives and children. A visit to Ireland in 1746-7 had given him a taste for druids and prehistory and then, probably on the recommendation of the Dukes of Kent and Portland, he began to make himself indispensable at Badminton, adding curiously indeterminate and style-less garden buildings in a vain attempt to fill its vacant acres. Castle Barn is his most memorable creation and stands in a farmyard looking as if it has arrived accidentally from some Hanseatic location on the Baltic. Massive square battlemented towers with round-arched openings flank the barn, its gable end crow-stepped and guarded by semicircular bastions. The low screen walls that link the towers to the barn have blind cruciform arrow slits with the remains of ochre limewash suggesting that the building was originally colourwashed ochre and white to act as an eyecatcher. Placed out of sight of both house and road it makes little contribution to the landscape commensurate with its size, though it may well have been visible from Swangrove. Wright's Ragged Castle, a small tower with a stair turret, is more conventional in design and makes a modestly effective park marker close to one of the few public roads that cross the park. Wright's rarest and most Rococo park building at Badminton, the Root House or Hermit's Cell, is, unfortunately, out of sight in a private area (**colour plate 13**). Despite its frail construction of branches, bark, roots and tree trunks it has been preserved because, in living memory, the Duke would entertain his guests sometimes by sending a servant to dress up in a cloak as the Hermit Urganda; thus affording an eighteenth-century Gothick frisson in the blasé twentieth century. A note by the Duchess describing an inscription, now lost, over the door of the Hermit's Cell, has been mistakenly thought to relate to a similar building, Bladud's Temple, which Wright constructed shortly afterwards at Stoke Park, Stoke Gifford, for Norborne Berkeley, the Duchess's brother.[16] The inscription was in Latin:

OBSCURUM VERBORUM UMBRAGE NOVORUM
URGANDA HIC CARMEN MAGICO DEMURMURAT ORE

The quotation from Ovid's *Metamorphosis*, Book 14, was 'English'd' by the Duchess:

Here Urganda in Woods dark & perplex'd
Inchantment Mutters with her magic voice.[17]

36 Thomas Wright's interpretation of the 'Savage Picturesque' was classicism in a bush surrounded by boulders. This illustration of 'the Abode of an antient Philosophical Druid', ornamented with honeysuckle and ivy, is taken from his 1755 Arbours

On the floor of the Cell, Wright had inscribed the famous words of Archimedes: *dos pon sto* – Give me somewhere to stand (and I can move the earth).[18] This last quotation came naturally from Wright with his scientific background, but the choice of a female hermit was distinctly perverse. The Cell's door resembles an agonised mouth.[19] What it needs today is a picturesque tangle of bushes around its ravaged walls. In 1755 and 1758 Wright published *Six Original Designs for Arbours* and *Six Original Designs for Grottos*. They were the first illustrations of their kind to show buildings in a natural setting of an undergrowth as contorted as the arbours and grottoes themselves (**36**). This indicates that the Hermit's Cell once had a leafy setting, not bare grass.

The design for what would have been the archetypal Rococo garden was offered to the Duke by Wright soon after he arrived at Badminton. It was never laid out and, for all his dextrous handling of the style on paper, Wright's work elsewhere in the county's gardens suggests that he preferred the Savage Picturesque of rocks, rough buildings and natural tree-scapes which would become fashionable in the 1770s. His Rococo garden plan is dated 1750, but by that time, in the north of the country, Benjamin Hyett, a rich Gloucester merchant, had already created an equally committed Rococo garden of eclectic buildings at Marybone House in the city's suburbs (**37**). It dates from at least as early as 1740 and, a few years later, probably

37   *The suburban Rococo garden at its wildest and most eclectic in Marybone House, Gloucester, painted by Thomas Robins in the late 1740s. A pagoda, possibly the earliest in the country, broods over wriggling paths, Gothick and classical mix in one pavilion and Gloucester's ships and chimneys provide the backdrop*

after 1744, Hyett had called an enchanting second Rococo garden into existence in a sheltered valley next to his country seat, Buenos Aires, now better known as Painswick House. Sadly the Marybone garden has left no trace on the ground, though its exotic terrain was recorded faithfully by Thomas Robins, the 'Limner of Bath'. Robins was a committed Rococo artist who may also have served as the designer to several of the gardens which he painted. His speciality in a painting was a symbolic bird, flower or animal border in the true Rococo profusion.[20]

In its prime the grounds of Marybone House must have been the talking point of polite Gloucester. From right to left in the Robins gouache, their space of perhaps six acres, heavily compartmentalised by walls, includes, below the house, a four-bay Gothick pavilion with classical side arcades, lawns and parterres from his grandfather's original seventeenth-century garden, a massive and genuinely medieval hall, which was a relic of Gloucester castle, a second garden house or lodge, and then, as its climax, a splendid four-storey pagoda towering over an axial path and a wooded garden of wriggling paths and secluded glades. Visitors throng the garden and children play at fencing games on a little plateau. The place brims with popular life and Robins's rampageous Rococo cartouche sets the tone of it all.

Hyett's Marybone garden will have inspired another essay in this cheerfully absurd suburban Rococo. Between 1749 and 1757 Dr Charles Grevile was enlivening the

12 separate enclosures of the Gloucester garden behind his house at 2 Barton Street with a remarkable collection of incidents.[21] There were topiary seats with mock classical pediments, pergolas with heraldic arches, a niche for a naked nymph, topped by a rose window and flanked by urns and, as a climax, a feature which, on 14 September 1757, captured Robins's attention. This was a tall obelisk 'inlaid with old broken china' and poised precariously upon ogee Gothick arches, the entire nonsensical structure set high on a garden mound planted with shrubs. Essential to this episode of the Rococo 'Gardenesque' was a mockery of styles, a deliberate flaunting of a classical obelisk by Gothick arches. But why the broken china?

The principal aim of a true Rococo layout was to divert, amuse and surprise any visitor with tightly packed events. Rough rocks and shellwork, the 'rocaille' and 'coquille' that would give the style its name, 'Rococo', in the nineteenth century, were secondary to Hyett but primary to Robins. The visions captured by Thomas Robins at Marybone and Barton Street are frustrating because neither survives, but there is still, by serendipitous chance and the determined restoration work of Lord and Lady Dickinson, Paul Moir and their committee, an opportunity to enjoy it all in Hyett's second garden at Painswick (**38**). As late as 1945 many of the features recorded by Robins in that hollow of the wooded Cotswold edge had been preserved by Hyett's conservative descendants. Five gardeners were still needed for just those eight acres as late as 1965, which may explain why so few Rococo layouts have endured the centuries.

What perhaps not all the visitors to Painswick Rococo Garden appreciate is that Benjamin Hyett did not intend this private, hidden valley to be so much a garden of Eden, as a place for gentlemanly revelries, presided over by the goat god Pan, whose statue by Jan Van Nost stood above the Cold Bath.[22] Timothy Gyde was a notoriously profligate bachelor, Richard Clutterbuck was another bachelor, Thomas Wright never married, though he had, late in life, an illegitimate child. Hyett was a member of a local drinking club and built for it, on the other side of Painswick valley, a club house, Pan's Lodge, hidden in woodland, a bizarre mix, like that pavilion at Marybone, of Gothick and classical motifs. Robins painted it for Hyett, adding a staffage of drunken nymphs and satyrs carousing around the figure of Pan.[23] So the question has at least to be asked, if not confidently answered, whether the mood of a Rococo garden in the middle years of the century may have had a particular appeal to bourgeois men of a free-wheeling sexual disposition. With that in mind visitors will be able to make their own interpretation of the Rococo circuit at Painswick.[24]

On first entry through the Melon Ground it seems that there can be no possibility of surprise. An entire circuit of paths, little temples, seats and groves is laid out in the fold of land below. Daringly, but authentic to Robins, the restorers have even planted a substantial diamond-shaped kitchen garden to make the centre of the garden homely and functional. A path up to the right leads to a pretty Gothick summerhouse with two façades, one topped by an ogee gable, the other with a jaunty concave Chinese roofline (**39**). The Red House, as its name suggests, is brightly painted, as were most Rococo garden buildings. It looks as if one wing of an original

*38 Benjamin Hyett crammed at least fifteen eclectic structures into this small fold of land
behind his house, Buenos Aires, at Painswick. Rococo in its frame, cartouche and spirit,
the 1748 painting by Robins contains, nevertheless, only one serpentine path*

tripartite structure has been lopped off, giving it that Rococo element of surprise.
However, it was built with only two façades and these are cleverly contrived to face
down two separate alleys: one commands the central axis, the other the perimeter
walk. There follows a a wriggling path through shrubberies, the only example in the
garden, down to a restored Gothick Exedra, a semicircular structure, backed by the
handsome grove of mature beech trees which dominates the garden. A side turning
to the right here leads to a modern maze. The main perimeter path leads down by
the Doric seat to that Cold Bath for Hyett's supposed naked revelry. The statue of
Pan, being valuable, has been moved inside, where it must create a sinisterly powerful
presence (**colour plate 12**). When first placed in the garden Pan was consciously
sited so that he could command every ornamental building and area in the open
section of the valley.

Now an entire hidden and wooded half of the grounds closes in. The Pergola
alongside the lake gives on to wooded glades where the Hermitage once stood near

39   *The Red House, visible on the extreme right of the Robins painting of Painswick Rococo Garden, proves that with the Gothick style at their disposal the English could afford to ignore the French Rococo*

a small cascade, surrounded in early spring by snowdrops. The whole area was once threaded with a tangle of dark paths prefiguring Wright's later designs for the woods at Cleve Hill and Stoke Park. Running parallel to this shady area was the Elm Walk, now replanted with beech, ending in a Gothick-arched stone screen. Up to the left is the path to the Pigeon House, next to which Robins drew himself in 1748 on the 'Buenos Aires' painting, sketching the landscape. The Pigeon House may well date

40   *Coerced, presumably by his patron, Benjamin Hyett, Robins has included Pan worship and an orgy in the bottom right of his 1757 painting of Pan's Lodge, a stylistic confusion of buildings for private revelry in the woods above Painswick*

from Charles Hyett's ownership (he died in 1738 when Benjamin inherited), but its floor has a six-pointed star pattern of possibly arcane significance. The Robins painting shows its porch which has since been removed and sited to overlook the kitchen garden as the Doric Seat. Now the circuit leads back along the Elm Walk, past the lake and the bowling green and then climbs up right to the Eagle House, restored from a Robins painting entitled the 'Gothick Pavillion'. Its Gothick hexagonal room for alfresco meals stands above a Gothick grotto alcove flanked by classical niches. These vantage points gave three separate sight lines across the valley: one obliquely left to the Hermitage, another obliquely right to the Exedra and the last centred on Pan at the Cold Bath. The house itself does not command any views of the garden or whatever went on in it: a topographical feature which Benjamin Hyett may well have considered a plus.

That then is the celebrated Rococo Garden of Painswick, a delightful toy of miniature vistas, but for what games was it constructed? It is no use searching out the woods east of Painswick (or 'Pans-wyke' as Robins liked to record it on his cartouches) for relics of Hyett's Pan's Lodge (**40**). A flowering of periwinkles in spring is the only trace of his den for more serious drinking and riotous escapades. But, in addition to the two painted views, Robins made a detailed sketch of it, showing two sizeable Gothick chambers, one on either side of a classical porch leading down by flights of steps to a semi-circular bastion garden crowded with chairs and defended with two small cannon. It even had a keeper's cottage to the rear. 'Pan Deus Arcadiae' Robins wrote beneath his drawing, and it is hardly surprising that, educated in little else but the classical authors and living in classical houses, these eighteenth-century gentlemen took the classical gods as seriously as the Christian, and patterned their moral conduct on Homer, Horace, Lucretius and Juvenal as much as on the Gospels. Naturally, therefore, their landscape aim, using eclectic buildings, was to create a classical 'Arcadia'.

Waterworks do not feature prominently in any of Hyett's gardens. The limestone Cotswolds are notably dry hills and Allen Bathurst had trouble gathering enough springs together to feed his small lake at Cirencester. Prince Frederick, the only real royal patron of Rococo garden styles, was, however, particularly fond of boating. William Kent's superb state barge, designed for the Prince's progress along the Thames, is a proof of this. So any park owner hoping to entertain the future king would try to provide a light-hearted nautical experience. The poet and wit Richard Owen Cambridge lived between 1741 and 1748 at Whitminster down in the wet lands of the Vale, and in that short period not only landscaped his flat park, creating a canal, but acquired a Venetian gondola or decorated boat. When Prince Frederick made his Gloucestershire visit he was treated to a Venetian ride down the Whitminster canal with musical accompaniment.

This could have inspired Robert Tracy of Stanway Manor in the north of the county to dig the most dysfunctional and implausible of canals as part of the death-centred Rococo garden which he had achieved by 1750. That was just one year before Prince Frederick died, blighting the ambitions of a host of Rococo-philes nation-wide. Whitminster's canal has vanished, but the garden at Stanway has recently been restored

41   *Thomas Wright put this plan for a Rococo garden at Badminton to the 4th Duke of Beaufort in 1750: an intensely artificial compression of apparently natural woods and streams. Above it are drawings of the intended garden buildings; the garden was never carried out*

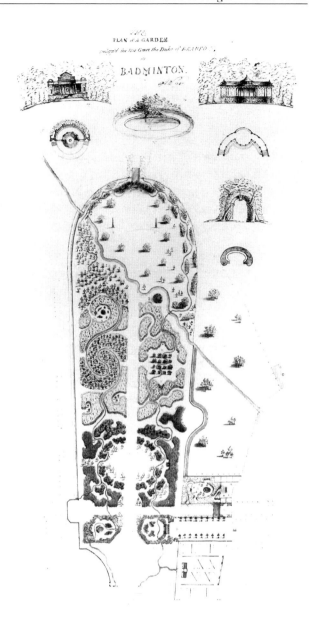

with its canal and is now open for inspection. The garden is centred on a sharp, elegant pyramid, the conventional eighteenth-century symbol of respectful mourning, but placed upon an equally elegant belvedere or garden pavilion of channelled rustication containing an octagonal room overlooking wide views of the Malverns. From a reservoir immediately behind this landmark the cascade flows under the belvedere for 200 yards down the hill to the canal which is dug laterally along the contour line. A 1748 painting in the house by William Taylor shows a rowing boat proceeding along this elevated waterway, so it was conceived as a canal with a view and is said to have included a statue to Neptune.[25] A Latin inscription over the west arch of the belvedere records that it was built in 1750 as a tribute to the memory of Robert Tracy's father, John; the Rococo mood brought cheerfulness even to mourning.

Down in the south of the county Thomas Wright was striking up a close relationship with yet another bachelor and Rococo gardener. This was Norborne Berkeley, the brother of the reigning Duchess of Beaufort and an engaging eccentric who managed, by the end of his life, to revive a lapsed medieval title in his own favour and become, not only Lord Botetourt, but a Governor of Virginia. He was so fond of Wright that he gave him his own apartment in Stoke Gifford House and left him an annuity of £100 in his will.[26]

Time can allot very different fates to gardens. Painswick lies intact, quiet and private. The grounds of Stoke Gifford, on which Wright spent so much time and Berkeley so much money, have been slashed through by a motorway. The faintly ugly 'King James Gothick' battlements which Wright added to the house are familiar every day to thousands driving in and out of Bristol.[27] Something of Wright's garden survives up there in the scrubby woodlands that cloak the hill, but an analysis of that rejected garden which he designed for the fourth Duke is needed to make sense out of those confused remains.

The Beaufort garden plan indicates that Wright's ideal was a central axial way cut through quite dense woodland to a final exedral-ended clearing (**41**). The woods on each side of that central spine should be threaded by devious winding streams and equally devious winding paths opening out to little clearings among the trees. For these 'Sylvan Saloons' Wright proposed a whole gamut of eclectic park buildings. There was to be an 'Orangerie with a double front', a 'Chinees Temple', which he illustrated, 'wing'd with umbrellos to shade the Auricula and other curious kinds of flowers', an 'open Temple of the Dorick Order dedicated to Hercules or Manly Fortune', 'Egyptian Obelisks' and a 'Rosarie' with 'a small Gothic Temple open and facing it on three sides'. Scattered about the woods were areas where the trees and shrubs themselves created events: 'an Evergreen plantation forming a Grand Area in the Centre', a 'variegated Thicket' and a 'Talisman or Magical Grove formed of Scarlet and Evergreen Oaks'. A 'Kitchen Garden', 'Apiary' and 'Menagerie' brought in a domestic element where the Duchess could play at an idealised peasant life.

The fourth Duke died in 1756 and the Beauforts were never among the hyper-rich aristocracy, so that particular plan got nowhere. But a simplified form of it with central axis, an exedral conclusion dramatised by an apsidal-ended orangery with a Roman Doric façade, and winding ways through the flanking woodlands was laid down by Wright at Cleve Hill House for Charles Bragge, a close neighbour and friend of Norborne Berkeley.[28] A few surviving fragments of it can be searched out among the villas of suburban Bristol at Downend.[29] The south lodge to the house, a cruciform thatched cottage at the corner of Downend Road and Croomes Hill, has been attributed to Wright in the past, but is now proven to be of Regency date.[30]

The similarities between Wright's proposed garden for Badminton and what he and Norborne Berkeley created together at Stoke Park are less obvious, but still exist.

42 *Stoke Park, the house Thomas Wright was soon to transform into a Jacobean-Gothick-style castle for his friend Lord Botetourt, overlooks the hillside where most of Wright's garden buildings were sited. Gentry pose as Arcadian peasants in the foreground*

At Stoke there were already two mature woods separated by a long, narrow clearing or axial way, Lawn Wood on the east, now called Hermitage Wood, and Great Wood, now Long Wood, to the west. Before Wright's arrival in 1749 Berkeley had already been underplanting these and Barn Wood on the ridge above the house with mountain ash and laburnum (**42**). Wright immediately began to create a complex system of winding 'Wood Walks' opening out into clearings, which he called 'Saloons' and furnished with seats. Apparently his favoured garden was the exact opposite of one with views out into the landscape, such as Kent designed. Wright wanted privacy where flowers and blossom could be enjoyed among enclosing shrubs. It was typical of him that he contrived a tunnel under the central axial way, to link the two woods together by a dark route out of the public eye. This charming absurdity survives today, a little threadbare, but with traces on one of its entrances of alternate vermiculated rustication.

Woodland gardens, by their nature of encroaching shade and grudging soil, have a short life, but Mark Laird, in his brilliant study *The Flowering of the Landscape Garden*, has used Berkeley's notebooks in the Badminton archives to describe, not only how these 'Wood Walks' must have looked, but also how they smelt.[31] With Wright's fondness for shades and Norborne Berkeley's wide knowledge of the flora of

America, in particular of the flowering shrubs and trees of the south-eastern seabord, these paths must for a few brief years have been coaxed into exotic colour and scent, forerunners of the American Garden which William Beckford would create at Fonthill in Wiltshire and of a thousand Victorian shrubberies.

A bill of 6 April 1751 records the purchase of strawberry trees, double almonds, sumac, Spanish broom and woodbine. The scented witch hazel, 'Oleaster', snowdrop tree, dogwood, sweet gum, sassafras, white and black walnut were all tried out in the woods of Stoke, though only the inevitable laurel, yew, holly and box have survived. Planted on the verges of the paths and in beds of the 'Saloons' was a wealth of flowers: 'Aster tripolyi', 'Yellow Thorn', 'White Laylock', 'Red Garden valerian', and 'Double Blossoming Bramble' with 'Bloody wall flowers'. All were given a chance to flourish, and in 1753 'Ever-green Rose', 'Double Sun Flower', 'Double Soapwort', 'Virginia Rose' and 'Double Fumatory' were added. George Mason, writing in 1795, recalled that 22 separate species of rose were planted in Barn Wood.[32] He added that Wright's management of them 'gave me, more than anything I had seen, an idea of what might be done by the internal arrangement of a wood'.[33]

When Mason rated Thomas Wright as the most important landscape gardener to work in the interval between William Kent and Capability Brown he was either joking or testing out his readers' awareness; there was no interval between Kent and Brown as they worked consecutively at Stowe. But, to be fair, Wright was creating a shift in garden fashions in those three woods at Stoke Park. At Barn Wood he was following the lead set back in the first ten years of the century at Wray Wood, Castle Howard. In a 'Saloon of Oaks', reached by five wandering paths, grassed over and planted with flower beds, he had a ten columned Ionic temple built. A little to the east in the same wood he created a stone walled reservoir from which a sluice could release a torrent of water to fall down a 30 yard tunnel and spill out in a brief cascade on the edge of the wood. The wreck of this waterwork can still be traced; possibly it could be revived.[34]

Lawn, or Hermitage, Wood was more Wrightian and innovative. Its 'Great Saloon' led into a smaller 'Wood House Saloon' where the trilobal Bladud's Temple was built instead of the usual hermitage.[35] John Wood the Elder of Bath had recently, in 1742, published his *Essay towards a Description of Bath* praising the role of King Bladud, the legendary father of King Lear, in discovering the healing qualities of the hot springs of Bath. Norborne Berkeley seems to have intended the monuments of his park at Stoke to be elegiac and solemn, not 'follies' in his usual wildly playful spirit, but more a reflection of the nation's heroes. Near the cascade a memorial, still intact, to the fourth Duke, Berkeley's brother-in-law, was set up.[36] Out on the hillside behind the Duchess's Pond an extraordinary monument of four obelisks was constructed, 'a model of ye Monument of ye Horatii at Albano', so Bishop Pococke noted on his visit of 1764, 'on ye Frieze round ye four sides is this Inscription, Memoria Virtutis Heroicae *S.P.Q.R.*'[37] Heroic virtue would have been a theme dear to Berkeley's heart. Not only was he an officer in the local militia, but on one occasion he virtually stowed away on a boat carrying troops to the siege of St Malo in order to get professional experience of war.

A third elegiac monument survives only as a blasted stump of stone. This was a star-topped obelisk to the memory of his sister's second child, Elizabeth, who died in 1750. It is possible that, in setting up these monuments high on the ridge above the open ground of the park and the Duchess Pond, Wright was compensating for the darkness of his 'Wood Walks' with a landscape in the new manner of Capability Brown. The motorway has devastated it, but originally it would have swept from Stoke House across to an ornamental castle-farm whose tall tower stands incongruously today in the grounds of a former hospital on the far side of the M32.

One advantage of Wright's rough style of garden designing was its relative cheapness. So much could be achieved by planting bushes, with little expenditure on stone, bricks and mortar. This will account for the number of gardens in the county planned by Wright for subscribers to his *Arbours* and *Grottos*. Charles Bragge's Cleve Hill has already been mentioned and Bragge's cousin, Thomas Bathurst of Lydney Park, a subscriber to *Grottos*, added a rustic umbrello and a Gothick temple to his groves.[38] Jerry Pierce of Lilliput Castle, a John Wood villa on the hills above Bath, was another subscriber to Wright's *Grottos*. Thomas Robins drew the Hermitage that Pierce had built in his garden.[39] It has some of the usual Wright characteristics, and one broken arch of the thatched cell stands in the grounds of the much altered villa, now called Battlefields. Another very Wrightian hermitage is oddly sited in the front garden of Chavenage House, crumbling away in a properly crepuscular grove, the extreme rugosity of its stones and gnarled tree trunks capturing perfectly the parody of wildness that Wright drew for his *Arbours* and his *Grottos*. Earl Berkeley not only subscribed to *Arbours*, before his death in 1755, but probably commissioned another root house from Wright, a smaller but vibrantly rugose version of the Hermit's Cell at Badminton. Under a spreading hat of thatch and with its stone walls still liberally covered with bark, it stands in the grounds of Berkeley vicarage and is said to have been the place where Dr Jenner carried out his small-pox vaccinations, a scientific connection which would have impressed Wright, the popular scientist.[40]

The best, however, of this chapter of Rococo-Arcadian gardens has been kept to the end. For someone who appreciates the need to pay an entrance fee before enjoying the light-hearted decadence and invention of Painswick, but who prefers the seedy grandeur of Kingsweston's woods or the bewildering mazes of Cirencester, then the bizarre complex of Rococo garden and industrial brass foundry which William Champion created between 1746 and 1769 in the coalfield east of Bristol is a rare and subtle pleasure. Champion, a Quaker like others in his trade, was not a Wright subscriber. He had, however, a more intimate contact with the garden designer. By persuading the cheerfully gullible Norborne Berkeley to invest heavily in his brass, copper and spelter manufactory at Warmley, he involved Berkeley in his own bankruptcy in 1768, thereby making it essential for Berkeley, now Lord Botetourt, to cajole the post of Governor of Virginia from the government. This led Botetourt to quit Gloucestershire and Stoke Park, to acquire a much needed income, enjoy the flowering of all the American trees he had been planting and, in 1770, to die of typhoid in Virginia, leaving the estate to his sister, who had been widowed since 1756.

Even without this unfortunate and disastrous connection, which robbed him of his best friend and patron, Wright, with his fondness for aggressive textures, must have been drawn to the iron hard, gleaming black slag which was a by-product of brass founding. Poured molten into moulds it produced indestructible building blocks, so horrid in appearance that when William Reeve of Arno's Vale, just across the Avon from Warmley and in Somerset, used them in 1764 to create a striking black and white stables and administrative block it was immediately christened 'the devil's cathedral' by Horace Walpole, thus keeping up the Rococo's long association with things unsavoury and bourgeois.[41]

The only reason why Champion's contemporary garden at Warmley, armed as it is with a frightening 20-foot colossus, is not better known nationally, is that it is so hard to find. It is a real treasure among gardens, admirably cared for by the local council and a group of interested friends. There is a car-park, but no charge for entry. Visitors will probably have its grottoes and echo pond, its giant and black walls to themselves, but they must also be prepared to enjoy the 'still sad music of humanity' rising from a large park of mobile homes and to turn a blind eye to new housing going up only feet away from choked canals and brambled paths. In the Bristol A-Z, find Tower Road and navigate to that along the eastern ring road. Soon a battered stone windmill tower and the Clock House, a last survivor of Champion's Battery Mills, will come into view and then a discreet sign to the left, pointing into a wooded garden, leads to the car-park.

This stands below Champion's surprisingly plain but correctly proportioned Palladian house, now a nursing home surrounded by lawns and mature trees, one of them a holm oak of Champion's original planting. What follows next is unavoidably complex and hard to explain, but rewarding to disentangle.[42] On the lawn below the house is the Echo Pond, an exact, bullrushy semicircle walled on its curved side with the purple-black slag blocks. There is still an echo but the rushes have dimmed it. Across the path behind the Echo Pond was once a 13-acre lake with an island on which the colossal Neptune statue stood. Neptune still rears up, but on an island of brambles (**43**). The lake is no more; two-thirds of it is a sea of mobile homes. Neptune is remarkably ugly. His huge body is made of white cement, he has a very brief costume of black brass clinker with a bulging codpiece and his face has been worn by the weather into an sinister snarl. One iron armature juts out to reveal where a trident-wielding arm was once fixed. Yet his aura is still formidable and the mobile homes actually increase it by their incongruity.

Further along the lakeside path the briars close in on one side, new housing on the other, and there on the left is the tall black and white 'summer house', the home of the sluice keeper who controlled the Warmley Brook which once entered the lake at this point under a big black arch of slag. Again there is a presence. Here it is necessary to return to the Echo Pond to explore the tangle of so-called 'grotto' tunnels which actually housed a Newcomen pumping engine and controlled an elaborate system designed to reuse the waters of the lake. It is all pleasantly but not wildly overgrown and grassy, with chequered patterns of black slag here and there on the walls and low, barred and locked arches leading down into dusty darkness.

43 *The Warmley Giant, three times the height of a man, poses in a revealing garment of industrial slag. Wright may have designed this 'savage' Neptune for the brass-founder William Champion in the mid-1750s. Originally the Giant stood on an island in a lake*

Next to these complex, tempting gates to the underworld stands a large artificial mound topped by a grove of trees. It has a Tudor air, but is far more likely to have been a viewing mound constructed from Champion's brass waste as it gives an excellent view of confusion, the windmill for alternative power and the dam that held up the lake. Somewhere in the engine passages a Gothic vault has been treated in the style of an Italian Mannerist garden like Bomarzo near Viterbo. By the addition of spots for eyes the arch has become a gaping mouth of Hell: all an imaginative extension of that savage version of the Rococo which Thomas Wright illustrated in his *Grottos*. There is no proof that Wright had any hand in the garden, the only link between Wright and Champion being Norborne Berkeley; but who else would have suggested a Hell's mouth for an engine channel and a hideous giant Neptune of slag for a garden ornament? The Echo Pond served as an overflow in times of flood, but to fashion such a sluice to provide a poetic reply to song is the kind of sophisticated notion that French kings toyed with in the royal gardens of early seventeenth-century Paris.

Back at the house, which has a barred vault entrance even under its terrace wall, the contrast between the garden and its calm, even bland, Palladian masonry is striking. This was an age when English houses played very safe and all the psychic head of repressed imagination had to escape safely in their gardens. Somewhere under those vaults and passages there was once a 20-foot waterfall pounding away, a pumping engine and a deep plunge pool. They foreshadow the lines from Coleridge's *Kubla Khan*:

> Where Alph, the sacred river, ran
> Through caverns measureless to man
> Down to a sunless sea

which would be written 29 years after Champion's bankruptcy and fall in 1769. The Romantic movement was waiting to be born, pregnant with the images of industry, but still obsessed by the giant gods of Antiquity.

1   Looking down from Thornbury's highest tower into the walled enclosure that contained
    the 'Privie Garden', where the embattled shadows lie, and the 'Goodly Garden', now
    covered by nineteenth-century topiary work

2   The deerherd's tower in Whitcliff Park, an early nineteenth-century successor to the
    Berkeleys' hunting lodge of 1329. Its viewing terrace commanded any deer hunt and its
    banqueting room housed subsequent celebrations

3 *With these slender columns and almost rounded Gothic arches of the Ambulatory at Horton Court William Knight tried, in 1521, to evoke the Florentine loggias he had seen on his embassies to Italy*

4 *Half villa, half hunting lodge and hawking tower, Newark Park was built in the 1550s by Sir Nicholas Poyntz with a roof terrace and corner turrets from which the old and infirm could enjoy the aerial and terrestrial sports*

5   *A view along the terrace of Campden past the fire-reddened wreck of the house to the west or garden pavilion, now (winter 2001) under restoration by the Landmark Trust*

6 *Earthworks of the Atkyns' former Sapperton Manor in the foreground and the bowling green set on its revetment high above the valley*

7 *The 'Ballroom', a last relic of Owlpen Manor's gigantic topiary overgrowth, where early eighteenth-century garden design has gone completely out of control*

8   *Claude David's statue of Neptune was intended to show the god as lord of Dyrham's unfailing springs, but now his waters have all gone underground*

9   *The Neptune at Westbury Court, set at a confluence of straight canals, has waters in abundance. The Tall Pavilion commands every corner of the compact grounds, laid out between 1697 and 1715*

10 *A rare survival of tentative garden informality at Hill Court; Sir Francis Fust's 'Curly Wurly' of the 1720s still winds tortuously up a hill between yew and box to a long vanished viewing pavilion*

11 *Allen Bathurst designed and built the Hexagon at Cirencester Park in the 1736, a confident classical temple by the man who had completed the first Gothic garden building in England four years earlier*

12 *Jan Van Nost's powerful statue of Pan was the inspiration for Benjamin Hyett's garden and gentlemens' club at Painswick. It is now kept indoors*

13 With a door like a distorted mouth and rough bark-clad walls, Thomas Wright's Hermit's
Cell at Badminton was supposed to house a female hermit called Urganda. This perverse
tradition was kept up by successive dukes of Beaufort well into the twentieth century

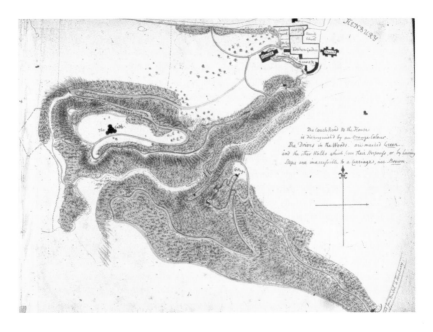

14 Humphry Repton's Red Book of 1796 for Blaise Castle Park illustrates the three routes
which he was preparing. The green and orange were for romantic coach rides to take in the
picturesque scenery, the brown route was for walkers. All three can be followed today

15   The Thornery or Stream Garden at Sezincote with its artificial rock ledges and rich
flower planting, inspired by Repton's similar garden at neighbouring Adlestrop

16   *The formal pool at The Rocks lies at the foot of a sheer limestone quarry face immediately below the surviving ranges of the Regency Gothic castle built between 1790 and 1838*

17   *Ferns, convincing Pulhamite grottoes and shallow rills in the Winter Garden, which was laid out in the 1850s at Highnam Court for Thomas Gambier Parry*

18 *A Jacobean vista of arch and pavilion in the supposedly 'Italian' garden at Westonbirt House, which Henry Hamlen designed in brilliant eclectic free-form in 1843*

19 *The Dam of the Seven Satyrs creates the upper lake at Cowley Manor and dramatises one of several sources of the Thames. It is only part of an imaginative water garden conceived in 1874 when the Manor was doubled in size*

20 *Built as a tennis pavilion at Abbotswood in Lutyens's convincing Cotswold vernacular, this building was intended as a casually asymmetrical balance to the Rose Loggia on the other side of the formal garden of 1902*

21 *The Red Borders at Hidcote with their twin brick pavilions were laid out for Gertrude Winthrop while her son, Major Lawrence Johnston, was serving in France in the 1914-18 World War*

22 The Herbaceous Borders at Rodmarton have a decisive linear and architectural composition. The topiary blocks around the central pool are cut with an Art Deco geometric solidity that punctuates the length of the enclosure most effectively

23 Crammed with all the engaging whimsicality of John Betjeman and the post-Arts and Crafts gardeners, this is the view down into Well Court at Snowshill Manor: a garden space created by Charles Paget Wade out of a few old farm buildings

24   *The Jekyll Border and Summerhouse at Combend, but not exactly as Miss Jekyll planned it in 1925. Originally the flowers flanked a wide gravel path, which soon poured itself away down the steep slope. Grass has proved more stable*

25 *A view through the wall into the water gardens of Middle Lodge at Avening. Before reaching this point the Aven stream has already been bridged five or six times in the atmospheric gardens created between 1899 and 1927 around Avening Court*

26 *The Doric Temple in the grounds of Barnsley House was rescued from the destruction of Fairford Park in 1962. Gloucestershire gardeners of the twentieth century have clung nostalgically to the eighteenth-century past*

27   *Prince Charles took the inspired risk, Julian and Isabel Bannerman thought up the*
    Savage Picturesque concept, and the Highgrove Stumpery is the result. Spiked chestnut
    roots and twin classical temples of oak compose memorably

28   *The new Water Garden at Kiftsgate Court is the 1998 creation of the the garden's*
    owners, Anne and Johnny Chambers: a horticultural Mondrian achieved with cropped
    grass, black water, paviours and golden philodendrons weeping tears

6 Lancelot Brown and the rule of shotgun and carriage

Lancelot (Capability) Brown set up business as an independent garden and park designer in 1751, after spending seven years replanting and settling the grounds of Stowe in Buckinghamshire to the direction of the absentee William Kent. It was only natural that, when Kent died in 1748 with his plans for the grounds of Badminton only partly achieved, the 4th Duke of Beaufort should have called in Brown in 1752 to advise him on the layout of the small pleasure ground immediately east of the house.[1] The plan which Brown then drew is so similar to Kent's garden at Carlton House for Frederick, Prince of Wales, in every detail of its open central axis, its two sylvan clearings and the serpentine course of its belt path, that Brown could well have been following an existing scheme bequeathed by Kent. The lower part nearest the house of the elaborate Rococo design for the same area, drawn in 1750 by Thomas Wright and described in the last chapter, is again very close to Brown's plan, though rather more geometrical in its planting. So it is possible that Adam Mickle, the Duke's head gardener, had begun to clear away the dense maze garden of the 1st Duke to a Kentian scheme as revised by Wright and Brown.[2]

Brown's next contact with Gloucestershire was at Dodington in 1764, by which time he had become a national figure. Dodington is the most forbidden and at the same time perhaps the most satisfying park in the county. It is forbidden because the southern half of it, Brown's only achieved work in Gloucestershire, is strictly private. But it is satisfying because its northern half, which was remodelled to the Brownian formula 50 years later by one of his imitators, William Emes, is crossed diagonally by a very revealing public right-of-way with glorious Brownian views. In its course this path also passes over a delightfully odd Gothick waterfall above a canal. This was constructed by the owner of the park, Christopher Bethel Codrington, who was an amateur architect in his spare time and a close friend of James Wyatt. The much larger Gothick Cascade House and serpentine rill between Brown's two lakes is another of Christopher Bethel's 'fancies'.

While that encapusulates Dodington's accessible charms there is much more to be said about one of the county's greatest and most inadequately researched historic parks. The Codringtons were a local family who had become comfortably rich by pioneering sugar plantations in Antigua and Barbuda. Their wealth explains why, when the Blathwayts' water gardens were falling into disrepair in neighbouring Dyrham for lack of maintenance, Sir William Codrington, Christopher Bethel's great-uncle, could afford to pay Brown £1368 for the work done between 1764 and 1767 in transforming the valley of the little River Frome that ran past the old Tudor house in a series of mill ponds and a small formal canal.

None of the usual Brown contracts, maps or directives to foremen have survived at Dodington, but it is known, from the careful ink and watercolour map of the park drawn by the surveyor James Maule in 1770, precisely what Brown's park looked like in its prime.[3] Its condition before its remodelling can be guessed from another map which James Spyers, one of Brown's advance scouts, had Stanley Gale draw for him in 1782 in preparation for another Brown reshaping of another Cotswold valley, that at Woodchester near Stroud.[4] Brown died in 1783, aged 67, so Woodchester had to wait for Humphry Repton's attentions, but Gale's map shows the valley below Lord Ducie's house as a complete patchwork of small hedged fields around a chain of five mill ponds, each with its dam. Maule's map of Dodington shows the Frome leaving Dodington's walled formal garden, with its straight canal, via 'Mill Close'. So before Brown's arrival Dodington's grounds would probably have been as hedged and strewn with mill ponds as Woodchester still was in 1782.

Brown did not have to create two 'lakes', only cosmetize the banks of the existing ponds; and he did not, as Dorothy Stroud claimed in her pioneering study, design the celebrated and poetic Gothick Cascade House between the two ponds with its serpentine streamlet.[5] Maps of the grounds as late as 1820 show only a sluice between the ponds,[6] though a note 'From A to B is a 11 feet 5 inches fall' proves that Christopher Bethel was planning those works at the 'New Water', 'Water head', or 'fish pond head', which litter the account books for the house between the years 1823 and 1826.

James Maule not only mapped Brown's park in 1770, but drew as a frontispiece to the estate book a careful picture of the old Tudor house taken from the south-west (**44**).

44   *The old house at Dodington drawn by James Maule for an estate book in 1770 shows Capability Brown's planting and pond of 1764-7 with a glimpse of the earlier formal garden canal to the right of the house*

The hills north of the house, which would be transformed in the 1820s, were still a patchwork of hedges (**45**). Brown had not been able to persuade Sir William to abandon his walled garden with its canal. Instead he had hidden it from the new drive by a dense planting of shrubs and trees. The drive then took a typical Brownian course. First it swung around the bottom of the 'Lower Great Pond' to wind its way back south, between seven artfully sited small clumps of trees, in a pleasure ground on the far side of the Lower Pond. It then turned back between the Lower and Upper Ponds, where the Gothick Cascade House and waterfall now stands (**46**), to exactly the course of the present drive from the house up to the Bath Lodge. Vineyard, Bailey and Pen clumps had been planted on the left (all Brownian and surviving today), Black Brake was on the right. The drive entered Dodington Wood on a steep curve to reach the carriage sweep at the main road.

The account books reveal that by 1820 the masons', carpenters' and gilders' work on James Wyatt's great new house at Dodington was coming towards a close. Christopher Bethel Codrington, robbed of his friend Wyatt's help by the carriage accident that killed the architect but left Codrington, who was sitting beside him, unscathed, was turning his attention to doubling the size of the park and revising the Brownian half of it. The accounts book D 1610/A78 was kept in perfect copper plate hand and meticulous detail. In 1820 there was an expenditure on 'the Pleasure Grounds', 'the Flower Garden' and 'For stones & sundries building of a Falling House £13.13.0'.[7] For the next seven years there was work around the ponds. A new

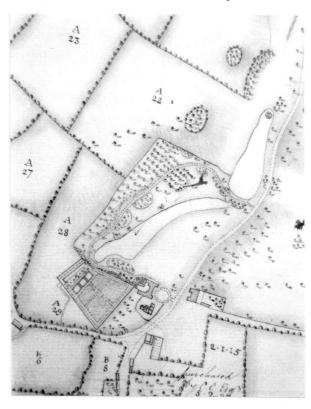

45 *Maule's 1770 map of Dodington park indicates how limited Brown's park work of the preceding decade had been. His drive winds among tree clumps and crosses between the two lakes where the Cascade House would be built later*

island was being constructed in 1823 in the Lower Pond, there was work on the 'New Water Head' and 'digging stones for the Ice House', which stands today with a Gothick graden seat above it.[8] The Dairy, to Wyatt's striking classical design, was begun in 1824,[9] and work continued on the island, the Ice House, a Boat House and the 'New Water Head'. Pennant stone from Bristol was being brought in for the 'Pond Head Wall' in 1825, and now the new lodge, the Chippenham Lodge, was begun together with the 'New Carriage Road' which would bring a whole new northern sector into the grounds of the park.[10]

Building the new Gothick 'Falling House' or 'Pond Head' meant that the drive could no longer be routed between the two lakes, so that entire sector of it on the far side of the Lower Pond was abandoned and run instead directly from the house up the valley. Above Brown's old pleasure ground a new 'Pleasure Ground Wood' was planted with a winding carriage road running on a circuit within it. The steep slopes of the Cotswolds in the extended northern reach of the park were landscaped to the old Brownian formula, possibly to the direction of William Emes and John Webb, who had done surveys in 1808.[11]

This is the area of the park where the Brownian landscape can be enjoyed today, albeit at Emes's second hand. The footpath starts at a stile opposite Coomb's End farm and climbs, gently at first, with opening views of steep pasture, Hammerdown Clump and the sweeping curves of Frenchpiece Wood. Then, after crossing

46 *Christopher Bethel Codrington, an inspired gentlemen amateur, designed this Cascade House between the two lakes at Dodington and built it in 1820-5. A sinuous raised aqueduct leads water into the central tower*

47 *The little Cascade Bridge at Dodington is another Christopher Bethel Codrington design, amateurish and old fashioned, hidden away in a remote sector of the park*

Christopher Bethel's drive, comes his charming miniature Cascade Bridge (**47**). He must have been, in aesthetic terms, a throwback to the age of Batty Langley's Rococo-Gothick. A clutch of drawings show him designing a greenhouse for a friend, Lady Garlies, that is pure Langley, all delicate ogee arches.[12] In another he has added, to a romantic drawing of a towered seat by F. Onslow, a taller pointed-arched tower close to that of his Gothick Cascade House between the two lakes (**48**). Another drawing in his own hand is for its twin side towers; it is undated but next to a drawing in the same amusingly crude style by Harriet Dawson, dated 1809.

There are no drawings for the Cascade Bridge in the northern park , but it is in the unmistakable Christopher Bethel manner. Above it was a little pond, now almost dry, by a leaning twisted oak. From this lost pond a trickle still runs under the Bridge over which the public footpath crosses. This has an accurately Perpendicular Gothic parapet, very Wyatt in style, over an entirely incorrect Gothic ogee arch, pure Codrington, above the waterfall. Above it is a clumsy gargoyle head with popping eyes and flowing locks, not unlike the Gorgon's head in the Roman Baths. The meagre streamlet then falls into a long, straight canal running down to another bridge at the point where the new drive breaks out of a wood of noble specimen trees underplanted with box. Christopher Bethel must have intended departing guests to look sharply to their right for a glimpse of the canal, waterfall, ogee-arched bridge and oak tree.

48 Above the left-hand tower of this romantic design by F. Onslow, Christopher Bethel Codrington faintly sketched in the ultimate form of the Cascade House centrepiece. So a Gothic seat mutates into a Gothic waterfall

Even so the drive from the Chippenham Lodge was always tame compared with the drive Brown had designed to run down from the Bath road. Inaccessible today, this approach was nostalgically evoked by Christopher Hussey, writing in 1924, but still in fruity Edwardian prose:

> I well remember the sensation of having left the world behind; of entering a valley of enchantment, narrow and deep at first, and hidden in woods, but broadening out into a kind of secret arena, with broad stretches of turf, clumps of aged oaks, and a curving lake, the sheltering woods watching from their hills around. We were not prepared for the strange and town-like group of buildings which a turning in the valley at length displayed. Our sentiments of romance and mystery were suddenly tripped up, by the sight of a very logical, precise building, very much fin de dix-huitième siècle. It was as if Talleyrand had strayed into Lorna Doone.[13]

Anyone who wishes for glimpses of that 'strange and town-like group of buildings' today can catch them, when the leaves are fallen, from the footpath a little higher than the Cascade Bridge.

Not all of the Capability Brown phenomena, that rage for his services which overtook king, aristocracy and gentry after he set up his own landscaping business in 1751, was to do with Arcadian aesthetics and privacy. He launched out with his technical expertise in draining and planting, his teams of skilled labourers and his Northumbrian charm at a time when two technological improvements springing from the Industrial revolution were subtly changing the average landowner's requirements for the land around his house.[14] Shotguns had become lighter, shorter and more accurate; carriages had become faster, more elegant and, therefore, more prestigious and covetable. They were also more comfortable to ride in as a result of superior springing. Two new experiences had, therefore, opened up for the wealthy. With the new guns, fat old men with a reasonable eye could bag quantities of pheasants as those birds rocketted up obligingly high from the belts of trees and undergrowth where they bred and flourished best. New carriages offered another thrill: that of speed savoured while lolling back luxuriously upon padded leather seats. The result was that wide expanses of lawn-like turf became desirable as areas where horse and carriage could move fast with virtually no jogging discomfort. Long, smoothly engineered driveways, often circumnavigating the park, became the expected treat for favoured visitors. Now scenery could be enjoyed in quick motion, so Brown obliged by creating dramatic turns and revelations of lake or house or distant hill. His circular routes nipped in and out of narrow belts of trees which afforded alternations of view and shade while at the same time providing ideal breeding ground for pheasants.

While Brown did give Dodington a long belt of trees beside the Bath road, good for pheasants and for privacy, the steep 250ft drop of the Cotswold edge made a circular drive round the park impracticable. But Brown, who must have revised and improved some 60 English parks in a 30-year working life (1751-83), was copied by a number of imitators. Batsford Park, near Moreton-in-Marsh on the Warwickshire border, had been given formal Bridgeman style avenues earlier in the century and in 1763 Thomas Edwards Freeman, who had recently become the owner, called in Samuel Driver to plan a modern park. It was a peculiar choice as Driver's recent, 1759, scheme for nearby Adlestrop Park had been in an old fashioned Rococo, with a winding canal, Chinese bridge, summer house and sinuous paths to a cascade, all very crowded.[15] However, Driver, a London trained surveyor and nurseryman, had sensed the way the winds of garden fashion were blowing and in three plans of 1763, 1764 and 1766, so temptingly drawn and carefully coloured as to appear more like aerial views than maps, he offered Freeman not one Brownian style park but two. One was to be laid out on one side of the house and one on the other, with the offices in front, stables to the left and woodyard to the right, both hidden behind lines of judiciously broken and occasionally clumped trees.

John Davenport was paid £40 in 1783 to liven up Driver's proposals with an enormous new plan (**49**). In this the stables and the woodyard were still sited one on each side of the entrance area with a dairy added to the woodyard. But all these buildings were now to be concealed in a mazy wood of crazily winding and turning carriage drives. The lake on Driver's plan has been galvanized into serpentine twists, inlets and peninsulas with two bridges and two garden pavilions. A greenhouse, lodge and barn enliven its rival circuit where a cruciform of Bridgemanesque straight avenues has been allowed to survive. For most of their courses these circling drives are shadowed within belts of trees by narrow paths for walkers. Behind the house is a large shrubbery with more sinuous paths, a pavilion, a pool, a parish church and a kitchen garden. Close to this and handy for the house is a cold bath.

Woodyards feature prominently in most of these post-1750 parks. There was one beside the old 'servants' route into Dodington next to the estate smithy. They were a sign that Gloucestershire landowners were absorbing the commercial lesson of Allen Bathurst's Cirencester Park and making the increasingly wooded areas of their parks pay their way. Simplification and utility like two twin plagues hit Kingsweston when the architect Robert Mylne was brought in by Edward Southwell III in 1763-72 and Brown himself was consulted during this period. Mylne produced a formidable technical and administrative centre for the estate on the other side of the public road from the house. Visually unrelated to the real park it stands today in a strange empty grandeur. The stable

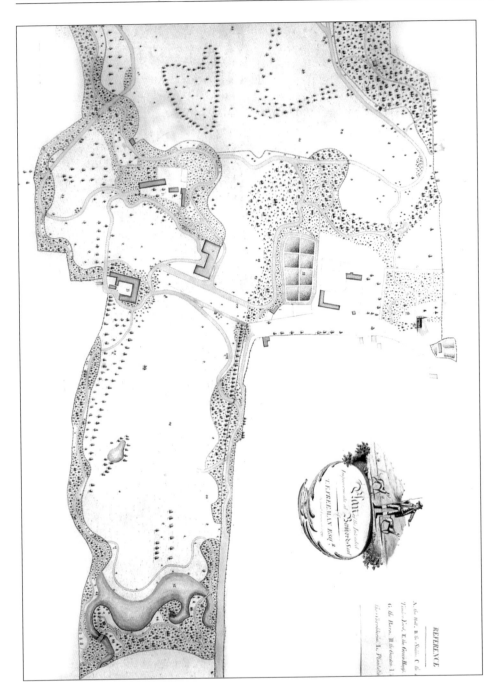

49 *John Davenport's ambitious new designs of 1783 for the park at Batsford prove him to have been a Capability Brown follower. The belt drive winds in and out of clumped trees affording picturesque views. All offices are discreetly concealed behind woodland*

block with wings flanking a courtyard has that air of solemn consequence that adheres automatically to any structure in even a modified Vanbrughian mood. Facing it the fish pond contrives to be magisterial; it is a huge stone square, crammed now with lily pads and flanked, to echo the stables, by the solid cubes of two gardener's houses. A massive ice house and the wreck of a formal garden is hidden in thick woodland behind the stables, while brick-walled kitchen gardens, appropriately ambitious in scale, once extended away to the side of the fish pond. Across the road Brown's advice, for which he was paid £84, seems to have been taken to gut the park of its avenues and create that hollow empty meadow or lawn which now reaches interminably away in front of the south façade.[16]

Disappointed that nothing was done at Batsford in response to his schemes of 1783, John Davenport took up employment at Daylesford where the ex-Nabob, Warren Hastings, was establishing himself as a country gentleman in the parish where he had spent happy childhood years at the rectory. Hastings's horticultural fixation, as befitted a Nabob, was with exotic fruit. He sent to Alipore for seeds of the custard apple, grew Mediterranean and tropical fruit in his greenhouses and attempted, with some success, to introduce lychees, which he thought delicious. On his farms he experimented with new methods of growing barley, and 'brought goats and yaks from Tibet and cattle from Bhutan to cross with his native herd'.[17] An estate map of 1786 proves that Davenport started planning with a completely clean sheet.[18] The old house was entirely surrounded by hedged fields, most of them small, with names like Great Sainfoin and Brook Furlong. There was a wood, an orchard, a warren and an abundance of springs feeding several pools. Topographically Daylesford park is not dramatic, though mildly undulating, and such a terrain always exposes the essential blandness of a Brownian formula.

In September 1788 Davenport was on site and began to direct the enclosure of Samuel Pepys Cockerell's grand semi-Palladian, multi-winged house with woods on every side where there was any danger that it could be overlooked from public rights-of-way.[19] In January 1789 he was instructed to build the 'garden walls, hot house' and to 'hurry to start on the pleasure and flower gardens'.[20] J.P. Neale's drawing of the house, engraved in 1823, shows plain lawns sweeping up to the front of the house in the approved Brownian manner with single specimen trees and a shrubbery.[21] The estate's administrative buildings were sited outside this pastoral claustrophobia, but the regulation slim, twin lakes were dammed into existence to create relief within the exclusive enclosure. In November 1790 Davenport was sacked for adding what was considered to be an unnecessary cast iron bridge over the upper of these two lakes to give access to the Walled Garden. It is possible to sympathise with him. His bridge, like the enchanting Gothick Greenhouse or Orangery which he designed for the garden, must have been an act of aesthetic defiance against the lifelessness of a landscape formula of 'pleasing simplicity'.[22] So too were the pleasure gardens that by June 1795 were in full bloom. The Orangery 'was rich with grenadillas, lychees, custard apples, alligator pears and mangoes, while the Walled Garden produced peaches, cherries, nectarines, plums, strawberries, gooseberries, currants, raspberries and grapes'.[23] An Arcady of water, trees tactfully sited, and wide-spreading lawns, usually fenced for cattle grazing, is often described as essentially English, but on a level terrain could be equally described as essentially artificial and boring.

Another major park created by another Brown follower, William Emes, surrounds Northwick Park, Blockley, that fascinatingly ugly complex where Lord Burlington's Palladian additions of 1728-30 sit so oddly among the taller, shaped gables of a misguided remodelling of about 1800. Emes followed the usual formula of the twin lakes, Upper and Lower, the Upper Lake terminating in that admired Brownian style of an indeterminacy among trees which suggests that there could be much more of it around the corner. A visit to Northwick today is interesting, both to judge the impact Emes made upon a very large park and to appreciate how much a developer, packing desirable residences into the immediate surroundings of an historic house, can in fact enrich and improve the site, contrary to what the Cassandras of statutory societies are inclined to predict. Emes's work is almost invisible, his long Lower Lake lies, as its name hints, so low as to be hardly noticed, but the drive winds tantalisingly about woodland to the east, with the main house appearing and disappearing to create higher expectations than it will, in the event, satisfy. What does satisfy is the variety and architectural quality of the developer's houses that suddenly crowd in after the security office. The estate is, of course, private, an enduring Cotswold tradition, but visitors who have driven in hoping to evaluate Burlington and Emes are more likely to come away with an ambition to join the happy band of modern residents in the walled enclosure of the 'William Emes Garden'.

There was nothing actively wrong with the Emes landscape at Northwick; it is simply that Brownian parks were designed for sportsmen who wished to rear flocks of pheasants and produced landscapes which could be easily absorbed from a speeding carriage, full of idlers who were reluctant to get out to enjoy the kind of features that stud a Rococo garden like Painswick or Arcadias like Stourhead in Wiltshire. It is significant that the Brownian craze was followed by sharp reactions; first by the enthusiasts for the 'Savage Picturesque', landscape connoisseurs like Uvedale Price and Richard Payne Knight, then by Humphry Repton who took over the mantle of Brown deliberately, first to embroider it over with enrichment and finally to turn it inside out into the Gardenesque.

Capability Brown was never much admired in the nineteenth century. It was only when cars had taken the place of fast carriages as the toys of the twentieth century, and landscapes could be enjoyed at even greater speeds, that Brown returned to favour and Dorothy Stroud could publish her pioneering biography in 1950 to a general chorus of critical approval. In the last three-quarters of the twentieth century simplicity was at a premium in architecture; detail and enrichment were considered an aesthetic sin. Brown's landscapes could have been designed for such an age; but it is a reasonable proposition that his formula only succeeds when, as at Blenheim in Oxfordshire, he had some tremendous existing artefact like Vanbrugh's imperial Roman viaduct to work around, or where, as at Dodington, the landscape was already full of incident and where an amateur genius like Christopher Bethel Codrington was prepared to come later and enrich the scene with structures of imaginative fantasy. Dorothy Stroud was understandably eager to attribute these to her hero on their supposed similarity to a known Brown courtyard screen at Burton Constable, Yorkshire. Before 1950 the Gothick Cascade House had been loosely attributed to James Wyatt. This book is happy to have done justice to a half forgotten amateur and now to move on to parks and gardens conceived in a more positive tradition.

7 Humphry Repton and the winds of change

Lancelot Brown and his followers were often catering for the Mr Toads of the Georgian aristocracy, the fast riding, fast shooting philistines of landscape. But Brown died with excellent timing just before his reputation fell steeply with hostile criticism mounting, firstly over the essential selfishness of clearing whole villages away to create vast open lawns, and secondly because of the actual tedium of many of the resultant parkscapes.

Opposition to smooth lakesides, velvety lawns and carefully clumped trees had been building up ever since Edmund Burke had drawn a distinction between the 'Sublime' and the 'Beautiful'. His treatise of that name was published in 1757 and was soon widely discussed.[1] Once a concept has been launched it has a life of its own, and before long connoisseurs of wild nature and tourists questing after the Picturesque became desperately precious, not only about rugged mountains, but about the subtle textural details of branches, bark, roots and hedgerows.[2] They followed routes clearly prescribed in specialist guidebooks, questing after particularly well composed views, which had to be enjoyed from exact viewpoints and looking in certain directions, preferably in favourable light conditions in order to catch a landscape just as an artist would wish to paint it. It was, in fact, a cult for the would-be superior. New parks and gardens had now, if their topography offered any kind of opening, to supply glimpses of the sublime as well as the beautiful. Romanticism was preparing a take-over from classicism.

With Uvedale Price writing at Foxley and Payne Knight turning out his verse treatise *The Landscape* at Downton, both in Herefordshire, the neighbouring county of Gloucestershire, sharing a bank of the river Wye, was well placed to catch the Picturesque infection early. A boat trip down the Wye from Ross to Chepstow had become a standard day trip for sophisticated tourists armed with Claude Glasses. These little instruments were telescopes in reverse, intended to distance the scenery and dramatise its composition.[3] William Gilpin was only one of several travel writers who made the voyage, but his *Observations on the River Wye and Several Parts of South Wales* (1782), illustrated with his oval sketches in imitation of Claude Glass images, sent Picturesque fanciers flocking to experience the sublime conclusion to the Wye excursion as the river swept around the cliffs and park of Piercefield.

Begun in 1752, long before Repton's time and indeed before Burke's formulation, Piercefield Park nevertheless makes a useful introduction to sublimity as all other attempts would necessarily lie in its tremendous shadow (**50**). Strictly speaking Piercefield, where Valentine Morris grasped the park potential of 200 foot cliffs, is

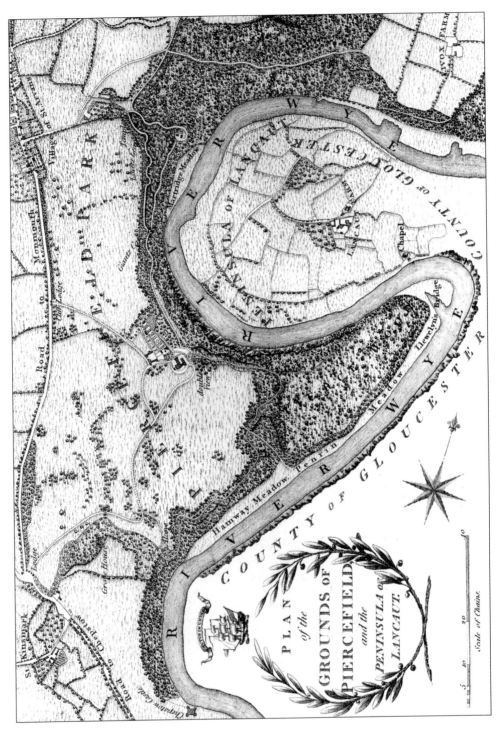

50   *The tourist trail for 'Sublime' or 'Beautiful' views at Piercefield Park extended along the cliff edge from the Wyndcliff further to the right to Chepstow Castle on the left. Boats sailing down the Wye landed on Martridge Meadow for the path to the Giant's Cave*

not in Gloucestershire but Monmouth (Gwent). However, an essential contrasting sector of its landscape, a model farm and ruined chapel overlooked by cliffs, is sited on the Lancaut peninsula, an authentic part of Gloucestershire within a dramatic loop of the Wye. Arthur Young, one of several travel writers of the time who praised Piercefield at length, wrote that the views of Lancaut from the Apostle Rocks on the Monmouth side, 'which are "beautiful" are all intermixed with the "sublime"; the farm beneath you [Lancaut] is superlatively so; the precipice you look down from, the hanging woods, and the rocks are totally different'.[4] Young meant that they were in contrast entirely 'sublime', and he found this confusing aesthetically.

If visitors today keep religiously within the county boundary and make their way down to remote and isolated Lancaut they are unlikely to be confused. Everything across the muddy tidal Wye is, in Burke's sense, 'Sublime': the towering limestone cliffs and the shaggy woods. The peninsula on which they are standing, mild pastoral farm land, represents Burke's 'Beautiful'. Viewing it all from high up on the cliffs Young was disturbed by the juxtaposition of the two qualities. Anyone anxious to walk those cliff paths that lie a mere hundred yards away across the river will have to make a detour of at least two miles. The stone giant that once poised a threatening boulder over his cave mouth fell down long ago, but it remains a most atmospheric park to visit and one well worth the journey.

Into this uncertainty of landscape fashions, when picturesque wildness was becoming a cult, the 'sublime' was a potent catch-word and flower beds were making a comeback, stepped the unlikely figure – balding, mild-eyed and polite to the point of obsequiousness – of Humphry Repton.[5] Born at Bury St Edmunds in 1752 and reared among the tame landscapes of East Anglia, he had failed in business and in a political career, then spent several years helping neighbours in Norfolk with their estate problems before, in 1788, when he was already thirty-six years old, a shortage of funds obliged him to set up as a landscape advisor. Lancelot Brown had been dead five years and Repton may have hoped to succeed him. He brought a sensitive eye and an imaginative mind to estate reshaping but very little else except a gift for accurate, appealing water-colours. Over the coming years his taste in landscaping would be directed far more by the wishes of his patrons than by any vision of his own. He was wide open to the influence of books and fashion and his servile charm would profit him until the long wars with France began in 1793. After that business slumped and he was ready to leap at virtually every possible commission.

Repton's first Gloucestershire park layout design, of 1795-6 at Blaise Castle estate, four miles north-west of Bristol, was not, however, an anticlimax, even compared with Piercefield. The county and Repton were both fortunate. Repton often lacked the drive to impose his sensitive perceptions upon a terrain. Only a minor artist but a persuasive writer, he had none of Brown's talent for organising teams to drain, dike, plant and reshape. But at Blaise he began with a dramatic valley between wooded hills, the property of a rich, forceful owner, John Scandrett Harford. This Quaker banker was a man who was prepared to listen to Repton's airy sensitivities, read the Red Book of ideas presented to him by Repton, then take things into his own highly capable hands and literally blast those proposals into practical reality with gun powder.[6] Repton made his first visit to Harford's new purchase in 1795. Work went on apace and by July 1799 Harford was able to drive a friend in a four-wheeled coach around Repton's cleverly devised orange carriage route in the morning and his wife around Repton's green route in the afternooon (**colour plate 14**).

The park is a successful confidence trick. Harford's house stands almost on a public road, virtually at the heart of Henbury, a commuter village. But Harford had bought a considerable estate of steep, wooded hills with a ravine and a pump house shaped as a Gothic castle, all designed for a different house, but on land contiguous with his own.[7] Repton saw that, by siting a new Gothic gatehouse at the point in this estate nearest to Bristol, a drive to the back of Harford's house could be contrived which would, by its devious route, give the impression that the house was surrounded by a huge Picturesque park far from any village. Driving guests in from Bristol, Harford would be able to pose as a major landowner and give them a thrilling experience of an almost, but not quite, terrifying 'Sublime', ending with the calmly 'Beautiful'.

This orange route on his map in the Red Book was only Repton's first ingenuity. A green route offered in addition a fast, exciting circuit entirely within the park for the entertainment of guests on the next day of their visit; while a third, brown route, provided walkers with a whole sequence of Gothic and 'Sublime' thrills, all within a quarter of a mile of the house.

Red Books with their overlays were the innovations on which Repton's reputation has been based. Not many of the parks which his Red Books projected were ever laid out because he had no workforce in waiting to realise his visions. Of those which were completed few have survived, as most of his patrons were middle class industrialists whose houses and parks – on the outskrits of large towns like London, Bristol, Leeds, Norwich and Hereford – have since been swamped by suburban sprawl. But the Red Books themselves have survived to delight garden historians and to give the impression of a far more important Repton oeuvre than ever actually existed. His tempting water-colours had flaps, showing the grounds in their unimproved state. These pulled back to reveal the grounds as they could exist if the owners were prepared to spend a fortune on earth moving, dam building and tree planting to Repton's direction.

Those overlays were not Repton's only lure. His style of writing is seductive to a high degree. He was genuinely 'picturesque' in his aims because he landscaped to create actual equivalents of pictures with highlights, shades and colour schemes. To make a picture out of the view from Harford's house, his Red Book required, firstly:

> the removal of a white rail fence which catches the eye and prevents it seeing anything but itself, secondly the taking away the tops of several tall trees which hide the opposite wood, and also a corner of the lawn where, thirdly a cottage is proposed to be built. This cottage will give an air of cheerfulness and inhabitancy to the scene which would without it be too sombre, because the castle, tho' perfectly in character with the dignity of the surrounding woods, increases rather than relieves the apparent solitude.[8]

51   *Blaise Castle was built in 1766 for Thomas Farr as a picturesque shell to conceal an unsuccessful pumping station. Humphry Repton disliked it but was obliged to feature the Castle in his park drives to humour the new owner, John Scandrett Harford*

The 'castle' referred to was the pump house (**51**). Repton disapproved of such shams but Harford had insisted on keeping his castle.

Repton's personal contribution to Picturesque theory was the notion that signs of human activity in the form of cottages, gate lodges, bridges and roads enlivened and improved a view. This was an idea in direct opposition to the demolished villages and walled sporting parks of Brown. Rene Louis Gérardin's *De la composition des Paysages* of 1777 had given him the notion, but Repton's particular slant was painterly. The Blaise Red Book claimed that 'the occasional smoke from the chimney' of his proposed Woodsman's Cottage, on a bend of the orange carriage route, would produce 'that kind of vapoury repose over the opposite wood which painters often attempt to describe', while 'a covered seat at the gable end' would excite '*la Simplicité soigneé*'.

The orange route opens with a gatehouse lodge (**52**) set back from and above the public road, a warning to prepare for a Gothic carriage ride, not to a rather plain

52   *The Gothic entrance lodge to Repton's ingeniously attenuated 'green' route to Blaise Castle House, proposed in 1795 and implemented by 1799*

classical house, but to some Castle Perilous. By well graded bends the drive plunges down through the woods, sweeping past a quaint, virtually uninhabitable thatched cottage.[9] This is the section where Harford's men used gun powder, and their bore holes can still be seen in the rocks. At the next house, the Woodman's Cottage, a design markedly inferior to the Nash-Repton cottages built later for Harford at Blaise Hamlet, the drive enters a dark wooded ravine, then rises on the other side from gloom to cheerfulness and widening views. A path to the left is the start of the brown route to a precipice walk with a cave and a Lover's Leap, but the orange drive breaks out from the trees and the 'Sublime' to a sudden 'Beautiful' view of wide lawns and Harford's sober house. As a Quaker he had rejected Repton's suggestion of a portico.

The green circular route begins at the house and climbs the castle hill in a zig-zag course. This originally offered an exhilarating series of glimpses of the Severn estuary and the Welsh hills, caught through prepared gaps in the tree cover. Finally, after a last sharp bend, it broke into a hill-top glade, open only to the western views of the sea, but centred by the trilobal tower which Harford had inherited from his predecessor, Thomas Farr. This was the Gothic treat, 'the oldest in the kingdom', that Catherine Morland had looked forward to visiting with the boorish Henry Tilney in Jane Austen's *Northanger Abbey*. Had she ever arrived she would have found it occupied by a steam engine which Farr had vainly hoped would pump enough water out of the earth to create a lake in the dark ravine. Lack of significant water is the one real weakness of Blaise Park. Repton swept away Farr's platform for miniature cannon, even though the firing of cannon to produce satisfactory echoes was an accepted park pleasure of the age. The Giant's Cave at Piercefield had one such platform.

In 1799 Repton was working on two very different garden schemes in the county. One, at the Royal Fort almost in the heart of residential Bristol, was a cosmetic exercise for Colonel Thomas Tyndall who had inherited a small park ravaged by 'large chasms in the ground . . . immense heaps of broken earth & broken rock'.[10] These were relics of a building scheme for 500 houses which had gone bankrupt in 1793. By subtle gradations and smoothings Repton created an undulating garden, the steep lawn of which still lies below the Royal Fort's west or garden front. A judicious planting of trees concealed a new suburb of the city on an opposing hill, and a public right-of-way was hidden behind a bank and a shrubbery. Slight remains of these survive amongst towering twentieth-century university blocks, which no tactful art of Repton could ever have obscured.

In the same year, at Adlestrop in the north of the county, he was brought in to carry through and render fashionable the union of two parks, owned respectively by an uncle and his nephew. Adlestrop Park, a Sanderson Miller house of some substance, had, as described in an earlier chapter, a Chinese-Rococo layout of 1759-63 by Samuel Driver; but Adlestrop House was, until Repton got to work, only a rectory with a small garden. It was, however, the Rector, the Revd Thomas Leigh, who was the guiding figure behind Repton's reshaping, not James Leigh, the Rector's young nephew, who was the owner of Adlestrop Park. Consequently Repton's visual drama tended to be directed towards Adlestrop House, not Adlestrop Park.

Several public paths cross these linked estates and give today the impression that Repton's solution to the task was conventionally Brownian and a trifle bland. There are the usual two slim lakes created by dams and sluices and linked by a cascade with a two foot fall. The upper lake, with three small islands, enriches the western views from Adlestrop House and from its lower end a belt of trees reaches back to the church. This effectively allows each of the two houses to pretend that it stands alone in extensive grounds. A lower lake gives Adlestrop Park its own water feature to enliven views to the west. So far the revisions seem to have been simple and predictable. In his usual ingratiating manner Repton appears to have been pleasing two paymasters while offending neither. The truth is, however, much more interesting. In its first condition after the reshaping the Adlestrops represented Repton at his most visually subtle and Gardenesque. He was playing tricks of diversion and optical illusion which make his device with the cottage chimney smoke at Blaise seem positively straightforward. His account of that first innovative layout at Adlestrop is given in his *Observations*, published in 1803 when the operation was still fresh in his mind. The passage is instructive as it throws much light on what Repton's role must have been when he was advising, in 1804-10, on the construction of the more important, but very ill-chronicled, gardens at Sezincote, seven miles away to the north-west. His work at Adlestrop suggests that he was largely responsible for Sezincote's most famous garden feature, the Thornery or water garden.

With his inimitable aesthetic self-confidence Repton related how, before he began work, there was a small pool near Adlestrop Rectory 'supplied by a copious spring of clear water'. Its 'cheerful glitter...gave pleasure to those who had never considered how much it lessened the place, by attracting the eye and preventing its range over the lawns and falling ground beyond'.[11] Repton congratulated himself on putting an end to that apparently innocent pleasure:

> This pool has now been removed, – a lovely stream of water has been led through a flower garden, where its progress down the hill is occasionally obstructed by ledges of rock, and after a variety of interesting circumstances it falls into a lake at a considerable distance but in full view of both the mansion and the parsonage.[12]

So the belt of trees between the grounds of the two houses must have been a post-Repton and discordant intervention. He had left both houses sharing the long tongue of a stream garden, full of flowers, an anticipation of such nineteenth-century features and also of the Victorian passion for rock gardens. 'It may perhaps be objected', he wrote, 'that to introduce rock scenery in this place would be unnatural, but if this artifice be properly executed, no eye can discover the illusion; and it is only by such deceptions that art can imitate the most pleasing works of nature'.[13] In much the same tone he had hailed Harford's rock blasting to create at Blaise a road 'where carriages now pass this tremendous chasm with perfect ease and safety . . . Where man resides, Nature must be conquered by Art!'.[14] Ingenuity or brute violence could solve all garden problems. He was writing in the confident spirit of the new century, anticipating at Adlestrop the picture postcard charm of many Victorian gardens, of rocks, running water and bright flower beds, while at Blaise he had planned like a Victorian engineer, a Telford or Brunel.

At Blaise those bore holes in the rock for gun powder charges are a reminder of this power-gardening; at Adlestrop there are livelier reminders. A clear streamlet still runs quickly downhill in the middle of that later belt of trees, half smothered in nettles and brambles where once there were garden flowers. But unexpectedly Repton's 'ledges of rock' have survived the gentle flow of two centuries and still offer miniature barriers of stones two or three inches high and at intervals of about five yards. The cascade between the two lakes is almost gone (**53**), but this very early rock garden, one of the first in the country and a clear anticipation of Victorian Gardenesque fashions, can still be visited and valued.

Though far less Gardenesque, Repton's work on Oldbury Park, which began with an inspection of the grounds in 1799, was another subtle achievement, a minor triumph of the Picturesque carried through on a site of some industrial squalor. Oldbury Court, a Tudor house which would be demolished in 1960, stood high above the wooded gorge of the Frome, a substantial, even on occasions a formidable river, which had been harnessed by three weirs to power mills on the opposite bank. The gorge itself had been extensively quarried for its Pennant sandstone, though Shiercliff's *Bristol and the Hotwell Guide* of 1789 mentions 'elegant rural walks' that were 'carved

53 *Artificial ledges of rock in the Stream Garden which Repton created in 1799 to unite the gardens of Adlestrop Park and Adlestrop House. The wood which has grown up since has frustrated Repton's purpose*

through the woods and precipices' and at least one 'beautiful cascade', so the scene was not total desolation.[15] Thomas Graeme, the owner of the Court, called Repton in, probably on the strength of his reputation at Blaise, to create a more substantial park. There are virtually no records and no Red Book, but enough remains, in what is now a large municipal park flanked by a council estate, to reveal Repton's methods.

As at Blaise he began a main drive to the old house from the most distant possible corner of the park, starting with the gloomy 'Sublime' and proceeding to the smoothly lawned and clumped 'Beautiful'. A new bridge over the Frome from Frenchay, Bristol's most polite suburb, led to a thatched gate lodge, now demolished. From this the drive climbs up through woodland and a dramatically shattered landscape of quarried Pennant stone, the trees seeming to grow directly out of the rock. This carriage route shortly breaks out into open lawns with two bold clumps, one of oak, one of sycamore and ash, before sweeping up to the site of the house. Alternatively a walker's path, carefully graded and trimly walled with stone slats, leads away from the site of the lost lodge to follow the river gorge in a contrived Picturesque route to the house.

This, presumably Repton's path, still offers a most curious park experience. It is shaded all the way by mature trees, it rises and falls alongside cliffs and fissures of the soft rock. Twice the path drops to near river level at brief meadows in order to draw a walker's attention to a weir or a rushy island. On the opposite bank there are steep woods where badgers burrow among broken mill walls, and above the tree line are the villas of Frenchay, Bristol's equivalent to London's Twickenham. It may sound Arcadian, and it is indeed beautiful with a theatrical wildness. Repton must have been aiming, with a classical boathouse and two frail bridges all now demolished, at something like Payne Knight's park-gorge at Downton in Herefordshire, which he had visited. But all the while the presence of a large city is felt. There were working mills on the river in Repton's time. Today the iron tops of storm drains punctuate the path and a whiff of sewerage blows up from the Frome. In summer, scores of happy local children splash in the dubious brown water – a very old fashioned spectacle in this age of city lidos and gleaming municipal swiming baths.

Rather than following the modern tarmac route close to the river bank it is worth tracing the twists and rises of the original Picturesque path by its stone slatted supporting wall, up to the point where a small stream comes down from the left. This is where Repton's boathouse once stood. Now his path climbs steeply up through an under-planting of holly and laurel, past a natural rock arch, with spectacular views down into the gorge, to reach the garden walls of the vanished Court. It is no longer possible, now the house has gone, to test out the truth of Repton's claim in his *Observations* that 'by a very trifling removal' of earth he opened a view from the house down into 'the romantic glen'.[16] It would however have been typical of his topographical tinkering in the surroundings of big industrial cities during that period of the Napoleonic wars when major commissions out in the country were hard to come by.

Repton built a complete villa, Brentry Hill, in 1802 for a Bristol merchant William Payne, siting its rooms to take advantage of those views of the 'picturesque assemblage of gardens and villas in Henbury and Westbury' and 'the mountains of South Wales' that he had captured on the green carriage route at Blaise.[17] With that delicate preciosity, which often makes it hard to take him as seriously as he deserves, he rationed these westward aspects, 'the most unpleasant for a house' by reason of prevailing winds, with moveable panels and Venetian blinds.[18] Another charming classical villa in Westbury-on-Trym, Cote Bank, may have had Repton grounds created in 1803, and he also worked for Dr Lovell at Stapleton in the same year.[19] His other major commission in the Bristol area was at Leigh Court in 1814, but that is in Somerset and was a chapter of frustrations. Repton never had Capability Brown's sure touch in handling clients. He was paid £66.3s in 1801 and £24.3s in 1803 by William Blathwayt for some service, possibly a naturalising of the banks of pools in the south-west garden at Dyrham; but a handsome classical pavilion, which he designed for a terrace there, was never realised.[20]

Further uncertainty surrounds the part that Repton played in the creation of the gardens at Sezincote after 1804. His innovative stream and rock garden at Adlestrop is important because it is our best indicator of the character of his work at Sezincote. And now, as so often when dealing with Gloucestershire gardens, a writer has to reach out for superlatives to appraise that exotic house with its equally exotic gardens. Are they the most original, most exquisitely contrived or simply the most memorable union of house and garden in Britain? Perhaps it is easier to describe Sezincote as the palace and grounds of Coleridge's *Kubla Khan*, but achieved by a relatively modest English gentleman; certainly there was Romantic poetry in their conception and the poem in question had been written only a few years earlier.

The grounds must have owed most of their Indian-Islamic and Regency English character to their Nabob owner, Sir Charles Cockerell, to the scholarly painter recorders of Indian architecture Thomas and William Daniell, and to the architect Samuel Pepys Cockerell, who was Sir Charles's brother. But somewhere there in the background as Sezincote took shape was the eager, compliant figure of Humphry Repton, ever helpful, always ready with a reference or an imaginative idea. The designs which Repton prepared for a new Royal Pavilion at Brighton in his Red Book of January 1806 are every bit as confident and convincingly oriental as the John Nash designs which were eventually built. Repton noted in the 1808 publication of his rejected scheme that just before his first visit to Brighton:

> I had been consulted by the proprietor of Sesincot, in Gloucestershire, where he wished to introduce the Gardening and Architecture which he had seen in India. Although I gave my opinion concerning the adoption of this new style, and even assisted in the selecting of some of the forms from Mr T Daniell's collection, yet the architectural department at Sesincot of course devolved to the Brother of the Proprietor.[21]

So, as usual, Repton supplied the ideas and someone else got the commission.

When visiting Sezincote it is worth making an effort, by negative visual discipline, to strip the grounds of the sumptuous planting by Sir Cyril and Lady Kleinwort during their occupancy from 1944 onwards. The Kleinworts were informed and imaginative, their recreation of the decayed gardens was masterly, an artwork in itself, making it a place of horticultural pilgrimage at virtually every season. Nevertheless the original intention and the true setting for the house was the garden as Thomas Daniell recorded it in his aquatints of 1810, and in those aquatints there is more than a little of Humphry Repton.

The drive followed by most visitors today, that leading off the Bourton-on-the-Hill to Moreton-in-Marsh road, is an un-Reptonian disaster: a long trail, screened from the dull scenery on either side by trees and only redeemed by the proliferation of white trellis work on the Indianesque Diamond Lodge half way along it. There is no attempt at any sequence of the sublime or the beautiful, and the house first shows up when it is quite close and viewed from the side.

117

Then, almost abruptly, with no warning, the drive comes to the Thornery, and here again the planning is perverse (**colour plate 15**). Left and right, as it crosses a bridge of verdigris-coloured metal topped by Brahmin bulls, there are fantastic vistas; but they do not unroll. They go by in a flash – complexities of flower colour, pendulous bushes, the glimpses of a pool, great trees – but leave no abiding impressions or views, only a strong temptation to go back on foot and explore. That is the significance of Sezincote: the Arcadian park of wide vistas, lawns, temples and well disposed trees planted to exaggerate small folds of ground, is over. Parks are passé, Gardenesque layouts for detailed plant examination and appreciation are in. Classicism is out; uninhibited eclecticism is permissible.

The house is built of orange stone, like a mosque made out of breakfast marmalade with a bulbous, verdigris-coloured dome, and as it sidles into view it emphasises this break with tradition. To be fair, it does face, across a standard ha-ha, a standard Arcadian lawn sweeping down hill to the typical Brownian lake, largely hidden by trees but pretending to be a big river; but that is the only concession to past landscape convention. At this point, intrigued by the unfamiliarity of the architecture, it is best to keep the Thornery in reserve, as essentially a separate feature, not one obviously linked with the house, and to move forward to the Orangery on the far side (**54**). This, as a garden feature, is without equal. The Palladian cliché of a curved office wing terminating in a pavilion has been transformed into an exhilarating Moghul pastiche, sixteen flimsy bays long of iron and glass, ending in an onion-domed octagon almost Gothick in style. Its entire scimitar-shaped interior is filled with perfumed greenery: jasmine, abutilous, hibiscus and whatever can be persuaded to climb up and hang down fetchingly. To walk its receding perspectives is pure pleasure and it fulfils to perfection Repton's ideal of the conservatory as an extension to an interior.

To front this miracle and the huge canted side bay of the marmalade house, the Kleinworts, Lady Kleinwort in this case, had the courage to impose a new formal garden centred on an old raised flower bed. It is meant to be an Indian 'Paradise Garden', full of symbolism, the material world represented as a square reconciled with the circle of eternity; but it does not work. These straight canals and Irish yews could easily pass as a 1920s imitation of a seventeenth-century formal English garden. With that intoxicating Orangery behind it the Kleinworts could have got away with spitting cobra fountains, pergolas of poisonous trumpet flowers and absolute asymmetry. Perhaps their grandchildren will be more bold. The steep bank behind, alive with the colour of copper beech, golden yew, silver willow and purple sumach, is more in keeping with Moghul excess, while the little grotto before the Kleinworts' tennis pavilion is an authentic relic of the earliest planting.

On the other side of the house is the north lawn and the Thornery, as the stream-garden is confusingly called. The path to it is not so much directed as distracted by the usual Sezincote outpouring of rare trees and shrubs. [22] Magnolia, dogwood and hybrid thorn grow below Sir Charles's bedroom pavilion where, in memory of humid Indian nights, he slept under a tent-like roof supported by wooden spears with, however, the comfort of a heating system. Maples, Chinese Dentzia, golden cypress, weeping hornbeam, Mountain Ash, Persian Iron Wood

*54 Palladian quadrant arms boldly reinterpreted in Islamic forms to create the Orangery at
Sezincote, a design by S.P. Cockerell, advised by Thomas and William Daniell*

and hardy Palm all cluster about the mounting path to the top of the Thornery
and, despite the glorious distraction of flowers in summer, the visitor will begin to
notice that the Thornery is articulated by large, often grotesquely misshapen trees.
It is a linear rather than a colour composition; something which those early Daniell
aquatints emphasised clearly, painted as they were before the flowers took over and
the bushes grew tall.

Whether Repton simply picked out architectural features from the Daniells' *Oriental
Scenery* (1795-1808) which could hold a water garden together and then left it to the
two Cockerells to order them, or whether he planned the entire Thornery himself, will
never be known. It is, however, worth recalling his self-congratulation over the prime
feature at Adlestrop: 'a lively stream of water has been led through a flower garden,
where its progress down the hill is occasionally obstructed by ledges of rock, and after
a variety of interesting circumstances it falls into a lake'.[23] Every twisting path of the
Sezincote Thornery lies within the sound of hurrying water. The stream begins at the
pool of the Temple of the Hindu goddess Souriya who is riding on her seven horses.
It then hurries noisily down, criss-crossed by paths and stepping stones, splashing over
man-made ridges of rock to the Indian bridge with the bulls (**55**).

This is a most insistently eclectic and un-English structure. The classical orders have
been abandoned for blockish columns copied from those in the caves at Elephanta
outside Bombay. Most exotic of all in these chilly Cotswolds is a stone seat placed in

55 The artist of Indian scenes, Thomas Daniell, designed this exotically un-English bridge to carry the Sezincote drive across the Stream Garden or Thornery

the shadows under the bridge and set actually in the water course for coolness (**56**). It looks down to the pool of the three-headed cobra, a fountain of water spitting out from their fangs. A repellant symbol of an aggressive alien evil, the great bronze snake has coiled itself up on a stake to challenge anyone who leans over that verdigris balustrade between the Brahmin bulls. Whoever decided on its placing, and it is unlikely to have been the mild-mannered Repton, was not intent upon conveying the charm of India but its menace. Chinese cowslips grow on a small island, foliage tends to copper rather than green, and the chemical purples of hydrangeas dominate. The next, steeper and even noisier, reach of the stream flows down into a pool around another great outcrop of rock recalling Repton's comment that 'it is only by such deceptions that art can imitate the most pleasing works of nature'. On this reach of the garden the grotesquely shaped trees completely take over the attention from the Kleinworts' planting. There

56 *To remind Sir Charles*
Cockerell of the summer
heats of India this stone seat
was built actually in the
Stream Garden and under
the shadows of the bridge.
Beyond is the bronze
fountain of the three-headed
spitting cobra twined around
a trunk

is one enormous umbrella, a weeping hornbeam, a weeping beech, a contorted willow, a twisted English oak, several superb Lebanon Cedars (always a Repton favourite) a Noble Fir and a weeping Pagoda tree on another rocky outcrop.

Finally the stream-garden calms down into the Island Pool with minimalist wooden bridges and a sinisterly crawling Juniper. Subliminally, China seems to have taken over from India and the Thornery ends with that unimportant, even evasive, lake. What the flowers do in this garden is to distract from the unity of it all. In Daniell's time the Thornery, now half lost in bloom, could all have been taken in from the bridge: the whole stream with its prominent rock outcrops, the distorted trees, Souriya's Temple, the cobra fountain and the Island Pool. It would have been far more linear, even rugged, with what Repton described at Adlestrop as 'the interesting straggles of the babbling brook, which soon after spreads/Into a liquid plain, then stands unmov'd/Pure as the expanse of Heaven'.[24]

But the novelty of Sezincote's grounds is the comparative insignificance and unimportance of the lake, the 'liquid plain'. Someone, Repton, Daniell or Cockerell, created here one of the earliest and greatest gardens of the nineteenth century. Gardens had found a new focus and so had plant specialists. The whole essence of the Gardenesque was that it provided showcases for plant experts and enthusiastic head-gardeners.

After all this uncertainty over the exact authorship at Sezincote, the Hamlet at Blaise fits naturally enough into Repton's cloudy oeuvre. It is a creation which can legitimately be squeezed into the garden category because its nine houses for 'aged persons who had moved in respectable walks of life, but had fallen under misfortunes',[25] are set with the most artful inconsequence around an undulating green whose humps and declivities have been calculated to produce soft shadows in the evening sun. A path in the same spirit of casual charm runs around this retreat for superior 'peasants', who were required to have 'sufficient income to maintain them comfortably when relieved from the expense of House-Rent'.[26] It was, in effect, a Garden Suburb: the little cottages and the planting were a unity.

John Nash, who collaborated unhappily with Humphry Repton on several occasions, usually to Repton's loss, claimed to have invented the notion of almshouses around a village green in 1797 at High Leigh in Cheshire, and carried it into realisation at Blaise in 1811. He was away in Ireland for most of the time when the benevolent Quaker, Thomas Harford, was actually building the nine cottages, and it is generally assumed that Repton's fourth son, George Stanley, supervised their construction to Nash's designs on a site which his father had laid out with careful simplicity.[27] Whoever was responsible, it is a feature of the Repton saga that should not be missed. The National Trust which rules the Hamlet has managed to keep everything wonderfully underplayed. It is easy to walk past the entrance to the place in Hallen Road, a suburban street of Henbury, without noticing it. A small path leads under trees and there Nash's apotheosis of the china mantlepiece ornament lies in a perfect picturesque succession of intensely individual creations. Each one of the nine cottages is linked to the others only by its enormous chimney stack, appropriate in size to a large Tudor house, or even Hampton Court (**57**). Nash lavished his invention of bows, canted bays, seats beneath loggias, variations upon the themes of thatch, dovecotes, bread ovens and cosy dormers. Repton may have sited the authoritative sundial on its column with his refined feeling for assymetry, just as he directed the dimpling of the green. It is perfect of its kind; no other garden village is likely to equal it for bijoux middle class retirement. To stand there absorbing it, preferably in the evening sunshine of a clear summer's day is to understand the entire, subtle, genteel Repton aesthetic.

Repton died in 1818, looking forward with his characteristic cloying and sentimental aestheticism to the time when his dust and crumbling bones would become 'the pabulum of Roses';[28] not for Humphry the pabulum of dandelions or lowly weeds. He was the last of the eighteenth-century landscape gardeners and the first of the Victorian flower gardeners, adept in both schools, a pliant, serviceable figure, visually most subtle with a keen eye for the potential of even the most unlikely sites. He would have loved, if he had lived in this century, floribunda roses and the planting out of roundabouts and motorway service stations!

At the end of the last chapter of his *Observations* he gave a little coloured vignette to prove his awareness of the cutting edge of optical science. It consists of a circle of six circles, each one a different colour, in the sequence: Red, Orange, Yellow, Green, Blue and Purple. As an infallible guide for flower planting he assured his readers that no colour should ever be planted next to its neighbour in the sequence. Gardeners

57 One of the nine cottages that John Nash designed and George Stanley Repton built in 1811 to form Blaise Hamlet: the apotheosis of the almshouse ranged, each one in dazzling spatial invention, around an ideal village green

should always move across his charmed circle to put red flowers with yellow, yellow with blue, blue with orange and so on. His trained eye as a painter convinced him of the rightness of this judgement, which would have meant that blue should never be put next to green! If only he could have lived to enjoy Cezanne.

In his time he was taken seriously. As late as 1850 William Andrews Nesfield, the arch apostle of a revived fashion for formal planting in *parterres de broderie* using box and gravel, was brought in to advise on the park at Estcourt, just to the east of Tetbury. His response, unlike his usual rigid layouts, was pure Repton with optical subtleties and a refined thinning down. In true Repton style Nesfield produced two delicate water-colours (**58**).[29] No. 1 shows the view from the house across a late eighteenth-century lake as Nesfield found it. No. 2 shows the same view as it could be improved to a Repton pattern. Repton could easily have written Nesfield's commentary himself:

> The faults in No. 1 are, that the existing lines are hard and artificial – The Belt A is not parallel with the lines of Nature, but with the point of sight at the House – the tall trees c c break the skyline, but not sufficiently so as regards the ground line.

58   The upper watercolour is William Andrews Nesfield's rendering of the planting he found
      at Estcourt Park in 1850. The lower demonstrates his very Reptonian proposals for
      adding dimensions and depth to the planting and picturesque interest to the lake shore

And Nesfield's solution:

> To remedy this latter a loose mass of thorns, Maple & etc should be placed
> at d d on No. 2 which will (by means of the large Oak at E) compose a
> vista towards f and thus display a very agreeable horison provided g No. 1
> is removed.

Repton's concern at Blaise, that the eye should perceive changes in distance, should
become aware of a deep valley by various tree markers and observe nuances of any
foreground, are equally Nesfield's concerns. The lake in No. 1 'by no means conduces
to the picturesque because it wants variety & is too palpably tame & artificial'. So in
No. 2 it has become a serpentine with irregular banks. This was the lesson that
Repton had learnt from the admonitions of Richard Payne Knight when he visited
Knight's Teme Gorge and was told the errors of Capability Brown's landscaping.
There was, therefore, even in the mid-Victorian heyday of Italian and French formal
gardening, some continuity with eighteenth-century traditions of landscape.

8 Gloucestershire Gardenesque – the eclectic Victorians

It was John Claudius Loudon, a confident and prolific Scottish garden journalist and practitioner, who invented the term 'Gardenesque' in 1832, but it would not be fair to either praise or blame him for opening that Pandora's box of commercialism, rampant variety and aggressive professionalism which settled over nineteenth-century gardens under cover of the term.[1] Long before 1832, gardens were run for the benefit of head-gardeners, with the evolution of prize blooms, greenhouse complexes, multi-styled gardens and efficient horticultural engineering. Repton's own career was evidence enough that, after the death of Lancelot Brown, fashions in garden design had been speeding up and Repton was far from being a lonely pioneer. At Temple Guiting, folded away in the high Cotswolds between Stow and Winchcombe, there is a curious little garden that exemplifies the absurd pace of change which modish-ness and literary advice were imposing upon an eager amateur: a warning of the productive chaos of gardens to come.

George Talbot had inherited his father's property at Temple Guiting in 1785, still well within the Brownian era. He built himself a handsome house down in the valley between two small streams and began, in the Brownian manner, closing down lanes and footpaths to create an illusion of privacy and to open up prospects.[2] The drive was routed to make an unnecessarily long approach and two ponds, token lakes, were achieved by damming the larger stream. Then, moving into the Repton mode, Talbot planted a small rosary and an even smaller French garden above a south-facing terrace and squeezed into the patch of land below it a 'Roman' bath and a ten foot precipice to evoke the Sublime, or mock terror, by its sudden drop. Cascades and rustic bridges enlivened the smaller stream and a path passed under the new drive through a Cyclopean bridge. A grotto tunnel was devised simply by roofing over one of the blocked lanes. Not content with this condensed Reptonian Elysium in his garden, Talbot took up the latest advice offered to estate owners in Loudon's *Observations on the Formation and Management of Useful and Ornamental Plantations* of 1806:

> A number of hedgerows, all properly interspersed with timber trees, will completely change the appearance of a country, improve its climate, and yield a considerable quantity of timber to the proprietors of the lands.[3]

Loudon even promised that such tree planting would improve 'the health of its inhabitants' with 'a few near houses or villages, to group with them and improve their appearance'.[4] Persuaded, Talbot constructed miles of carriage rides by planting belts of trees and coppices along the local lanes of the largely tree-less Cotswolds, turning Temple Guiting into the bowery hollow which it still remains. As fashions moved on another stage the 'precipice' was modified by a rockery.

Temple Guiting is a private house, but Talbot's creative tree planting can be readily experienced along the roads about the village, and through the trees below the church two of his ponds, a little waterfall and a small peninsula of yew trees can be glimpsed, suggesting the miniature scale of it all. Particulars of the sale held in 1836 after George Talbot's death extolled the 'happy admixture of all the wildness of Hafod scenery, with the Claude-like landscape of the far-famed Piercefield', and praised 'the never-ending peeps' of the grounds, 'the cascades and hollow glens – the embowering shades and rockwork'.[5] Loudon had urged such busy 'peeps' in his 1812 *Hints on the Formation of Gardens and Pleasure Grounds*, while tree planting was becoming, not so much a fashion as an obsession with the gentry of the county. If one thing dominates Gloucestershire's nineteenth-century gardens, not always happily, it is the tree, used not in the Georgian way as part of a clump or plantation to shape a landscape, but as a specimen to be admired in itself for its rarity or its angular silhouette. There are four large arboreta in the county: Westonbirt, Tortworth, Batsford and Highnam, and such was the Victorian fondness for redwoods, Wellingtonias and monkey puzzles, there are few parks without a restless scatter of alien specimen trees disturbing the skyline, usually near the house where they can be easily admired and do the most visual damage. The park at Ashwicke Hall, high at the southern end of the Cotswolds near Marshfield, is typical of these mid-Victorian half-hearted arboreta. It was laid out after 1860 for John Orred, a wealthy Liverpool lawyer, with the usual noble but alien profiles from the coast of California rising around the tall castle keep of the house.

In such a tree friendly century it was natural that Picturesque gardens were still being laid out. It was during the occupancy, from 1821 to 1859, of the MP William Noel that Clanna, a remote and architecturally undistinguished house on the southern slopes of the Forest of Dean, changed its name to Clanna Falls on account of the Picturesque cataracts linking the long thin lakes Noel had created to thread its woodlands. Only the stable yard and a few Swiss-style cottages still stand as reminders of the much larger house that Captain Walter Marling built after 1884 on the site of Noel's house, but much of Noel's park survives in the stewardship of the Forestry Commission.

It is easy to see why the Captain adopted a Swiss style for his estate buildings. The whole park is completely un-Gloucestershire in feeling, far more like a valley in the Jura. The upper waterfall, which can be reached up a tangle of narrow lanes behind Alvington, is more readily heard than seen, thundering away in a dense undergrowth below the remains of an iron footbridge which once gave safer access (**59**). A path winds down from the waterfall beside the hidden stream to the upper lake, crossing it first on top of a long narrow wall with no handrail and then by a series of stepping stones: an unusual experience, a watery equivalent of the vertiginous. The lake itself is a green mirror to the trees that crowd in on all its banks except at its foot where the dry stone steps, of what was once another impressive cataract, lead down into brambles. A circular sluice out in the lake now acts like the hole in a bath tub to carry water on to the next two lakes with their further small falls. The landscape is enclosed

59 *During his long occupancy, from 1821 to 1859, the MP William Noel transformed the grounds of Clanna by a chain of narrow lakes linked through woodland by picturesque waterfalls. The house was renamed Clanna Falls; this is the upper cataract*

and, even in its Noel prime, Clanna park must have been a claustrophobia of trees and waters with only limited prospects.

The Rocks, in Marshfield parish, high up in the cold, wind-smitten hills to the north of Bath, even in its present enchantingly dilapidated and divided state offers an altogether more bracing and even a nationally important Picturesque experience. It is, however, one of Gloucestershire's problem gardens, under-recorded and overgrown. In the early seventeenth century it was called Southernwood, the three-bay, gabled Jacobean house of the Meredith family. John Jacob bought it in 1691 and had changed its name to The Rocks before his death in 1728. It must have been this first John Jacob and his wife who turned the old house and its rugged grounds into a Picturesque pleasure park visited and enjoyed by residents of Bath as early as 1738. That was before Valentine Morris had realised the Picturesque potential of Piercefield or Edmund Burke had published his treatise on the Sublime and the Beautiful.

The first proof of this is a poem by the Bath poet, Mary Chandler, entitled: *To Mrs Jacob On her Seat called The Rocks, in Gloucestershire*, published in her book *The Description of Bath* in 1738.[6] By that date the Jacobs' house was already 'An hospitable Seat',

> Securely seated on a Rock,
>   Whence silver Streams descend,
> From Cliffs, the Ruins of old Time,
>   And murmur as they bend.

The poem makes it clear that the grounds and not the house itself were the attraction. They offered 'Romantic Views' and were 'Diversify'd a thousand Ways,/And beautifully wild'. It was a place to 'feed poetic Fire;/Each broken Rock, and Cave, and Field,/And Hill, and Vale, inspire'. But the experience is more awesome than conventionally pretty, a clear foreshadowing of Burke's concept of the Sublime:

> When we, amidst the Shades below,
>   From the steep Hill descend,
> Where Crystal Stream in Mazes flow,
>   That tow'ring Elms defend;
>
> Like PLUTO's Regions, wrapt in Gloom,
>   We think the darksome Way,
> That ends in the *Elysian* Plains,
>   Fair, flowr'y calm, and gay.

So here is an early eighteenth-century park being seen in terms of the classical underworld. As the second John Jacob grew up he inherited his parents' tastes in landscape, buying Thomas Gainsborough's 'Hilly Wooded Landscape', an intense little painting. Between 1758 and 1774 Gainsborough was living in Bath, often setting his portraits in woodland surroundings and occasionally venturing into such pure Picturesque studies.[7]

On this evidence The Rocks should have featured in a much earlier chapter, but this is not a simple garden site. The property passed by marriage to the Horlock family and they, between 1790 and 1838, transformed the house into a Gothic castle. That was partly demolished when the estate was divided and sold up in 1957, leaving the grounds in an intriguing confusion. A lime avenue, planted in 1761 by the second John Jacob, still links the handsome relics of the Horlocks' castle to the main road, but the castle itself stands quite literally on the edge of a cliff, and all the wooded grounds lie below this, out of sight until the castle is reached. The views out over this last southern reach of the Cotswold escarpment are sensational, but immediately below the fifty-foot sheer cliff, the result of seventeenth-century quarrying, there is a large formal pool (**colour plate 16**) surrounded by terraces with plinths for statues or urns, an entirely unpredictable feature to find in the wild woodland that drops steeply down into the St Catherine's valley.

At some stage, whether under the Jacobs or the Horlocks it is not clear, the entire wooded slope was made into a Picturesque garden. Three sets of steps lead down to it. If the southernmost flight is taken, a terrace path leads back beside a craggy limestone cliff broken with fissures and grottoes and dark with twisted trees growing from cracks in the rock. The formal pool is a problem. It hardly fits a Picturesque park of broken rocks, but would the second John Jacob, the planter of the lime avenue, have carved out such a water garden in such a surrounding?

A romantic path leads further down from the pool to Oakford Lane through a valley of the rocks, with a rustic bridge over a hollow-way up to the Home Farm. There on the northern reach of the escarpment is another and bolder rocky staircase which must once have featured in a Picturesque circuit. It would be satisfying to attribute all these garden remains to the Jacobs and the 1730s, but there are no records to clinch the matter and, by its surviving outbuildings, the Horlocks' castle was an ambitious structure which would have required a bold setting.[8]

In earlier chapters it has usually been possible to write chronologically, garden following garden in a sane stylistic sequence; in the nineteenth century, with the flowering of the Gardenesque and its consequent free-for-all of Picturesque, Italianate, Elizabethan revival, arboreta, rock gardens, French formalism and bog gardens, that becomes impossible. At Toddington Manor (1820-35) for instance, the domestic model for the Palace of Westminster, Charles Hanbury-Tracy created, contemporary with the Picturesque mood of Clanna Falls, yet in an entirely different spirit, a rigidly formal garden which could be described as Italian crossed with a scholarly Perpendicular Gothic.[9] It survives today, but only just.

The main drive to the house winds down from the village, turns a bend by an enchanting, life-size stone statue of a Dresden shepherdess, and there the thunderous orange stone pinnacles and turrets of Toddington Manor make a sensational surprise view. Burberry Hill, the wooded knoll behind the shepherdess, was once a pleasance, but its paths have grown over. To the north a few specimen trees dot the flat, empty park before the tame conclusion of a tree belt. The infant Isbourne has been widened to justify a bridge, but the woodland around it cuts half the park off from the Manor. The flatness of the terrrain has defeated the imagination. Only west and south does the landscape come to life. An unusually animated reach of the Cotswolds creates a backdrop and the sharp-edged spire of G E Street's intensely Early English, Victorian Gothic parish church of 1873-9 strikes a suburban rather than a rural village note. In the fore-ground are two formal gardens, the western one level, the southern sunken, both confined in balustrades, steps, groups of statuary and dry fountains, as sharply chiselled and angular as the broach spire just across the fields (**60**). Some flowering bushes hang on to life among overgrown knots of box, but the statues and the steps are the keynotes. The quatrefoils of the balustrades are Gothic, as is the arched fountain of the western garden, but the later statues of muscular, half-clothed maidens improbably restraining enormous animals defy stylistic categories: they are Edwardian in character rather than early Victorian. The south garden is similar but has been sunk into an excavation to achieve a stately descent. Far out of sight on the perimeter of the dull, 6000 acre park are late nineteenth-century lodges, four of them built for Hugh Andrews in token

60   *For his ambitious High Gothic palace of Toddington Manor (1820-35), Charles Hanbury Tracy devised a superficially Italian formal garden, but set amidst its box parterres this Tudor-Gothic fountain. The massively sculptured maidens on twin plinths are later additions to the layout*

Cotswold Gothic. Toddington lies in summer sunshine like a sleeping, though far from beautiful, Princess, waiting to be woken by the kiss of some corporate training enterprise or country house hotel chain. 'I know not', John Britton wrote in a flattering monograph aimed at Hanbury-Tracy, who had become in 1838 Baron Sudeley of Toddington, 'of any parallel instance where a house of equal extent, diversity of parts, richness of decoration, and harmony of arrangement, has been the work of an amateur architect'.[10] Its gardens betray that amateur status by their heavy uncertainty.

To appreciate the very real virtues of the Gardenesque – its variety, its ability to surprise and divert at every turn of an estate – it needs to be seen brushed, combed, well watered and generally in apple-pie order. There had been a subtle change in aesthetic values as the nineteenth-century succeeded the eighteenth. Loudon offered a redefinition of Burke's analysis of Beauty that was coldly acquisitive, capitalist and even male chauvinist. Beauty, he claimed, could be found in

> such objects only as excite our love of possession, whether from their rarity, or suitableness to our ideas of communicating pleasure. Supreme beauty, to the mind of man, is only found in a lovely woman…the most beautiful women, either in form or colour, are always tender and delicate.[11]

Translated into horticultural terms this meant that a garden should rouse envy by its show of rare exotics that a neighbour would wish to rival, and by a show of tender plants which could only flourish in a heated greenhouse. The Gardenesque was, consequently, a high-tech style, not the result of an aesthetic movement or an historic revival, but of maximum expenditure. Unfortunately high-tech does not age attractively. Consequently the gardens of Highnam Court, a mile to the west of Gloucester, which were at the cutting edge of technology in their time, are something of a minor miracle in that they can be enjoyed today in their Gardenesque perfection, thanks to their regeneration through the scholarly care and hard cash of one man, Roger Head, a communications executive turned dedicated gardener.

Highnam's gardens really began when the Court was bought in 1838 by Thomas Gambier Parry, a young man fresh from Oxford and very rich. He found the gardens around the house, a Commonwealth build of 1658, in an arid part-formal, part-Brownian condition. The multiple stew ponds and the 'Great Pool' shown on Ferdinando Stratford's map of 1757 had been reduced to a series of rectangular canals below the house, flanked by two standard, slim lakes bordered by tree belts with an S-shaped belt of trees cutting down and through an expanse of bare grass land.[12] Parry was a hyperactive artist, collector and philanthropist. He had the local church rebuilt with a rectory, a school and five lodges, then re-routed the drive to make the blank north side of the house its entrance front. The old entrance front of 1658 became the garden façade facing south with an 1843 balustraded terrace by Lewis Vulliamy. A formal east garden with a conservatory, a sunken South Garden, a Winter Garden Terrace and a Winter Garden were added, the latter being one of the earliest and most successful Pulhamite gardens in the country.[13] It was a garden that required much care and many gardeners.

By 1992 a detailed survey and report found the house unused, the lakes silted and eroded and the gardens sadly neglected and overgrown.[14] Today Roger Head's transformation is virtually complete, and in sunshine the gardens almost dazzle in their colour and orderly perfection. Driving in by the Chepstow Lodge there is the cheerful sound of a Picturesque Pulhamite waterfall under the bridge over the river that waters the grounds so generously. Because the terrain is generally level the lake to the left makes little landscape impression. To the right is typical Victorian parkland with Gardenesque specimen trees: pinus, sequoia, fraxinus, acer, liordendron, cedar of Lebanon, the usual restless muster of green silhouettes. Highnam's importance lies in its gardens, not its park. It works intimately.

Entrance is through a brick wall into the East Garden. Set into a niche which was once within a demolished conservatory is Oliver Cromwell, half-nude, half-Roman, posing as Hercules. The statue should stand in the niche over the south door, but political considerations banished him after the Restoration of 1660.[15] He was brought here from exile in the stable court in 1920 and looks out over a correctly gaudy formal planting of geraniums with a punctuation of Parry's Irish yews. The South Garden is an immaculate sweep of grass down to the lower lake. Every path at Highnam is now of golden gravel, its grass borders are shaved to perfection and a wonderful neatness and cleanliness, as in an old-fashioned municipal park, refreshes every view. Municipal parks of the old style were, of course, all Gardenesque. The Broad Walk leads west towards the walled former Kitchen Garden and passes on the right a new orangery which has been added to the house as an exact match to the billiard room on the east side. Palms wave inside it and coi carp sport their sickly beauty in a tank seven feet deep. In the orangery there is also a survivor of one of the Pulhamite urns which once punctuated the Winter Garden Terrace; the statues that line the path today are modern replacements.

James Pulham was brought in by Gambier Parry in 1849 and worked here until 1862. The Pulhams had devised an ingenious process for making lightweight but natural-looking boulders by applying Portland cement to bricks and clinker, colouring it, spraying tiny pebbles to imitate sedimentary deposits and then laying out 'rocks' in imitation of natural stratification. One of the pleasures of Highnam is trying to distinguish Pulhamite from real Forest of Dean sandstone. It is not easy. James Pulham was so proud of one of his rocks at Madresfield Court in Worcestershire that he signed it as a work of art.[16] Round the corner of the former Kitchen Garden is a Pulhamite mini-mountain: climb this and a genuine surprise view opens up. Water cascades down from your feet into the walled garden, which is the exclusive realm of Roger Head's business partner and developed with idiosyn-cratic panache. Two more fountains, one very large and dolphin-ridden, play away, making three in this one limited area quartered by laurel paths. In Gambier Parry's day Irish yews bordered the paths with a patriotic display of blue lobelia, calceolaria, two shades of geranium and blue salvias, the foot soldiers of the Gardenesque army.

Beyond the rocky outcrop a Pulhamite rill brings water down to the Winter Garden and a new lake has just been completed from the withy bed where was, again in Parry's time, the Hawkins' Pond. This new creation with its graceful wooden bridge is a replica of Monet's lily lake at Giverny; to the side will be a Wild Wood Garden and beyond a very large Wild Meadow bordered by mature trees.

A gravel path back through the trees leads into James Pulham's masterpiece, the Winter Garden, really a vast rock garden of mazy paths (**61**). It is threaded by tiny streams crossed by rockwork bridges; there are two grottoes with ferns and seats and a cave (**colour plate 17**). Shrubs and flowers are present but not intrusively so; there are swamp cypresses, bamboo, acers and eucalyptus. The charm of it all is to follow the slab steps and golden gravel to glimpses of the outside fields and then, by arms of water, down to another lakeside. The excellence of the planning is that it draws a visitor in to lose all sense of direction and make sudden discoveries. A garden should work and divert, not act merely as a county flower show or a museum of trees. Highnam fulfils this objective perfectly.

After revived Highnam, Gloucestershire's other Gardenesque example comes inevitably as an anticlimax. Tortworth Court, seat of the Earls of Ducie, should have had a tremendous park around the characterfully monstrous jumble of Gothic motifs that Samuel Sanders Teulon put together in 1849-53 as an implausible residence for the 2nd Earl. But its first planning was uninspired and time has not been kind to it. To have moved over to the south side of the village from his old house by the church was a perverse decision by the tree-loving Earl. He had in his garden there what was,

61 *The Winter Garden at Highnam Court is a children's paradise of Pulhamite boulders, slab bridges over narrow green streams and Pulhamite grottoes, all laid out in the Gardenesque style for Thomas Gambier Parry in the 1850s and 1860s*

and still amazingly is, reputedly and plausibly the oldest tree in England, a sweet chestnut which was ancient in King Stephen's reign (1135-54). It deserves a pilgrimage today before going on to Teulon's Tortworth, which is now a hotel.

After deserting this ancient family retainer the 2nd Earl predictably planted an arboretum to compensate, but the Gardenesque gem of his new garden is the conservatory. It began life as a chapel with agonisingly pointed Early English arches and floral capitals designed by Teulon for the 2nd Earl. The 3rd Earl employed Ewan Christian in 1874 to turn it into a domed conservatory in a concord of iron and glass. Now the hotel uses it for conferences. There should be a subtle landscape planting down to the lake and over the hills beyond, but a tip, planted over with trees, has cut off most of the lake from the house, losing any sight of Teulon's actively three-dimensional Gothic boathouse. Beyond the lake the hills are densely planted with a thick, featureless rug of trees. All that can be enjoyed is a terrace with a great scarlet circle of formal planting on green, and a pets' cemetery large enough to suggest that the Ducies took pot-shots at their dogs.

Earl Ducie's arboretum was inspired and enriched by Robert Stayner Holford's arboretum at Westonbirt, begun in 1829 and now probably the most celebrated in the country. This is a complex of glades and drives and avenues, visited for some particular excellence every month of the year except December, when only peace and quiet are promised. January and February offer scented witch hazels and Christmas box, March camelias, April primroses and blossom, May rhododendrons, June mock orange and lilac, and so on. October draws the biggest crowds, for the maples in full array and the usual autumnalia of dying colour.

Across the road the gardens of Westonbirt House are more interesting but open to the public only on a few advertised dates when the girls' school is on holiday. Architecturally they are unique exotics and they were built, surprisingly, before the gargantuan Jacobethan palace that stands behind them. In front of the house there is the standard unadventurous park, more native in its planting than American. As the visitor rounds the house on its west side a giant stone conservatory looms up on a sweeping exedral arm of the building. From that point onwards, though there is good formal planting and excellent order, the interest and the excitement, which is the correct word to use for this prodigy, comes not from the trees, shrubs, flowers or the lawns, but from the garden buildings. They were designed by a pupil of Vulliamy, Henry Edward Hamlen. He contrived these extravagancies in a Moorish Rococo in 1843, but the palace-house that towers behind them was not rebuilt until 1864-74 when R S Holford tired of the more modest Tudor house which his father George, founder of the arboretum, had built in 1823.

The terraces of the central garden on the south front are grandly Italian, lively with urns and cherubs, but upstaged by the church, St Catherine's, part-fourteenth-century, part-Vulliamy. There is a Pulhamite rockery to the west with a small lake, but the gardens' greatness lies to the east. A long arbour of honeysuckle leads to Hamlen's garden, Italian more in name than actuality.

It is difficult to convey the style and character of this rectangular enclosure, cut off from the other gardens by yew hedges and a circular pool with fountains where a lion's head spouts over water lilies. To some extent Hamlen has anticipated the glorious outdoor rooms of the post-1890 Edwardian gardens, but with the grandeur more of a Portuguese palace than a relaxed Tudor manor. Its entry points are under richly pinnacled arches, marginally Jacobean (**colour plate 18**). These lead axially to two heavily carved and fretted pavilions with fish-scale domes, both subtle variants on the one mysterious theme, dream-like and slightly oppressive in their dusty interiors (**62**). Between these a glass vaulted conservatory leads back into the house. The formal bedding is tightly constrained within swirling symmetrical stone borders, tensely controlled. It is a space that needs to be peopled and is probably at its best when the school is in session. Empty it feels decadent and overwrought.

In complete contrast the Queen's Garden at Sudeley Castle, Winchcombe, is devoutly historicist and self-consciously appropriate to its site. When it was planted between 1856 and 1859 next to St Mary's church and supposedly on the site of the castle's original Tudor pleasance, it was among the very earliest of such Tudor revival gardens and marked a significant loss of Victorians' confidence in their right to lay out gardens of their own often manic devising, regardless of the period architecture standing nearby.

62   Henry Edward Hamlen
devised two of these
pavilions in High
Victorian Jacobean to
enrich sumptuously,
together with ornate
Jacobean arches, the
'Italian Garden' at
Westonbirt House.
Built in 1843 these
may have inspired the
rebuilding of the house
in 1864-74

Sudeley Castle was virtually rebuilt by George Gilbert Scott with an unusually appreciative eye for the charm of ruins, long reaches of which range evocatively about the grounds. Two bachelor glovers from Worcester, John and William Dent, had bought the estate in 1830 and begun the restoration, but it was their heir, John Coucher Dent (who succeeded in 1855) and his wife Emma who took direction for the period gardens from W A Nesfield. Their Queen's Garden has survived intact, as architectural in form as Hamlen's work at Westonbirt, but composed from solid yew, not stone. Two great double hedges of dense greenery have been trained and clipped into alternating round arches and portholes leading into a claustrophobic corridor. An arc of the same massive strength fronts St Mary's tower. Dotted at random along these barriers are rounded puddings of the same topiary, golden alternating with green.

As in Hamlen's strange garden this Queen's Garden appears to be moving towards the Edwardian ideal of an outdoor room but not quite grasping the possibility. Were those grim corridors intended for assignations, as in the later gardens for the 'Souls' of Balfour's period?[17] An octagonal pool centres the space between the yew walls, and the formal beds around it are solid with roses of recent planting. It works in a nursery catalogue manner, but it would never be surprising to hear 'Greensleeves' sobbing out in piped music.

In the rest of the county Stancombe Park and Cowley Manor remain, both intensely atmospheric and memorably beautiful, but entirely different in style, as is the way in this disparate period of garden history. The house at Stancombe is sited, like The Rocks, on the Cotswold edge, but here the land falls away not in a wooded cliff, but into a steep green combe. There is an upper garden of the 1960s and 1980s, open, conventionally flowery and belonging to a later chapter. But its Folly Garden, a macabre evocation of the classical Underworld, the habitation of the dead, lies some 200 feet down the hill, out of sight around a bend in the valley. Young Bransby Purnell created this secret water garden, using the labour of retired soldiers soon after Waterloo:[18] a place of dank and decadent enchantments, more Wagnerian than Regency in spirit.

A narrow path, the Menagerie Walk, curved against the side of the combe, leads down into Hades, flanked by topiary animals, shrub roses and comfrey. From a circular enclosure, with a font and a mosaic panel set above it, a stepping-stone walk winds through ferns and almost tropical gunnera leaves dripping with water. Brick side-walls close in upon the narrow path and water rushes under the flagstones. A dark tunnel entrance beckons, and as visitors are growing used to the dim light they are surprised by a huge stone dog – Cerberus guarding the Underworld – and a series of 'moral' choices of ways (**63**). Tame Cerberus with cakes and honey and the rivers of Hades can be explored. The tunnel divides and the right-hand turn leads to a lake, the Styx, with views across to a Doric Temple (the Elysian Fields).

Another tunnel containing a fossil collection opens up and then, in welcome open air, comes the Egyptian Court. Three ways, or decisions, lead out of it. To the left is a landing stage where Charon's boat could ferry dead souls to Elysium. Another leads through a whale's jawbone to an Ice House, while the third is a keyhole opening to yet another tunnel and a yew walk. This is inhabited by a bronze boar, a cast from Il Porcellino in the Uffizi gallery in Florence; the family call him Cornelius. The embattled yews lead to carefully composed views out of the garden, a gardener's cottage and the Temple, which can only be entered by a concealed door at the side (**64**). It has a new sybaritic interior but is not open to the public. A flagstone path leads on to two pagoda-roofed greenhouses with their original leaded glazing and shelves for exotics. One has a fountain in the centre and another swan fountain plays in a clearing, or would play if the original water system had not dried up, though water drips down every wall. An arched pergola leads back to Cerberus and the way out of the Underworld.

Cowley Manor in the hills behind Cheltenham has a quite different water garden, Italian this time; one which is all the more precious because, at the time of writing (September 2001), it feels threatened, not structurally, but in the richly delicate textures of decayed stone and the plants that have colonised it. On the steep slope above them is the Manor, a swaggering Italian palazzo, built over two phases, 1855-7 and 1896-1902, and in two different limestones. It is being turned into a very select and expensive hotel.[19]

63 *In the years after Waterloo Bransby Purnell decided whimsically to recreate the Hades
and Elysium of the Ancient World in his Cotswold valley at Stancombe. Here the dog
Cerberus guards one of the gates to the Underworld*

64   *The Temple in Stancombe's Folly Garden was meant to represent the Abode of the Blessed and fitted up accordingly in sybaritic luxury. It should be reached by a boat trip across the River Styx with Charon as the oarsman*

A team of almost a hundred skilled workmen has cleaned and scraped its superb stonework so that it looks as if it was built yesterday. The result is that, embarrassingly, its garden façade is in two distinctly different colours where R A Briggs added, in the wrong stone, six supposedly matching bays to George Clarke's original five. Everywhere about the palazzo there is life and activity. In contrast the lakes below the terrace and the great fountain-dam of the Seven Satyrs are wonderfully dead, textured and decayed, a lost garden of the Renaissance that could have been sketched out by Raphael and matured through three centuries.

What makes the fountains so important as well as so dramatic is that they are arguably the true origin of the Thames. The Seven Springs above Cowley are one of the two putative sources. They feed the Churn, and the Churn seems, at its union with the Thames further east, to absorb that river rather than vice versa. The small dark source-pool brims out below overhanging trees and runs immediately under a rustic bridge into the Upper Lake. This has been contrived by the dam of the Seven Satyrs, symbolising those Seven Springs (**colour plate 19**). The lake and its ornate dam lies overlooked by the palazzo and its terraced garden, the balustrades of which are decorated with four exquisite reliefs of the Seasons as young maidens. The Satyrs on the dam spout vigorously (**65**), long beards of weed dangle from their chins and their water falls noisily into a deep pool, a tempting cold bath flanked by stone eagles. From this, steps with couchant lions lead the substantial flow into the grey, melancholy Lower Lake. Its banks and its island are overgrown and richly textured with a fragile beauty that the inevitable repair of its crumbling margins must damage. The Cockleford Brook pours out from the lake to flow pleasantly through a small park with 'shallows for the deer',[20] but after the two lakes and the Seven Satyrs, the eagles and the lions, there can only be a visual anticlimax.

Particulars of the sale of 5 July 1892 [21] mention a 'Rustic Summer House', a 'Boat House', 'Coniferae on the banks', a 'Tennis Lawn' and 'a newly built Skittle Alley roofed over with Iron and filled with a Fire Place and lighted by Gas'. The complexities of such a virtually self-supporting estate at that period are listed proudly: piggeries, dog kennels, a 50 acre deer park, red and fallow deer, four paddocks, private telegraph wire, three 'Vineries', a 'Peach House', and 'Cucumber, Melon and other Firing Pits'. There was a 'Gas Engine House and Wigham's Patent Atmospheric Gas Machine providing sufficient Gas for 80 lights for 6 hours without replenishing', a 'Paved Glass House with coloured tiles', 'Stove House', 'Palm

65 *A satyr mask of Raphaelesque grotesque work pours out one of the supposed seven source springs of the Thames on the Dam of the Seven Satyrs at Cowley Manor. These Italian water gardens were laid out after 1874*

House', 'Passages for Fern recesses', but 'all erected about 19 years ago'. That would date the offices to 1873 which was when the first owner, James Hutchinson, a London stockbroker, died; so Robert Richardson-Gardner MP, who bought the estate, may have improved the grounds. The illustration of the lakes, fountain and house preserved in the Gloucestershire Record Office is dated to 1874, [22] which casts an uncertainty over the architect for the Seven Satyrs and an agreeable mystery as to which Victorian owner and architect could have conceived a project so poetic.

9 Gardens of stone and outdoor rooms – Cotswold Arts & Crafts

Even if superlatives of praise had not been exhausted on the gardens of earlier chapters it would still be inappropriate to describe Gloucestershire's top four Arts and Crafts gardens – Hidcote, Rodmarton, Kiftsgate and Snowshill – as the county's 'greatest'. Greatness is not their quality. Apart from two errors in the direction of Versailles at Hidcote where, in any case, an American not an English Arts and Crafts enthusiast was directing operations, these gardens are modest and human in their scale. But of all Gloucestershire's gardens they are the most enjoyable to visit, the most practical and the most covetable. Catch Snowshill, that admirably presented National Trust property, on some late autumn afternoon and its empty grounds come very close to the Platonic ideal of the perfect garden. This is only the book's penultimate chapter, but it has also to be its natural climax. After the marvellous four the remainder of the twentieth century is all gently downhill, even when an heir to the throne moves onto the scene.

Why, between 1900 and 1939, which is rather longer than the 'golden Edwardian afternoon' of popular legend, was the time so right for gardens of magical quality, and why were the Cotswolds, as opposed to the county as a whole, the place for them?[1] The last question is the more easily answered. There was not just limestone readily accessible, varying from cold silver at Painswick to hot orange at Toddington, but multiple skilled masons able to work it. At the opening of the century the Cotswolds were still natural Arts and Crafts country; that was why the Guild of Handicraft left London in 1902 and settled in Chipping Campden. Even today the cost of rebuilding a Lutyens pergola at Abbotswood would not be astronomical. Quarries are still open and close at hand. The answer to the first question is more complex.

The Gardenesque was a response to the Industrial and Agricultural revolutions, so were Arts and Crafts gardens a delayed response to the Gothic Revival?[2] The Pre-Raphaelites were such a response in art, and pre-Raphaelitism was one of the rare, even unique, artistic movements that turned England back upon its own historical and topographical heritage rather than reaching out after continental models: French Impressionism or Viennese psychological insights as dramatised by Catalans. A logical concomitant of this unusual aesthetic insularity was a feeling, not for medieval gardens, since none had survived, but for the nearest approach to them, the romantic walled enclosures of the Elizabethans and Jacobeans: a Tudor Renaissance Revival in default of a Gothic one. This led to a sharp clash of interests: a tendency towards planting with simple native flowers appropriate to native gardens at just the time when Gertrude Jekyll, while paying lip service to tradition, was actually applying colour insights from French Impressionism to the enormous range of new flower species which the Gardenesque had made available to her.[3] It is fascinating today to walk around the garden enclosures of Hidcote and observe the gardeners of the National Trust straining to satisfy both interests, the native traditional and the Jekyll colour symphonies. They are not always happy flower-bed fellows.

Historicist gardens were being planted in the 1850s, like that already mentioned at Sudeley Castle; but it was William Morris who really orchestrated this garden preference, with his feeling for the functional needs of the middle-class as well as for the craft and traditional in garden design. He had moved in 1857 into the Red House, Bexleyheath, built for him by Philip Webb, with a homely walled garden that acted as an extension to the rooms of the house. Then in 1871 Morris rented Kelmscott Manor, Oxfordshire and that, with its dream-like, melancholy, walled gardens in the damp headwater country of the infant Thames, became something of an Arts and Crafts archetype. Morris expressed the place in poetry and prose, conveying an insidiously attractive atmosphere of decadent, *Roman de la Rose* adulteries and intrigue which reflected his own love-life. This appealed to an influential (and adulterous) section of the Victorian elite, the self-styled 'Souls', who were socially and politically prominent. Historicist gardens satisfied their desire for both a patriotic identity and an emotional yearning: that 'greenery yallery Grosvenor Gallery' mood which Gilbert and Sullivan mocked in *Patience*.

Morris insisted that enclosure and privacy were prime qualities in a garden. He wrote in 1882:

> It [the garden]should be well fenced from the outside world. It should by no means imitate either the wilfulness or the wildness of nature, but should look like a thing never to be seen except near a house. It should in fact look like a part of the house.[4]

That was written nine years before John Sedding, a founder member and sometime Master of the Art Worker's Guild, published his *Garden-Craft Old and New* (1891), a passionate plea for a return to the herbs and simple flowers, the mounts, terraces, clipped yews and gracious confinements of the traditional Elizabethan and Jacobean gardens. A year later Reginald Blomfield published his trenchant polemic, *The Formal Garden in England*, urging much the same thing. Both writers poured contempt upon the idea that

> two heaven-directed geniuses – Kent and Brown – all of a sudden stumbled upon the green world of old England, and, perceiving its rural beauties….. these two put their heads together, and out of their combined cogitations sprang the English garden.[5]

Sedding and Blomfield were united in their dislike of casual eighteenth-century landscape gardening, and any attempt to make a garden appear like an idealised tract of normal countryside. Sedding declared that

> It were a palpable mistake, an artistic crime, so to speak, to follow the wild flights of Salvator Rosa and Gaspar Poussin, and with them to attempt a little amateur creation in the way of rent rocks, tumbled hillsides, and ruins that suggest a recent geological catastrophe.[6]

The two books represent an attack on Arcadian gardening and a defence of historicist gardening, a return to architecture in the layout and more stone walling. But it was another founder member of the Guild, the architect John Belcher, who had almost given Gloucestershire its first of these walled and hedged enclosure gardens as early as 1889.

When Belcher was virtually rebuilding Stowell Park, near Northleach, for the Earl of Eldon, his assistant, Arthur Beresford Pite, produced a beautiful engraving proposing an ideal form for the new house and its gardens. If this had been realised in full it would have anticipated the Arts and Crafts gardens of the next thirty years in every detail. Whether it was Belcher or Lord Eldon who modified the proposed layout is not recorded, but the six small enclosed gardens west of the parish church never materialised and a lake below the house would have required a fifty foot dam. The little gabled garden house drawn by Pite at the north end of the terrace axis before the garden front of the house was altered in execution to a dovecote, and none of the gazebos or grandiose flights of steps were built on that terrace (**66**). In one respect, however, Belcher did improve on Pite's design. At the southern end of the long green entrance court he built a pair of daringly angular two-storey entrance lodges in the Elizabethan manner.[8] These are set diagonally, in a dramatic clash of styles, to tall gate piers topped with ornate classical urns creating, with flights of balustraded steps up to a higher terrace and a system of narrow cobbled ways, something close to a Jacobean garden complex.

Before the real flowering of Cotswold compartmentation came Gloucestershire's only garden by Sir Edwin Lutyens, Abbotswood, near Stow-on-the-Wold. The new owner, Mark Fenwick, had commissioned Lutyens in 1902 to rescue his plain, heavy Tudorbethan house of 1867. Fenwick was a Newcastle banker who had taken early retirement to devote himself to his real love – planting. Lutyens obliged him by devising a tactful but characteristically witty wing of Artisan Classicism with a roof gable pretending to be a pediment. Lutyens contrived one real signature garden in a fountain court and added two grand formal terraces as a frame for his patron's planting, attaching these last to the house by a massive pergola which has, regrettably, been taken down.

This is not a four-star Lutyens garden, but even a two-star Lutyens leaves an average garden looking commonplace.[9] The fountain court below the west side of the new wing is a classic instance of his carefully considered invention (**67**). He took the design of a domed water-lily pool which he was building in the same year, 1902,

66 *When John Belcher was rebuilding Stowell Park in the late 1880s his assistant, Arthur Beresford Pite, drew designs for a complex garden of terraces with hedged and walled enclosures. This terrace looking towards the Dovecote is one feature that was realised*

at The Hoo, Willingdon, Sussex, and set a replica of it within the wall of his new wing.[10] Its keystone features a head spouting water into a long circular pool giving on to a rectangular pool between the buttressed enclosing walls of a paved court. Bullrushes in the pool, hydrangeas in tubs along the pool-side and a cloud of sedum on the steps leading up to it are the only relief to stones and green water. It is enclosed, but not in the homely cottage style of the Arts and Crafts.

When it came to the two terraces of the main garden Mark Fenwick must have told his architect to subordinate everything to the south view, down across a great sweep of lawn into the valley of the Dikler. The upper terrace immediately before the south or garden front of the house is divided into three parts. The Blue Garden on the right and the Rose and Lavender Garden on the left are separated from a lower Central Garden by thick yew hedges cut into gabled shapes to reflect the profile of the house. An axial way runs through the middle of the Central Garden with its quartered beds, past a sundial, and down into the lower terrace where it is aligned upon a wrought iron *claire voie* set in the bottom wall. As Lutyens first designed the layout a rose pergola on the far left and a handsome tennis pavilion in Cotswold vernacular style (**colour plate 20**) standing alone at the right-hand corner of the

67   *The Fountain Court of 1902 by Sir Edwin Lutyens at Abbotswood reproduces a semi-domed lily pool which he was building in the same year at The Hoo, Sussex*

lower terrace gave an asymmetrical relief to the balanced formality.[11] But the pergola has been taken down and the tennis court which occupied the lower terrace has been replaced with formal bedding and a rectangular pool, where a bronze Donatelline Pan stands bewildered in the water. The Blue Garden opens with a narrow semi-circular fountain pool before a Doric temple seat, and its blue salvias are planted around another fountain pool in a geometry of low clipped box. Mark Fenwick's highly professional herbaceous border alongside the Blue Garden still flourishes. It attempts no Gertrude Jekyll subtleties, though she and Fenwick were friends. There is no intimacy, no enclosure, only a confident, lordly openness.[12]

All gardens are at the mercy of the weather, and I was in Abbotswood late in September on a miraculous day of late summer. But autumn was already colouring the trees that tower north above the house. On the slope below them the Heath Garden, Fenwick's memento of Northumbria, was breathing out pure honey. This had drawn down a flight of red admiral butterflies, four or five fluttering heavily on every bush. In a stroke of garden genius, that Fenwick may have planned, the autumn crocus had taken over all the garden's woodlands with an infestation of frail stars on long weak stalks. Pink is an uneasy colour, but here the union of heaths, crocus and red admirals was in animated accord. In spring apparently a similar assault is staged in this unusually favoured garden by wild orchids and fritillaries. These flowers also appear in a stream garden of Pulhamite rocks above the entrance drive, and there is a second, fully-fledged, water garden of nine pools which runs down a valley in the lower woodland to join the lake which Harry Ferguson created in the 1950s. Ferguson bought Abbotswood after Mark Fenwick's death in 1945 and retained the Fenwick planting, so Abbotswood represents a Lutyens garden designed without the help and advice of Gertrude Jekyll.

Most of the other early twentieth-century Gloucestershire gardens were formal and sub-Lutyens in their layouts.[13] Guy Dawber's Eyford Park, created over two periods (1911-12 and 1920), has the usual balustraded terrace with summerhouse, a round garden pavilion and a punctuation of gate piers. Dawber was working earlier in the county, between 1901-2, at Burnt Norton, Aston-sub-Edge, where he was reviving the terraced early seventeenth-century garden for the 5th Earl of Harrowby. The rose garden which he created to the west of the house and the semi-circular pool at the exedral end of the main axis would inspire T S Eliot in August 1935 to write the first of his *Four Quartets*: 'the roses/Had the look of flowers that are looked at' and 'Dry the pool, dry concrete, brown edged'.[14] An eighteenth-century garden pavilion stands in the grounds.[15] John Campbell's gardens of 1924-5 at Great Rissington Manor are much the same, though his gazebo risked a rustic thatched roof.[16] At Notgrove Manor, east of Bourton-on-the-Water, A N Prentice's garden of 1908 has an octagonal thatched dairy, and his heavy pergolas climb up around formal lawns set with stone French vases brought from Orleans House, Twickenham. [17]

Chronologically the next important garden after Abbotswood has to be Hidcote because, though much of the work on it dates from the 1920s and 1930s, it was begun in 1908, and photographs of about 1910 prove that its most clearly Arts and Crafts enclosures were by then already laid out and maturing.[18] Hidcote is a garden of some historic significance, as it was the National Trust's first major garden acquisition and it set the Trust onto a severe learning curve in management.[19] Now in its opulent prime Hidcote is perhaps easier to admire than to love. Its rival garden at Kiftsgate Court lies literally on the other side of the lane from it and Hidcote suffers a little from the inevitable comparisons. Of the 'marvellous four' Hidcote is the only garden with no natural topographical advantage. Kiftsgate includes a steep, almost cliff-like, woodland, Rodmarton has views across Wiltshire to the line of the Marlborough Downs, and Snowshill pitches its garden buildings and minute terraces headlong down the Cotswold edge to overlook Worcestershire. In contrast Hidcote has been laid out, with no advantage of a previous older garden, on essentially level ground tilting slightly upwards to the west, while its parent house, a converted farm, offers no architectural support or even much contact. Nevertheless, Hidcote has become an undoubted success, the National Trust's Gloucestershire flagship garden, visited on an average year by 125,000 people, more than its narrow paths and grassy verges can easily accommodate.[20]

Considering that Hidcote's grounds were all laid out in the twentieth century, curiously little is recorded about their origins. The rich, twice widowed American, Gertrude Winthrop, bought it in 1907. Her only son by a first marriage, Lawrence Johnston, had become a naturalised British citizen in 1900, and his life thereafter reads like something out of Henry James: long but not very interesting. He joined the British army and fought in the Boer and 1914-18 wars; which suggests that he could have had little influence in the early years of Hidcote when the attractive maze of small gardens, cut off from each other by high yew and box hedges, was conceived. So could his mother, a very resolute old lady, who specified in her will that Lawrence could not touch her capital but only live off the income, have been the real garden genius? That point deserves to be considered during any tour of Hidcote's incident-crammed and gloriously bewildering ten acres.

Then there is the mystery of the planting. Major Johnston kept no records, although he was an enthusiastic plantsman who travelled to remote regions of the Earth – Yunnan and Tanganyika – to find rare flowers, attended by his valet and his chauffeur (he never married). Very few of his rarities survived the Trust's takeover, which allowed his ingenious pergola-greenhouse to collapse and made no record of what was planted when it became the owner. The Major himself described his layout as 'a wild garden in a formal setting', and Miss Norah Lindsay, a disciple to whom he left his beloved villa on the Riviera, spoke of this 'jungle of beauty'.[21] Yet two thirds at least of Hidcote is completely formal, though a formal maze of oddly related parts.

As a result of the Trust's curious stewardship virtually all the overwhelming beds of flowers that now delight its visitors have been planted at Hidcote by the Trust's head gardeners and curators since 1948, when the Major beat a semi-retreat to the south of France to nurse his dermatitis. We need not, therefore, be too reverential about their authenticity. The wise course is to thread the mazes, appreciating that names like the Fuschia Garden, the White Garden and the Maple Garden are recent inventions, and find favourite regions in a delightful wilderness of choice. It is not an easy garden to absorb, and in her shrewd introduction to the first guidebook Vita Sackville-West abandoned any attempt at an itinerary. At least three visits at three separate seasons are required to do it justice.

In the heart of this maze is a large, green T-shape of two grassy avenues: the Theatre Lawn and the Long Walk. They were not planned, but simply evolved during the war years, 1914-18, which was when the twin brick gazebos, linchpins of the avenues, were built. This again points to Mrs Winthrop as the planner, though the Long Walk was not pressed beyond the Central Stream Garden to meet the horizon until after 1927, by which time the Major would have been back in control.

68   The Pillar Garden is, by its austerity and aggressive linear definition, the most committedly classical and Italian of all the many garden enclosures at Hidcote Manor. It was laid out after 1920 when Major Johnston had severed his ties with the army

Both avenues are best ignored as they only lead to what guidebooks describe as 'superb views of the Vale of Evesham', actually a broad tract of featureless country-side which Bishop Pococke would rightly have scorned. The more rewarding course is to bear to the left on leaving the ticket office and the Garden Yard to explore the fifteen distinct gardens.

Various axial routes, none of them particularly dominant or authoritative, connect these hedged enclosures. The Old Garden, Circle, Red Borders and Stilt Garden axis can lead, rather like a map of the London Underground, to another axis: Circle, Bathing Pool and Poppy Garden. Do not expect too much from the Bathing Pool. It is raised, circular and the colour and consistency of mulligatawny soup, unlike Kiftsgate's two pools which are black and spotless. Another axis could take in the Stilt, Terrace and Pillar Garden (**68**) with Rock Bank, and would then lose itself in the more open Spring Slope and Lower Stream Garden. An entirely separate area north of the Theatre Lawn has the Camelia, Pine, Rose and Kitchen gardens. The popular favourite, with those two charming brick gazebos, which are more Hampshire than Cotswold in profile, is the Red Borders (**colour plate 21**). Unlike the White Garden, which is not very white, these Borders really are red. The planting is inspired by Vita Sackville-West not Gertrude Jekyll; there are no subtle colour symphonies, just surges of bronze and scarlet. At other points, when in doubt, the National Trust has successfully hurled in regiments of phlox.

In its early years, before the Major returned from his wars, there must have been a general Arts and Crafts feeling to the enclosures of Hidcote, though local stone never featured much. Once the green hedges became overwhelmed by flower colour that Arts and Crafts mood was diminished. Banks of flowers are the crowd pullers so, for almost three complete seasons, Hidcote is a long running flower show set, not in marquees, but in a delightful maze of hedges and limited vistas.

At Rodmarton, in bracing contrast, the house and its gardens interact very closely and preserve with remarkable fidelity that spirit of extreme romantic liberalism, part paternalistic, part idealistic, which impelled the Arts and Crafts movement before Socialism made its aspirations look condescending. Incised upon the house wall in a quotation from Oliver Goldsmith's *The Deserted Village* the house boldly states its innocent, impossible ideal:

A time there was, ere England's griefs began,
When every rood of ground maintain'd its man;
For him light labour spread her wholesome store,
Just gave what life required, but gave no more;
His best companions, innocence and health;
And his best riches, ignorance of wealth.

Rodmarton is that rare thing: a true time trip back into an early E M Forster novel, say *Howard's End*. Thanks to three generations of dedicated care by the Biddulph family, an earnest amateurism lives on: uncommercialised, upper class and gently eccentric. Its interconnected garden rooms seem only to be waiting for the visitors to leave at five, and then a tea bell will tinkle and ladies in long green dresses and craft jewellery will come out of hiding and decide whether to eat their cucumber sandwiches in the Winter Garden, the Sunken Garden, the Leisure Garden or by the alpines at the edge of the Croquet Lawn, where dark walls of immaculately clipped yew will shelter them from every wind except that from the south. Rodmarton is true Merchant-Ivory land.

A young stockbroker, Claud Biddulph, who had a very rich father, retired here with his wife Margaret, a lookalike for William Morris's wife Janey. The young couple were intent upon pursuing those ideals of simple living, integrity to materials, local crafts and Christian responsibility that were the essentials of the Arts and Crafts movement. Claud meant to build a home for himself where he could play the benevolent local squire, use local labour, local stone, local oak and create over several years a team of men who would improve their own craft skills and at the same time pass them on to others. He chose as his architect Ernest Barnsley, a Birmingham man who had been restoring and building houses in the Cotswold vernacular tradition since 1894. Having worked as an assistant to John Sedding, Barnsley believed, like Sedding, that a house and its garden should be tightly integrated and mutually

69   *The Troughery at Rodmarton Manor is one of Ernest Barnsley's original enclosures, laid out, or rather built, as it is principally stonework, before 1914*

complementary. The basic structure of the gardens at Rodmarton was to Barnsley's design. The garden walls went up at the same time as the walls of the house, but the actual planting was controlled by Margaret Biddulph and her old tutor from Studley Horticultural College for Women, William Scribey, whom she brought in as head gardener. Margaret's life span, ninety years from 1880 to 1970, would ensure an enchanted continuity to the grounds at Rodmarton.

An earnest functionalism has shaped the planning. Immediately outside a Chapel for morning prayers is a long alcove within a south-facing wall where, on a very warm day, breakfast could be taken. High up on a corner of the house is a balcony with an open-air bedroom where health fanatics could sleep out in all weathers, protected only from the rain. The Leisure Garden below it is paved with stone so that it can be used in wet weather. Flowering trees, abrupt topiary, and a pyramid of small flower pots around a huge vase, all rise angularly from the flagstones. There are flowers to control weeds, but little grass. Around one corner, sheltered from every wind but again paved with stone, is a Winter Garden. Round the corner from that is The Troughery. Ranged with stone troughs like a miniature rectangular Avebury (**69**), it merges into The Topiary, which is equally geometrical in its clipping. Next to this angular pair is The Terrace, stone paved again with cypressus spires and more blockish, perfectly clipped topiary.

Then comes relief. The next garden is sunken and has vines climbing its pergola, forming a civilised sun-trap, and the Daffodil Paddock below this is wild meadow for most of the year offering no distraction from the views out to the Downs. A Cherry Orchard to the right, planted in 1958, is equally relaxed and unassuming. But, after the almost ritual White Border Garden of the period, comes an uncertainty of high dark hedges and walls where the surprises set in. Through an arch in one wall is a superbly contrived perspective shock of double herbaceous borders, tightly confined between a stone wall and rigid yew forms (**colour plate 22**). These direct the eye so firmly to a perfectly composed stone Summerhouse that the flowers become almost irrelevant. Half way along the vista is a fountain pool with seats set around it, each crushed between solid blocks of yew. For all its date this garden has no feeling of Art Nouveau sinuosity. Like the chip carving and the geometrical inset patterns of the Gimson, Barnsley and Peter Waal furniture which fills the entertainment rooms of the house, it is a garden looking forward to the Art Deco, to open air living, health and sport.

The stone Summerhouse is shadowed by trees. Beyond it the grounds become relaxed and unkempt with a Hornbeam Avenue deep in grass and a Wild Garden. But on a return path parallel with the Herbaceous Borders tall hedges close in again shutting out first the Tennis Court, then the Swimming Pool (both of 1974), and lastly the great Croquet Lawn of 1993. This has pink alpines covering the unexpected Rockery at its head and dark hedged walls solemnising every side except the one open to the south. As a final addition, there is a large Kitchen Garden and, at the entrance front, a circular lawn and lime trees distract the attention from Ernest Barnsley's diversity of façades.

After the first World War Snowshill and Kiftsgate Court garden got off to a start at much the same time, and, though the Muirs bought Kiftsgate in 1918, one year before Charles Paget Wade bought Snowshill, it seems stylistically logical to deal with Snowshill first because Wade was a William Morris man, as intent upon crafts and medievalising as the Biddulphs, while the Muirs were friends of Major Johnston, planting enthusiasts, into colour and eventually into abstract expressionism. With garden design there is always this conflict between flowers and form. Flower lovers are not necessarily lovers of gardens; garden lovers are not necessarily besotted on flowers. The architect M H Baillie Scott, who designed the gardens of Snowshill Manor for Charles Wade, warned that 'it should always be borne in mind that the flowers are for the garden, not the garden for the flowers'.[22] Wade echoed him:

> a delightful garden can be made in which flowers play a very small part, by using effects of light and shade, vistas, steps to changing levels, terraces, walls, fountains, running water, an old well head or a statue in the right place, the gleam of heraldry or a domed garden temple.[23]

This is no more nor less than a compressed description of what he created at Snowshill. Visitors should be warned, Snowshill garden is outrageously, loveably twee, a fantasy game of mock medievalry. Visitors must either play that game as they walk around, up and down and in and out of the garden's carefully contrived nookery, or else reject it, embarrassed and irritated by the arch contrivance of it all and its piled up 'antiquities'. What is endearing, however, is the way that the National Trust has succumbed to the Wade charm, rather as it surrendered at Hidcote to the Major's fever for planting. Sensibly it takes on a protective colouring from its various properties retaining their original spirit. Here at Snowshill the Trust has gone rapturously ecological. A handout, for reading on the long trek from the car-park and restaurant to the Manor, points out 'our friendly kestrel', 'a thriving rabbit warren', 'a local shepherd' with 'his flocks of Jacob and Clun Forest sheep'. A pile of dead wood has been left to provide 'dead wood habitats for insects', and the grass is grown long 'to encourage bugs and butterflies', while a stream 'provides a wetland habitat for frogs and newts'.

After this Cotswold menagerie of living creatures the first garden may seem tame: a long plain lawn leading to the front door. It is down the steps to the left that the drama begins of steep slopes and one small, walled enclosure piling in upon another in breathless succession. Wade's intention was clearly to outpoint Morris's garden at Kelmscott with religiosity and medieval nostalgia. St George and his dragon, brightly coloured, stand on a gable to the right. Down one set of steps is a long herbaceous border of dominantly blue planting. If anything wooden comes up at Snowshill it is painted turquoise blue. That was Wade's favourite colour and it accords admirably with grey stone and green yews. Down an alternative flight of steps is the Armillary Court with its gilded sphere and ten columnar yews (**70**), but the prime attraction here is the balcony view it offers down into the complexities of the Well Court (**colour plate 23**). Packed into that small space is a turquoise coloured astronomical clock, a medieval dovecote cooing with white doves, a lily pond, a Venetian well head, an exquisite little hidden pool full of live minnows and a converted byre with a statue of the Madonna in a turquoise blue surround. What was originally a small farmyard has become a compression from Kipling's *Puck of Pook's Hill*; olde England, with flowers attached.

An intense miniature kitchen garden teeming with vegetables lies down yet more steps below Well Court, but the best direction is through the byre along a radiant flower garden then up and back, past some billowing topiary enclosing a seat and a sheep dip pond with more fish, to the Armilllary Court again. That covers most of the garden; Snowshill is almost suburban in size, but so full of incident, carts, fire-engines, pumps, rustic implements and little poems: 'Hours fly/Flowers die/New days/New ways/Pass by/Love stays', that a tour can easily take at least an hour. And the visit should end in Charles Wade's bedroom, which is not in the Manor but in a cottage within the garden (he had a second bedroom over the byre for summer-sleeping). The cottage bedroom is the place to absorb his piety and his Emmett-like ingenuity, with his box bed, painted crucifix, its hanging lamps and travelling trunks and the prayer inscribed on a beam: 'Jesu for ye Moder sake save al ye sauls that me gart make'. There was once a contraption that allowed St George, or his dragon, to ring a bell in here. Wade must have quaked with Betjemanesque glee as he fitted it all up.[24] Wade, like Betjeman, was introducing a destructive note of mid twentieth-century whimsicality into the seriousness of the Arts and Crafts.

70　*The Armillary Court at Snowshill Manor represents Arts and Crafts garden design at its best: quirky, strongly linear and more dependent upon an interaction of stones, water and greenery than on flowers. Charles Paget Wade reshaped the old gardens of the Manor after 1919*

There was one other false note to his life, and it was a late one. After all those years of concentrated nostalgia for an England lost and gone, Wade, very recently married, retired in 1951 to the West Indies to spend the last five years of his life in the Caribbean sunshine. It does not fit in with the image he had projected before. But then Major Johnston did much the same by his retreat to the Riviera. The Biddulphs were made of sterner stuff. For them the crafts and lore of old England were not a dream fantasy but a creed, which even now they still live and garden.

If Snowshill's gardens are steep, then Kiftsgate's are precipitous and there is something about its soil, or possibly the sheer planting zeal of the three generations of Muir ladies who have gardened it, which encourages height. Everyone knows the Kiftsgate Rose, *Rosa filipes*, which has grown fifty feet high by eighty and ninety feet across, and is in danger of pulling down the copper beech up which it has climbed. But so many other plants at Kiftsgate grow tall or spiral enormously. Viburnums tower, magnolias become trees and the Heather Muir rose, *Rosa sericea*, flowers twelve feet high. Gardeners who think they know hydrangeas should see the Bridge

71   *The swimming pool in the Lower Garden at Kiftsgate Court seems to hang dramatically suspended over the valley: clear black water against green lawns. It was built in 1963 and unlike most such amenities it improves its setting*

Border at Kiftsgate in August. It is all too easy to lapse into lists of superb specimen flowers, roses in particular, flourishing on wonderfully controlled, but never regimented, beds, only to miss the strange geography which makes the place so memorable.

Up on the hill top fronting the two Ionic porticoes of the house are the Four Squares and the Wide and North Borders. After admiring these the visitor should turn down to the left, by Simon Verity's statue of 'Mother and Child' on its plinth of dry stones and cyclamen, and make for that black, semi-circular swimming pool far below on a green lawn. The stone steps lead down through angular Scots pines. This is one section of a brilliantly successful garden that fails, by its dryness and poor soil, yet it comes as something of a relief after the abundant flower orgies up above. In contrast the Lower Garden is visually stunning with its optical illusions (**71**). The black pool, built in 1963, appears to end in mid air because a ha-ha cuts down immediately behind it and then the ordinary farm fields drop so steeply into the valley that the water edge seems to lap against a distant perspective of Worcestershire. Swimming in that dark basin could combine exercise with a touch of vertigo. The changing room of 1984 has a Greek temple portico and works admirably against the pool's sleek modernity.

Back up on the hill top is what many might consider to be the most sensational garden feature of any in the Cotswolds; but as this is a very recent addition to the garden it will be reserved for the last chapter and the Kiftsgate tour will conclude with the White Sunk Garden before the house, the two Rose Borders and the Yellow Border. These, as their names suggest, are Vita-esque in their concentrated colour impact rather than diffuse and subtle in the Jekyll style.

Gertrude Jekyll is known to have designed a plan for Combend (or Combe End) Manor in the windy uplands of Elkstone parish. The owner, Asa Lingard, paid Miss Jekyll for a planting scheme for the new downhill herbaceous border in 1925, when Sidney Barnsley was fitting up the house. Jekyll never visited Combend and if she had she would surely have advised a revision of the plan to make the border follow the contours rather than drain down into the valley. Her scheme, which is being restored, was the usual one, with cool colours at each end and warm to hot pinks and reds in the centre, achieving together the typical cottage garden cluster (**colour plate 24**). The gravel walk which it once bordered, with shrubs on the other side, has been grassed over and now fades easily into a water garden, half wild, with Jekyll's curvilinear pond and a chain of little falls running down a thin woodland with ferns, irises and gunnera. The way back up the hill is through a parallel garden of stone walled and hedged enclosures with a garden house in the vernacular on one lawn, and a small orchard leading up to two broad terraces and a new lime tree avenue of subtly diminishing perspective. So a garden which freewheels fast downhill has then to lure its visitors back through a steep climbing sequence of discoveries. Four columns from the Roman villa lower down the valley have been incorporated to express the continuity of the site.[25]

There are a host of other gardens in the county from this period. Pinbury Park, between Stroud and Cirencester, was where the Barnsley brothers had their first experience of a Gloucestershire garden when they were repairing the house for Lord Bathurst after 1894. Its terraced garden and the 'Nun's Walk', an old yew avenue of uncertain date, may have given Ernest Barnsley a feeling for such sites and layouts.[26] Upper Dorvel, the house which he devised for himself later, next to Sapperton churchyard, has a garden with a similar feeling for topiary in an avenue.[27]

Batsford is interesting because its Wild Garden, which Lord Redesdale created after the new house had been completed in 1892, survives within the later arboretum. It aimed, by using Japanese artefacts and huts, at producing some of the effects of a Chinese garden. Having been *en poste* at the Tokyo embassy for some years Redesdale was more familiar with Japanese than with Chinese models. But in reality he achieved the kind of wild, natural garden that Reginald Blomfield's stylistic opponent, the Irish gardener, William Robinson, was proposing. Bronze Buddhas (**72**) and statues of those oriental lions which look suspiciously like Pekinese dogs stand near Gothick grottoes, a Japanese Rest House, a very English stream garden and the Simon Verity statue without which no modern Gloucestershire garden seems to be complete. As a final comment on the eclecticism of the new century Lord

72   *The grounds of Batsford have been through so many changes that its present garden-arboretum is hard to characterise. Lord Redesdale tried after 1892 to create a Chinese garden by setting up Japanese artefacts, like this Buddha, in the remains of an English Wild Garden*

Redesdale added around the house a neatly enclosed Arts and Crafts garden with the essential vernacular pavilions at the corners. The grounds of Batsford, controlled now by an arboretum trust and open to the public, should be experienced if only to understand the multiple cultural influences to which the county's gardens would be subjected in the remainder of the twentieth century.

10 'When in doubt, look backwards' – the later twentieth century

Modern garden design as the avant garde would recognise it: those chaste geometrical compositions of stone slabs, ruthlessly horizontal hedge lines, ingenious water effects and abstract or severely stylised sculpture, reached Gloucestershire only in the very last two years of the century. It might, however, have appeared much earlier, in June 1936, when Geoffrey Jellicoe and his partner Russell Page designed a masterplan for the garden at Kingcombe, the house which Gordon Russell had commissioned in 1925-6 from Leslie Mansfield in a restrained vernacular style on an exposed hillside outside Chipping Campden.[1]

Pitched immediately on the roadside, above a steep slope and with an abundant water supply, the house and its site suggested an Italian response from Jellicoe. As first built Kingcombe was two houses, the Russell residence and a smaller servants' cottage facing its entrance front across a paved courtyard. Jellicoe created a long lawn parallel to the road, overlooked by a high terrace punctuated by stone seats and leading up to the garden front of the house. There are tree peonies in the herbaceous border and a large catalpa of the original planting at the far end. Alongside this, but separated from it by a yew hedge, he laid out a long, narrow Italian-style enclosure with an axial path, now made more informal by a mazy path conducted through concrete planters with palms. At right angles to these two spaces, at their far end from the house, a flat-roofed summerhouse was built and, bursting from a 'green man' carving on its side wall, a stream of water filled two chains of stone troughs, laid down either side of a flight of steps, their leaden spouts intended to conduct the rivulets from trough to trough in an Arts and Crafts version of the water staircases of the Villa d'Este at Tivoli. By ingenious interchanges and conduits these runnels were meant to fill a square pool at the end of a Spring Garden Terrace, running parallel to the other two enclosures but some eight feet below them.

A second water garden was planned running down from the servants' cottage at the other end of the house in a geometrical zig-zag channel crossed by bridges, but Jellicoe then retired from the site and left Russell to amplify and enrich the layout as a leisure-time hobby. 'To have seen him at home, up to his knees in mud', his son-in-law and daughter wrote, 'excavating his garden canal next to an Irish labourer and an expert joiner, was to experience something almost feudal in character'.[2] Russell was also an expert stone carver and it is his stonework – owl tables, compass points in the pavement, door arches, gargoyle heads, T-square symbols and Celtic-style enrichments to benches – that catch the eye at every turn (**73**).[3] While Charles Wade gave the grounds at Snowshill grace notes of mock medievalism, Gordon Russell

73 *Water should spout from the mouth of this Green Man mask at Kingcombe House to fill a chain of stone troughs down three terraces. Whether this was Geoffrey Jellicoe's intention in his 1930s masterplan or an improvisation by Gordon Russell in the 1950s is uncertain*

gave Kingcombe the leaf, fruit and geometrical patterns of the Art Deco 1930s, continuing to work with them well into the 1970s.

Often building and digging himself, Russell presided over three major extensions to Jellicoe's original three Italianate gardens.[4] Below the Spring Garden, with its overarching, pollarded flowering cherry trees, its helebores and fritillaries, he dug a long, deep canal, straight for most of its course, but disappearing mysteriously at its eastern end into a grotto tunnel next to a crude Gothic folly tower, now covered with ivy, and stepped to make a children's play castle. Overlooking the water are thirteen parabolic arches above a wall entirely composed of bottle ends, collected from the Russells' Lygon Arms at Broadway and set in concrete, a bizarre arcade asserting those uneasy stylistic compromises of the 1960s so favoured by Basil Spence (**74**). On the wall is a row of terracotta pots specially designed for the garden. Next, down the hill, a great green terrace was hewn out, supported by a ten foot stone wall and ending in a bastion that served Russell as his hedge-ringed gazebo, commanding a lane where processions from the Dover Games marched down to Campden.[5] Lastly a series of concrete pools, overhung by rugged tufa rocks, replaced the zig-zags of Jellicoe's intention. By a charming conceit the water for this course can be made to

74   *Concrete parabolic arches and empty glass bottles from a Russell hotel line this formal canal below the Spring Garden at Kingcombe. Here the inspiration is definitely Gordon Russell rather than Geoffrey Jellicoe*

flow from Russell's own be-spectacled carved head. A black mulberry tree overhangs the first of three pools, and red willows pattern, but do not conceal, the splendid views over the town.

Long before these terraced gardens had been completed the original twin houses were linked and a 'Chinese' garden, actually very Japanese in character, was subsequently created in what had been the paved courtyard between the three wings of the house and the road. Steps lead down beside the pool to the porch and front door of the house, now rarely used.

Beech trees of Russell's planting have grown to produce a western grove sheltering the house from the prevailing winds that funnel down the valley. The seven distinct garden spaces compose exhilaratingly into a whole that is half bracing and view commanding, half private and enclosed in the regular Arts and Crafts manner. What is hard to convey is the mix of hedge, Cotswold stone and lawn with Russell's favourite material, concrete. Sometimes used raw in planters, sometimes attractively patterned with the impress of wattle hurdles or cabbage leaves, it works surprisingly well, firm proof that Gloucestershire Arts and Crafts design could adapt comfortably to the later twentieth century.

However, the only truly modern garden of significant size and advanced design would not be laid out until 1998 – a mere two years before it would have had to be classed as a twenty-first-century achievement – in the old hard tennis court of Kiftsgate Court. Gloucestershire had responded to the innovations of Arts and Crafts garden design with open arms, but then let a remarkable 63 years pass before venturing upon its successor. As Jane Brown remarked despairingly in her recent study of the modern garden, an appropriate slogan for English garden designers of the twentieth century would be 'When in doubt, look backwards'.[6] Admittedly Kiftsgate's new water garden, when it eventually arrived, was so intensely abstract and brilliantly pure in line that if Piet Mondrian could have lived to see it he would have been dazzled by its commitment. But one such garden in 63 years was a firm vote of no confidence in modern design from the county's gardeners and it needs to be explained.

The success of the earlier Arts and Crafts gardens provides the reason. Those pre-1939 gardens were seductively beautiful and entirely functional with their private spaces, their whimsical poetry and their reassuring historicism. Above all they were feminist in an increasingly feminist century. They returned flowers and the scholarship of horticulture with its set texts of seed catalogues to the forefront; they encouraged pottering by their scale and even raised pottering in a garden to an art form open to the least talented. A true modern garden as understood by Christopher Tunnard, Erich Mendelsohn or Oliver Hill, the generation of the 1930s, was an achieved and static work of art that defied pottering or Jekyllesque improvisations of planting.[7] There was nothing to be done with such a garden except to preserve it. Yet change all the flower planting in a garden like Rodmarton and add new features, as Simon Biddulph has done over the last few years, and the splendid bones of the place, its essential impact, survives. It is a frame whereas, enclosed in its hedges, the Kiftsgate water garden is the whole, breathtaking picture. There can be no graffiti, even of dead leaves.

Gloucestershire's gardeners of the later twentieth century had every right to feel self-satisfied and to conduct a fighting retreat against innovation. The first decade of the century had created a virtually infallible recipe for making gardens in a Cotswold landscape. Avening Court was sold in 1935 and the sale particulars for its gardens tell it all.[8] There was a 'Nun's Walk', borrowed from Pinbury Park, a 'Seven Springs' from Cowley Manor, a pergola out of Lutyens's Abbotswood, a herbaceous border courtesy of Miss Jekyll, a 'Bathing Pool' for that healthy outdoor living beloved of Arts and Crafts disciples, and a 'Fairies Pool' for addicts of J M Barrie's Tinkerbell. They sound trite but the garden they compose is hauntingly beautiful. In that almost sunless valley, narrow and hung with great trees, the Aven stream runs through a chain of clear, dark pools, crossed by a maze of small bridges, each pool a perfect setting for the drowning of Millais's 'Ophelia'. Then it flows out past a ruined horse-wash into the sunlight of Middle Lodge with cottage charms and yet more small bridges (**colour plate 25**). Much of this can be enjoyed, by the kindness of its creators, through a generous round *claire-voie* cut through the walls of an obscure lane in that tangle of ways east of Avening village. Two women shaped this archetype of Cotswold plesaunces: Mrs Pollock, between 1899 and 1914, and Mrs Lewis, between

1918 and 1927. These were the years when garden makers of the county could hardly put a foot wrong.

When G H Kitchin and the Countess of Westmorland came, in the late 1920s, to revive the dilapidated grounds of Lyegrove House near Badminton they took an eighteenth-century summerhouse and shell-niched seventeenth-century gate piers from neighbouring Little Sodbury Manor and improvised the new gardens tradi-tionally around their cultural loot. The result was predictably gracious and histori-cist, warmly commended in *Country Life* which, as the house magazine of the affluent landed classes, had far more influence on garden design in the twentieth century than any garden or architectural journal.[9] In a country whose last three centuries have been an historical success story historicism in gardens has a well merited cachet.

The war of 1939-45, the subsequent Labour government and West End plays by Douglas-Home worked together to create a nostalgia for the aristocracy which the Harold Macmillan years soon gratified. In 1958 Gloucestershire gardens moved on a tentative – but still traditional – step further. This was the year when Rosemary and David Verey settled in Barnsley House, a pleasant seventeenth-century yeoman house in the middle of Barnsley village, just north of Cirencester. Three years later another middle-aged and equally upper-middle class couple, Alvilde and James Lees-Milne, took up a residence that lasted from 1961 to 1975 in Alderley Grange, an elegant mid eighteenth-century classical squire's house. Any revolution which the two couples launched in their restyled grounds would be modest and undisturbing to *Daily Telegraph* and *Country Life* readers. The two wives, Rosemary and Alvilde, would be the prime movers, so in any changes flowers would, therefore, be prominent; but as both husbands were distinguished architectural historians garden buildings would not be entirely excluded.

Because it was planted with an imaginative flair, and on a scale perfect for the large suburban or country retiree garden, the Barnsley House garden caught a feminist mood in this affluent county of an increasingly affluent country. As the front for a commercial enterprise (a superior garden centre and consultancy), the Vereys' garden invited imitation and received it. Flower arrangements in vases are transient; Rosemary Verey demonstrated that flower arrangements with roots were not simply more enduring but an accessible art form in an age of leisure. Those quite limited grounds behind and to the right of the house have been among the most influential in the country and deserve a thoughtful analysis.

More than half the acreage of the Barnsley House garden is taken up with the large lawn and the small wilderness which offer a conventional green setting. The important gardens are concentrated at the back of the grounds and behind the house and sales area. A double axis links the Doric Temple, an import of 1962 from the destruction of Fairford Park (**colour plate 26**), and a Gothick summerhouse of about 1775 native to the grounds. The Grass Walk is separated by just a few feet from the parallel Lime Avenue which turns into a Laburnum Walk. Their double axis is crossed by the Yew Walk which also bisects a small lawn bordered by four herb and parterre beds; and that, apart from a small Knot Garden and the L-shaped bed in a corner of the big lawn, is everything. Manageability is the essence of Barnsley's attraction. A subliminal message goes out that one well-organised woman could become a garden artist by planting thoughtfully and getting a little soil on her hands.

In a series of cleverly illustrated publications Rosemary Verey made the art of Gertrude Jekyll and Vita Sackville-West accessible to every woman, and to the Prince of Wales. Leaves, shapes and textures were as important, if not more important, than colour. Following Verey's lead, subtle tapestries of green where, 'Softly variegated *Salvia officinalis* "Icterina" with matt-felted leaves looks perfect encircling *Euphorbia cyparissias*',[10] have become appreciated by amateur gardeners who, in an earlier generation, would have settled for gladiolae, dahlias and a nice splash of colour. Since Rosemary Verey's writing, if colour is allowed it has to be 'a classic harmony in the warm (not hot) purple-crimson colour range', where 'the silver foliage of the artemisia in the background sets off the composition'. That particular caption concludes with the giveaway: 'a composition as beautiful as a seventeenth-century Dutch still-life painting'.[11] Planting now can literally rival high art without the pain of mastering paint. Aesthetic sophistication lies at the end of everyone's fork and trowel.

Amidst this subdued subtlety the Barnsley House garden kept alive the Arts and Crafts tradition of whimsicality and written messages, as at Snowshill. Two stone gardeners by Simon Verity stand at the Iron Gate to the Potagers (**75**); the Hunting Lady with a sinisterly veiled face stands in an angle of the Wilderness and at one end of the Laburnum Walk is a Frog Fountain supported by two fighting rams. A copper plate on a column offers John Evelyn's advice in that Charles Wade mood of cosy religiosity: 'As no man be very miserable that is Master of a Garden here, so will no man ever be happy who is not sure of a garden here after'.

Verey-style gardens have proliferated in the county: decorously pretty variations upon her themes of knot gardens, filled conventionally as at Badminton with roses,[12] or less conventionally with herbs, in those Verey symphonies of green – combinations of sage for instance with parsley. Marsh gardens of gunnera and hostas, potagers where balls of golden privet catch up the roundels of cauliflower and where red cabbages grow side-by-side with blue borage have become almost standard features. Rosemary Verey educated thousands, even tens of thousands, of part-time gardeners to cast convention aside, to look anew at improbable combinations and to search out the real complexities of beauty. Few people can have given more honest creative pleasure to their fellow women and men, even if we are not all converts to the charms of fat purple heads of *Allium aflatunense* roofed by dangling yellow laburnum. Like all art forms the art of planting is subjective and arguable. She created a garden idiom for her time and made a good living out of it.

Alvilde Lees-Milne's garden at Alderley Grange was to the Verey pattern: green herbs in green and gold box knots, a lime walk, a white garden of 'Iceberg' roses and the saving architectural note of a Doric gazebo, dating from about 1710.

There are gardens in the Alvilde or Rosemary manner at Hodges Barn, Shipton Moyne, at Bourton House, Bourton-on-the-Hill, The Old Chapel, Chalford and Daylesford House, where the White Garden flies high on a metal pergola.[13] In the post-1964 planting of their Upper Garden at Stancombe Park, Gerda and Basil

75 Whimsicality runs like a thread through the late twentieth-century gardens of
Gloucestershire. At Barnsley House, the garden-shop of Rosemary Verey, dwarfish stone
gardeners guard the entrance to a flowery potager

Barlow stressed informal compositions of silver and gold, more Jekyll perhaps than
Verey. Even ducal Badminton followed the Barnsley House formula, though none of
the new box and yew beds there can hold a candle to the late Duchess's superb lake
of shimmering silver-purple crocus, planted on a truly patrician scale south of the
churchyard and unforgettable in the rare hours of February-March sunshine.

Not all of Gloucestershire's gardeners gave in to feminine feasts of colour and
softly rounded shapes. Over the county border in Oxfordshire David Hicks's garden
offered a masculine alternative with its unyielding straight lines of grass and stilted
hornbeam hedges, photographed for preference in a hard white frost or deep snow.[14]
Sheepbridge Farm, Eastleach has tortuously clipped topiary against grey rubble
masonry. At Ablington, near Bibury, the Manor plays with the same mountains of
yew and Robert Cooper has added two new garden buildings, one Gothick and
whimsical, the other, of 1991, by Oswald Brakspear, shaped like a grim Jacobean
powerhouse. These are set with no feeling of enclosure along a wide reach of the
Coln, but Rosemary Verey's two borders are safely confined within a new walled
garden. Another of her plantings, the Chapel Garden at Sudeley Castle, is similarly
cut off within walls behind the church, where her ingenuity in providing new scents
and new combinations of the unexpected can be enjoyed in isolation.

Her influence is also felt at Sudeley in the new knot garden designed by Jane
Fearnley-Whittingstall for the Small Courtyard. This was conceived in 1995 as a

celebration of Queen Elizabeth's visit to the Castle in 1592. The knot design is taken from the dress which Princess Elizabeth is wearing in the allegorical portrait of 'The Tudor Succession', which is often attributed to Hans Eworth and hangs at Sudeley. The tiled central pool and mosaic ornaments add an exotic Persian reference to an otherwise traditionally English garden form.[15]

Some of Rosemary Verey's garden paths lead to Highgrove and the Prince of Wales's celebrated garden there, the first hands-on, genuinely personal royal garden in this country since Prince Frederick Louis's Kew of the 1740s. What is so satisfying about Highgrove is that, as well as being royal, ambitious and still growing, it is essentially of Gloucestershire rather than of England as a whole. It has a major Rosemary Verey planting, there are whimsicalities, quotations and religious undertones, and it has any number of enclosed areas, in the Arts and Crafts pattern. Above all, it is human and entertaining in its scale, not grand.

In this country, where royal matters are concerned, the writing tends either to cautious flattery or malicious spite.[16] So it needs to be recorded initially that Prince Charles has, over the last ten years, made Highgrove one of the five best gardens in the county, the other four being Westbury Court, Cirencester Park, Painswick Rococo Garden and Kiftsgate Court. It is, in addition, a potent, controversial example of land usage for the rest of the country. That being noted it should be added that it is the creation of an idealistic, wilful, multi-millionaire who has been prepared to spend money lavishly and been able to surround himself with eager advisors. The Prince's true character is exposed more clearly in his garden than in any number of TV interviews and newspaper articles. His grounds brim with successes, and are imaginative, even poetic, but never quite pull together as a whole. But then neither does Cirencester Park, which was another creation of a confident individualist.

Like Hidcote, Highgrove has no natural topographical advantages. When he was considering a Gloucestershire home the Prince might have bought Ozleworth Manor, a more characterful house, set romantically among deep woodlands on the Cotswold edge, with a Regency bath house and a twelfth-century Norman church in a circular graveyard left over from the Celtic Dark Ages. Michael Stone eventually bought Ozleworth and it will be interesting to see later in this chapter what he made of its grounds by handing them over to be completely redesigned by Antony Young. In contrast, at Highgrove Prince Charles has never trusted any single garden designer for too long, sometimes scrapping his own old ideas for new projects in a learning process powered by his idealism and spirituality.

What first charmed the Prince about Highgrove was its sheer ordinariness. In his introduction to Candida Lycett Green's book on the garden he says he 'relished the challenge of starting with a blank canvas and seeing if I could fulfil my own dreams for the garden'.[17] The house, a dull Regency box of 1796, gutted by fire in 1894 and then largely rebuilt, stands on level ground, protected by narrow tree belts. Consequently, like Hidcote, it has limited views. The topsoil is thin and poor except for a richer section where the Walled Garden stands. Unlike Hidcote, whose even duller house shrinks away from its gardens, Highgrove stands foursquare and inescapable in the midst of them. Conscious of this visible presence the Prince made, in my view, a miscalculation, commissioning Felix Kelly to dramatise the existing main façades with bold Ionic pilasters and to add a broad classical pediment to the east roofline. The appliqué effect is mildly pretentious and unauthentic for a Regency building.

The estate buildings lie on the north side, with the Prince's shop, business park and centre for entertainment. That leaves the house itself as a modest private home. The entrance front faces east out onto Tetbury and the park, where a 1995 lime avenue, unrelated to the drive, is growing up. Only two gardens connect directly with the façades of the house. South is the Prince's first effort, the Sundial Garden, yew hedged and intimate where, helped by Lady Salisbury, in 1981-2 he planted six flower beds which had grown into a pleasant riot of colour and scent by 1998, whereupon he grubbed them all up and planted a black and white garden. Lady Salisbury took this philosophically, but the scheme involves nipping the buds from Bishop of Llandaff dahlias to enjoy their bronze leaves the better. Overall the prevailing colour is still green.

Next came the west garden, Highgrove's nearest approach to a grand axial layout, though in reality the axis proceeds along a chain of several intimate, richly detailed episodes. Its first fountain forecourt, the Terrace, has one huge cedar and William Bertram's Gothick pepper-pot pavilions perched at two corners. The paving is busily textured with flowers creeping from every crevice, and pots are set in plinths of box. Next in the axial sequence comes the Thyme Walk, then a geometric stone pool, the Bronze Gladiator, a lime tree avenue and ends with, not some classical temple, but a cosy vernacular pigeon house. That is only the central spine. Flanking the Thyme Walk are bulges of golden yew which the Prince inherited and, ignoring Sir Roy Strong's advice to root then all up, set his gardeners to clip each one into a different abstract pattern. Flanking these bushes are squares and rectangles of pleached hornbeams and here, at least, Sir Roy's advice was taken. In one of the garden's few conventional strokes, stone seats and statues of the Seasons were imported from Italy. Yew hedges, clipped to a Strong design to resemble castle walls, strengthen the axial line on either side. The Gladiator is traditional and formal, a copy of the bronze which once stood in Inigo Jones's garden at Wilton House, laid out for the Earl of Pembroke.[18]

At that point the Prince became more confident, found new advisors and abandoned formality. Everything else, including the most beautiful and exciting features at Highgrove, is unrelated to the house and must be searched out, after the Arts and Crafts manner, in hidden enclosures and groves. The ways that link these pass through Bertram's quirkily individual painted wooden gates and are scattered with enormous pots. Once it became known that the Prince liked pots he has been showered with a storm of these fat-bellied shapes. Gifts are one of the burdens of kind hearted royals and an entire Wall of Gifts in a shaded part of the grounds is hung with a chaos of assorted carvings.

There are four stars at Highgrove: the Cottage Garden, the Sanctuary, the Walled Garden and, most romantic and gloomily atmospheric, the Stumpery. But to find these, visitors will have to pay their respects to lesser gardens. There is a Laurel Tunnel, a Savill Garden, an Italian Azelea Walk presided over in the Roy Strong spirit by Diana the Huntress, a dismal Southern Hemisphere garden, Bertram's Hollyrood Tree House and, inevitably from an ecological Prince, a Wild Flower Meadow where, helped by plug implants, simple common flowers of the meadows like *Camassia leichtlinii caerulea* have been persuaded to grow, the first crop of dandelions being judged unsatisfactory.

The Cottage Garden was Rosemary Verey's mark upon Highgrove. She planted most of it herself, aided by Princes Charles and Harry. Its serpentine path leads to a white seat clasped around a *Sorbus thibetica* 'John Mitchell', and the beds give a most professional blast of bloom. Even a few staddle stones have infiltrated in the Rodmarton tradition. More princely and characterful is the Sanctuary (**76**). This strange little building is hidden furtively away in the new Arboretum, which was planted to the advice of John White, the curator at Westonbirt. The Sanctuary is a chapel to the Prince's pantheism and it was blessed, though not apparently consecrated, by the Bishop of London who confirmed the Prince's sons. In shape it hints at a cuckoo clock without a cuckoo. Keith Critchlow conceived it on the sacred geometry of harmonic proportions; but no one would ever guess that. Charles Morris actually designed it and it was constructed traditionally of cob (packed mud). Inside the walls are pargetted with vegetable forms and the capitals of its columns are carved into leaf shapes. A true shrine of the Green Man of legend, it indicates that the Prince, like William Wordsworth and the great Romantic poets, sees God most directly in the works of Nature. While in the Arboretum it would be a pity to miss Frederick Hart's exquisite Art Nouveau bronze of the Four Daughters of Odessa: one gift at least which the Prince must have welcomed.

The Walled Garden is a return to earth after the mysterious groves of the Sanctuary, though even here a bronze plaque of the Green Man by Nicholas Dimbleby is affixed to one of the walls. This is the overwhelmingly fruitful, flower-filled, brassica-bountiful descendant of that little potager at the back of Barnsley House. Its warm brick walls hold in the scent of roses and honeysuckle and its four great beds, two with St Andrew's and two with St George's cross-paths, are separated by tunnels of apples, sweet peas and runner beans. The gardener, a genius with vegetables, raises with strictly organic mulches and manures a cornucopia of exotic salads, Charlotte potatoes and strawberries. Brick-lined grass paths lead to a central fountain pool with coi carp, and outside the walls, in a Standing Garden, rows of plants and small trees queue up for the privilege of entry. If the Sanctuary was the private chapel of ecology then the Walled Garden is its stately home and showpiece, a demonstration of wholesome gardening triumphant.

But what is the Stumpery? Only a man as self-confident in his whimsicality as the Prince would have entrusted Julian and Isabel Bannerman with the task of designing this atmospheric evocation of the primitive pagan world (**colour plate 27**). On the strength of his Stumpery alone Charles's name will be secure in garden history. Like William Kent's Worcester Lodge and William Halfpenny's Frampton Orangery it creates the true frisson of a garden masterpiece. To enter its charmed circle in the

76 *Hidden away in Highgrove's small arboretum is The Sanctuary, a chapel to Pantheism, blessed by a bishop but not consecrated. Charles Morris designed it, the walls are made of cob, or packed mud, and vegetable shapes decorate the interior walls*

woods the visitor must tread a path of amonites (the Prince is always alert to the textures of a floor), then duck under an arch in the ferocious *chevaux de frise* of savagely spiked chestnut stump roots that form the walls of the circle. These bare roots shelter hostas, ferns, hellebores and all the dank greenery of the Prince's fancy. There in this ominous glade he has built solemn twin temples to prove the Abbé Laugier's scholarly theory that Greek temple architecture had its origins in huts constructed of tree trunks. Isabel Bannerman designed these two 'Doric' temples of green oak, with driftwood instead of carving for their pediments. In the Snowshill tradition both have inscriptions on their rear elevations: Shakespeare's 'Find tongues in trees, books in running brooks, sermons in stone and good in everything', and

Horace's scorn for those who dismiss sacred groves as mere sticks: '*Virtutem verba putant et lucum ligna*'.

The temples have a remarkable presence. Coleridge's lines from *Kubla Khan* about 'A savage place! As holy an enchanted/As e'er beneath a waning moon was haunted/By woman wailing for her demon-lover!' would have been an equally appropriate temple inscription because there, squatting on the grass, is the love-lorn woman. David Wynne's 'Goddess of the Woods' is nude, brooding and so sensuous that she is occasionally waxed so that admirers may run their fingers smoothly down her stone spine. The Bishop of London is unlikely to have blessed the Stumpery, but it is great garden architecture and, with William Bertram's Tree House just peeping into it, the whimsical thread of feeling is maintained.

It is fascinating to drive from Highgrove to Ozleworth, a journey of no great distance, to see the difference between the gardens of an inspired amateur Prince and an assured professional. Charles seems to have needed a spiritual and ecological play-ground where souls could be soothed and at the same time sewage could be processed, through bark and willow beds, into pure water in a pond where dragon-flies can breed. It was a pioneering aim for his century and before the century was out he had achieved it. Another hundred years may pass before Highgrove's signifi-cance has been nationally understood. At Ozleworth Antony Young had a simpler task: to tie an existing house, church, service area and a unique bath house together into an organic working whole with a squirearchical presence (**77**).

It was typical of the times in which he was designing that he has succeeded with everything except the church, with its hexagonal Norman tower set within a round pagan graveyard. The Prince might have encircled it with a Woodhenge and turned its paths into dark tunnels of climbing flowers; Antony Young, while handling the other units of his composition with calm assurance, has left it unchanged but never-theless subtly aligning one of the oblique walks of his Rose Garden on the church tower to give a visual if not a physical connection. When John Evelyn settled in 1651 in a similar, existing, run-down manor house and service complex with old gardens at Sayes Court, Deptford, he gardened to much the same plan as that produced by Young for Ozleworth. The exposed west front of the house has been deftly tied into its landscape by a formal Repton-style parterre of grass bordered with lavender, enclosed in a stone balustrade and accessed by steps down into the park. But the main focus of the planning has gone into the southern sector of the pleasure grounds and the service area of potting sheds, greenhouses, vine house and gardener's cottage at the back. These last make an inner service court around a circular Herb Garden. They, in their turn, are surrounded by a tennis court, Walnut Grove, Soft Fruit Garden and Ozleworth's set piece: a big pear and apple orchard walled around, orig-inally flanked by a Nut Walk crossed by espaliers and centred upon that remarkable relic, the circular Bath House of about 1800, half plunge pool, half open-air swimming bath.

The western walk of this enclosure leads down axially through the middle of the Rose Garden, bordered on the south by two formal Lily Pools at whose mid-point is sited a bronze statue of a naked huntress by David Williams-Ellis (**78**). The axis

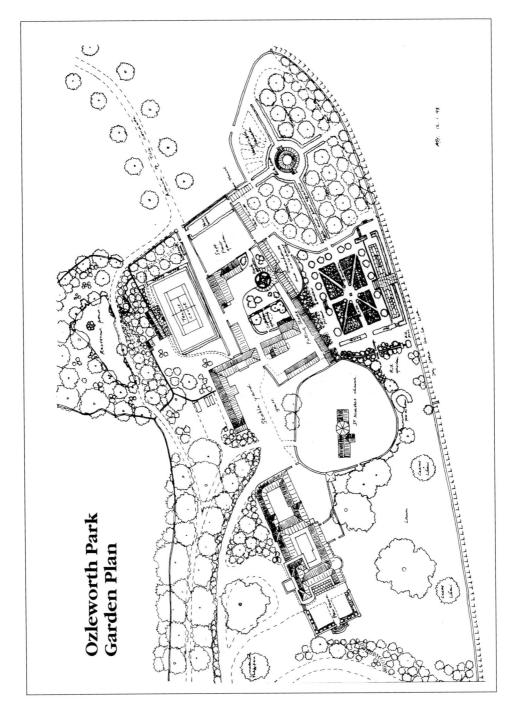

77 *Antony Young's masterplan for the revival of the gardens at Ozleworth Park which was completed in 1995. The pre-existing elements were the house, the rill, the Regency bath house and churchyard*

78 *Formal lily pools, enclosing walls and hedges with David Williams-Ellis's bronze of a naked huntress: the new gardens at Ozleworth*

then crosses an oak bridge to the Rill Garden. The rill itself runs like a relaxed connecting thread through the grounds. It starts from the reservoir pond in the woods above the house, falls into a stone trough, feeds the Bath House, then emerges above the oak bridge to run through the dense planting of philadelphus, syringa, deutzia, exochorda, peonies and daphne of the Rill Garden. A broad, sturdily re-built ha-ha, from which horses can look amiably over the lawns, ensures that this whole tightly clustered squire's garden lies in a green lap of pleasure ground with no apparent barrier between the ordered and the wild.

Ozleworth was essentially complete by 1995 and still conservative Gloucestershire abstained from 'modern' garden design. In 1991 David and Lucy Abel Smith had agreed to stage the biennial Quenington Sculpture Show and in 1997 took to running it themselves, turning the watery grounds of their Old Rectory on the banks of the Coln into a light-hearted Statue Garden which approached the modern via the usual route of whimsicality. When I last visited the show was entitled 'Fresh Air 2001' and the result was delightful with sculptural events in stone, metal, wood and plastic at every turn of the paths. Stainless steel insects lurked up the trunks of trees and ingenious devices in the fast-flowing green waters of the Coln reacted in complex ways to water pressures (**79**). From some lawns a whole troop of charmed

79   As the Coln flows past the Old Rectory with its seventeenth-century privy at
     Quenington the river is enlivened with water sculptures and unpredictable jets. This is
     only one section of Lucy and David Abel Smith's biennial Quenington Sculpture Show,
     dedicated to garden art

monsters appeared to pop their heads from non-existent burrows. One path was set
with white paviours that spelt out a message to walkers, distracting them from the
bizarre birds of wire and coloured glass strung from the branches above them. It was
undeniably modern; but as most of the exhibits could be bought, was it a garden or
a commercial enterprise?

And at last, in 1998 at Kiftsgate Court, in a garden which previously had dared
nothing more modern than the half-moon swimming pool and a Simon Verity
'Mother and Child', Anne and Johnny Chambers took the plunge into absolute
abstraction. This step was taken partly through sheer courage, with a husband and
wife team designing in mutual support; partly inspired by Geoffrey Jellicoe's stepping
stones across the moat at Sutton Court, Surrey; but chiefly due to the compelling
restriction of the site. Those tall, impenetrable walls of dark yew in an exactly defined
rectangle around their old hard tennis court demanded a geometrical response.

Even the entrance is magical in its drama: a Simon Verity statue seat in the form
of a wildly gesticulating woman appears to bar the way (**80**). Left and right of this
are hidden gaps in the hedge leading to the visual shock of the Water Garden

171

80   The woman in Simon Verity's sculpture seat gestures ambivalently: right, left or dead-
end? This is the entrance to the enchanted geometry of the new Kiftsgate Water
Garden, and a perfect preparation for its impressive introversion

(**colour plate 28**). The long rectangular pool has black painted walls that impart a sinister clarity of apparent bottomlessness. Pale silvery stepping paviours lead out to a square island of lawn set in the black water. The sides of the pool are silvery slabs, everything else is plain, unrelieved grass except that at the far end of the pool, on metal stalks nine feet high, a bed of silver and golden metal philodendron rears up from the water that exactly reflects them, and from each golden flower a trickle of water flows.[19]

There is nothing else; but where a normal abstract painting may leave the viewer cold, this abstract is interactive. The stepping paviours and the island of grass demand a response, yet the darkness of the water threatens it. The metal flowers are kitsch and sentimental, but everything else is harsh and unresponsive. After waiting 98 years Gloucestershire has gained a modernist masterpiece in garden design. The intriguing thing about it is that, like so many abstracts, but unlike the other four Gloucestershire 'star' gardens, it reveals nothing about the nature or the intentions of its creators. It simply reflects viewers back upon themselves.

Notes and references

1 An uncertain spring in the gardens of south Gloucestershire

1 *Country Life*, 16 November 1907.
2 *Ibid.*
3 John Chandler (ed.), *John Leland: Itinerary* (Stroud, 1993), p.186.
4 *Country Life*, 16 November 1907.
5 *Ibid.*, spoken to his son-in-law, the Earl of Westmorland, at Thornbury.
6 For an architectural history of Thornbury Castle as for all other houses mentioned in this study see Nicholas Kingsley's trilogy of volumes: *The Country Houses of Gloucestershire*. Volume 1:1550-1600 (revised edition, Chichester, 2001); Volume 2: 1660-1830 (Chichester,1992); Volume 3:1830-2000 (Chichester 2001). There are very useful surveys of the gardens in the introductions to each volume. Subsequent references to these volumes will be abbreviated simply to the author and volume number. *The Victoria County History of Gloucestershire* is also a prime resource of information on houses and gardens, and relevant articles will be found in *Country Life*, cited hereafter. The *Pevsner Buildings of England* volumes for the Vale and the Forest of Dean (Verey, 1980) and the Cotswolds (Verey, 1970) are invaluable. The latter volume has been thoroughly revised by Alan Brooks (1999). For Thornbury see also Robert Cooke, *West Country Houses* (Bristol,1957), pp.46-9. For gardens specifically see John Sales, *West Country Gardens* (Gloucester, 1981).
7 By a license of 2 August 1514: Public Record Office, c53/200, no.4.
8 For a full archaeological account of the castle see *Transactions of the Bristol and Gloucestershire Archaeological Society*, vol.xcv, pp.51-8.
9 The gardens at Thornbury are extensively covered in Avray Tipping, *English Gardens*, 1925, pp.337-42, which gives illustrations showing how the gardens might have appeared in Buckingham's time.
10 Public Record Office, E36/150, f.26; quoted in Tipping, *English Gardens*, p.339. Subsequent quotations from the Inventory will be given from Tipping for ease of reference.
11 David Verey, *The Buildings of England, Gloucestershire: The Vale and the Forest of Dean* (Harmondsworth, 1980), p.380.
12 Staffordshire Record Office, D641/1/2/202; quoted in Tipping, *English Gardens,* p.340.
13 Tipping, *English Gardens*, p.339.
14 *Ibid.*, p.339.
15 *Ibid.*, p.339.

16 Sylvia Landsberg, *The Medieval Garden* (British Museum Press, no date), pp.5-7.

17 Tipping, *English Gardens*, pp. 341-2.

18 See Timothy Mowl, 'From a View to a Death', *Country Times and Landscape*, November 1989.

19 See Timothy Mowl, *Elizabethan and Jacobean Style*, 1993, p.79.

20 Christopher Morris (ed.) *The Illustrated Journeys of Celia Fiennes c.1682 – c.1712*, 1982, p.54.

21 For the excavations of 1985 see *Bristol and Avon Archaeology*, vol.5, pp.55-6.

22 *Ibid.*, p.56.

23 Rob Iles, writing on the excavations in *Bristol and Avon Archaeology*, vol.5, p.56, suggests that it may have been one arm of the moat. This is unlikely.

24 The sundial is illustrated in Stewart Harding & David Lambert, *Parks and Gardens of Avon* (Bristol, 1994), colour plate 6.

25 Brooks, *The Buildings of England, Gloucestershire 1: The Cotswolds*, p.419.

26 For a discussion of the original architectural form of Newark see *Country Life*, 3 October 1985.

27 Matthew P McDiarmid (ed.), *The Kingis Quair of James Stewart*, 1973, p.84, lines 31-5.

2 Lost gardens of the Elizabethan-Jacobean continuum

1 See Kingsley, vol.1, Introduction.

2 *Ibid.*, plate 36.

3 There is a Caroline walled enclosure of 1632-41 at Doughton Manor with a later corner pavilion of early twentieth-century date. The garden still has paths dividing it into four quarters.

4 Gervase Markham, *Countrey Contentments, or the Husbandsman's Recreation*, 1633, pp.57-8.

5 Lines 25-32.

6 Kingsley, vol.1 includes two variant illustrations of the house and gardens in their prime (figs.7 & 52). They are both said to derive from a single lost original; see Kingsley's footnote 7 on p.65.

7 See Sara Paston-Williams, *The Art of Dining: A History of Cooking & Eating*, 1993.

8 A word used by John Evelyn for a place where he could carry out his experiments with hybrids; see Timothy Mowl, *Gentlemen & Players: Gardeners of the English Landscape* (Stroud, 2000), p.43 and Chapter 4.

9 For a discussion of Markham's planting schemes see Judith Roberts, 'The Gardens of the Gentry in the Late Tudor Period', *Garden History*, vol.27, no.1 (Summer 1999), p.108.

10 Gardens like those laid out for Henry IV at St Germain-en-Laye and Fontainbleau: see Roy Strong, *The Renaissance Garden in England*, 1979, pls.40-2.

11 Henry Wotton, *The Elements of Architecture*, 1624 (Virginia: Facsimile reprint, 1968), pp.109-10; see also Timothy Mowl, 'New science, old order: the gardens

of the Great Rebellion', *Journal of Garden History*, vol.13, nos.1&2 (January–June 1993), pp.16–35.

3 Vegetable formalism – the reign of pretension and utility

1 For the Franco-Dutch formal garden see David Jacques and Arend Jan van der Horst, *The Gardens of William and Mary*, 1988.
2 For the Kip of Hill Court see Kingsley, vol.1, p.242, plate 187. For subsequent Kip engravings discussed in this chapter but not illustrated see the same Kingsley volume under the alphabetical heading.
3 See 'Paradise in Gloucestershire', *Country Life*, 19 July 1984 from which all subsequent quotations are taken.
4 For Temple see Mowl, *Gentlemen & Players*, pp.64–5.
5 Reginald Blomfield, *The Formal Garden in England*, 1901, p.45.
6 This and all subsequent references to the Owlpen accounts are taken from Gloucestershire Record Office, D 979 A/E3, folio 16. Further citations of documents from the Gloucestershire Record Office will be abbreviated to GRO.
7 Molly McClain, Beaufort: *The Duke and his Duchess 1657-1715*, (New Haven & London, 2001), p.xiii; the seventeenth-century estate is also shown in drawings commissioned from Hendrik Danckerts which are included as plates 12-13.
8 *Ibid.*, Introduction, p.xiii.
9 Noted by Celia Fiennes in the Wilderness at Ingestre, Staffordshire; see Christopher Morris (ed.), *The Illustrated Journeys of Celia Fiennes c.1682-c.1712* (Exeter, 1982), p.155.
10 Quoted in Jacques & van der Horst, *William and Mary*, pp.158–61.
11 McClain, p.212.
12 *Ibid.*, p.212.
13 A page from the Duchess's 'Florilegium', painted by Kickius, is illustrated in Harding & Lambert, *Parks and Gardens of Avon* plate 7.
14 *Ibid.*, p.213.
15 Quoted in Anthony Mitchell, *The Park and Garden at Dyrham*, 1977, p.1.
16 *Ibid.*, p.11.
17 *Ibid.*, p.5.
18 *Ibid.*, p.5.
19 National Trust, Westbury Court Garden, Gloucestershire, 1977, Appendix, p.50.
20 *Ibid.*, p.50.
21 *Ibid.*, p.51.
22 Blomfield, *Formal Garden*, pp.84–5.

4 Formal gardening in Arcadian decline

1 The design, formerly at Elton Hall, is illustrated in Kerry Downes, 'The Kings Weston Book of Drawings', *Architectural History*, vol. 10 (1967), pp.9-88; fig.28. Colen Campbell's more formal Palladian design of May 1723 for 'Penpole Gate' is fig.29. A photograph of the building as executed is fig.30. 'The Kings Weston Book of Drawings' is in the Bristol Record Office, 33746. The several garden buildings were the subject of a conservation report commissioned by the City of Bristol Planning Department in 1985 from Niall Phillips Associates. An article based on this report by the present author appeared in the same year: 'The Surviving Vanbrugh Garden Buildings at Kingsweston', *Georgian Group Annual Report*, 1985, pp.37-49. See also Tim Mowl, 'Rescue Imperative: The Future of the Kings Weston Garden Buildings', *Country Life*, 29 August 1985. Nicholas Pearson Associates Ltd prepared an Historic Landscape Survey and Management Plan on the estate in 1994 and I am grateful to Simon Bonvoisin for access to this document.

2 Downes, 'The Kings Weston Book of Drawings'. The drawings for the forecourt gate are reproduced as figures 17 and 18.

3 The Stewart drawing is in the Bodleian Library, Oxford, MS. Gough Somerset 8, fol.36.

4 There are two austerely Doric designs for the Loggia in the 'Book of Drawings', one dated June 1718 (figs 25-6) and the executed design which has no date (fig. 27).

5 There are several designs for small castellated houses in the 'Book of Drawings', but none exactly resembles the Brewhouse as executed.

6 The west wall of the Loggia has a blocked window, but this appears to be a later insertion and the main visual axis of the building is due south, across the formal western terrace.

7 The 'Book of Drawings' has a design for the roof and ceiling of the 'Banqueting House at the end of the Terrace next the Roade' (fig.20) and a rusticated Garden Door, very close in style to the Echo, inscribed 'Sir. John Vanbrughs Door for the End Wall of the Middle Way at Kingsweston: by the Banqueting House Loggia' (fig. 21). This last is dated 26 March 1722, Vanbrugh's last known connection with the estate.

8 The orangery and the formal gardens had disappeared by the time Isaac Taylor surveyed the estate in 1771 and prepared a map dated 1772.

9 The 'Book of Drawings' includes a 'Pedestal of Hercules' which may possibly have been intended for the Echo (fig. 31).

10 John Symes Berkeley's siting of the Banqueting House at Stoke Park, just outside Bristol, in 1715 is in the same mood. The building was set at the end of a long formal terrace to the east of the house with no visual access to the spectacular views out to the east. The building survives in a dilapidated state (though under restoration in August 2001) and there are variant designs for it in the Victoria & Albert Museum (D. 126-1891) and in the Clarke collection in Worcester College, Oxford, the latter by Sir James Thornhill of a 'Banquetting Room' for 'Mr Berkeley's Terrace'.

11 Fig. 85.

12 *Ibid.*, figs. 81–4.

13 I am indebted to Mrs Richard Jenner-Fust for allowing access to the map and the garden feature.

14 Bridgeman was paid 'for journeys and plan of the New Park £71 14s'; see Clive Aslet, 'Lodge Park, Gloucestershire', *Country Life*, 13 March 1986.

15 Bodleian Library, MS. Gough Drawings a.4 No.68.

16 A 1740s birds-eye view by Lambert of Lodge Park is illustrated *Country Life*, 13 March 1986, fig.1.

17 For the Serpentine and another contemporary serpentine at Longleat see Timothy Mowl, 'Rococo and Later Landscaping at Longleat', *Garden History*, vol. 23, no.1 (1995), pp.56-66.

18 For Spring Wood see Mowl, *Gentlemen & Players*, pp.76-8.

19 The best account of Bathurst's landscape works and his close relationship with Pope is given in James Lees-Milne, *The Earls of Creation: Five Great Patrons of Eighteenth-Century Art*, 1986.

20 John Dixon Hunt & Peter Willis (eds.), *The Genius of the Place: The English Landscape Garden 1620-1820*, 1988, pp.204-8; p.205. See also Mavis Batey, *Alexander Pope: The Poet and the Landscape*, 1999.

21 *Eloisa to Abelard*, lines 163-4.

22 George Sherburn (ed.), *The Correspondence of Alexander Pope*, 5 vols. (Oxford, 1956), 3, p.500 (8 October 1735).

23 *Ibid.*, 3, p.134 (19 September 1730).

24 *Ibid.*, 1, p.515 (8 October 1718).

25 *Ibid.*, 1, p.476 (5 July 1718).

26 *Ibid.*, 2, p.50 (20 July 1720).

27 *Ibid.*, 2, p.82 (15 September 1721).

28 *Ibid.*, 2, p.207 (21 October 1723).

29 *Ibid.*, 3, p.299 (20 July 1732). See also Christopher Hussey, *Country Life*, 23 June 1950.

30 Quoted in *Country Life*, 23 June 1950.

31 *Correspondence,* 4, p.25 (14 August 1736).

32 *Ibid.*, 4, p.25.

33 For the Robins sketches see John Harris, *Gardens of Delight: the Rococo English Landscape of Thomas Robins the Elder*, 1978, plates 92-3.

34 'Windsor Forest', lines 17-21.

5 Thomas Robins and Thomas Wright – Rococo rivals

1 For Rococo gardens see Timothy Mowl & Brian Earnshaw, *An Insular Rococo: Architecture, Politics and Society* 1999, chapters 3 & 4; Michael Symes, *The English Rococo Garden* (Haverfordwest, 1991); Mowl, *Gentlemen & Players*, chapter 11.

2 Shakespeare Birthplace Trust Record Office, Leigh Papers, DR18/25/1.

3 *Ibid.*, Leigh Papers, DR18/8/7/4 & 5.

4 *Ibid.*, Leigh Papers, DR18/8/7/4.

5 *Ibid.*, Leigh Papers, DR18/8/7/9.

6 See Howard Colvin, 'Georgian Architects at Badminton', *Country Life*, 4 April 1968. Bridgeman's drawing and a related canvas by Wotton are illustrated as figs 4 & 5.

7 Kent's designs are in the Badminton archives and are reproduced in John Dixon Hunt, *William Kent: Landscape Garden Designer*, 1987, cat. nos. 1-5; see also *Country Life*, 4 April 1968. Kent may also have designed gatepiers for the park at Great Barrington where the landscape was remodelled in the mid-eighteenth century with perimeter tree belts, a circular temple and a Gothick seat.

8 Canaletto's view of the park from the house is reproduced in Michael Liversidge & Jane Farrington (eds.), *Canaletto & England*, 1993, fig.5.

. 9 Worcester Lodge appears in sketchy outline in Dixon Hunt, cat. no.4; The Lodge was built after Kent's death by Stephen Wright and completed in 1750. It was seen by Bishop Pococke in 1754: 'At the further end of the Park is Worcester Lodge, on the highest ground in the Park; it is the design of Kent, and is a grand gateway, one arch in the middle and one on each side, one leading to the stair-case, the other a room for servants; over all is a grand room which commands a most glorious prospect. It is all built of fine freestone. Here the Duke often dines in the summer': J Cartwright (ed.), *The Travels Through England of Dr Richard Pococke 1750-57*, Camden Society, 1888-9, 2 vols., I, pp.31-2.

10 Canaletto's painting is usually dated to 1748 (Liversidge & Farrington), but it was perhaps commissioned in 1750, after the construction of the Worcester Lodge, to record the completion of Kent's landscaping.

11 Dixon Hunt, *William Kent*, cat. no.2.

12 W S Lewis (ed.), *The Yale Edition of Horace Walpole's Correspondence*, 48 vols. (New Haven & London, 1937-83), vol.18, p.255: Walpole to Horace Mann, 20 June 1743.

13 Dixon Hunt, *William Kent*, cat. no.5.

14 There is another charming Gothick gazebo of late eighteenth-century date at The Sevillowes, Chalford, and a Gothick gateway of similar date at Amberley. The Gothick summerhouse by the lake at Newark Park is part of the 1790 remodelling of the Tudor deer park.

15 The map (GRO, D149 Pc 788) dates from the 1770s and shows the layout with a *patte d'oie* of tree avenues radiating from the garden front and orchards flank-ing the house. The canal is strictly rectangular, without the semicircular projec-tion that exists today, and the Orangery is clearly marked as three interlocking octagons at the head of it.

16 The inscription is quoted in David Lambert & Stewart Harding, 'Thomas Wright at Stoke Park', *Garden History*, vol. 17, no.1 (1989), pp.68-82; p.78.

17 *Ibid.*, p.78.

18 *Ibid.*, p.78.

19 This is most apparent in a drawing of the Cell by Thomas Robins: see John Harris, *Gardens of Delight* plate 54.

20 Most of Robins's extant paintings are reproduced in Harris, *Gardens of Delight*.

21 See John Harris, '"Gardenesque": the Case of Charles Grevile's Garden at Gloucester', *Journal of Garden History*, vol. 1, no.2 (1981), pp.167-78.

22 See Timothy Mowl, 'In the Realm of the Great God Pan', *Country Life*, 17 October 1996.

23 For Pan's Lodge see *Country Life*, 17 October 1996 and Harris, *Gardens of Delight*.

24 For Painswick see Roger White & Timothy Mowl, 'Thomas Robins at Painswick', *Journal of Garden History*, vol. 4, no.2 (1984), pp.163-78. The author is also indebted to Jean Manco's unpublished report prepared for the Painswick Rococo Garden Trust, November 1992.

25 See *Country Life*, 17 December 1964, fig.5.

26 For a biographical profile of Wright see Eileen Harris, *Thomas Wright Arbours & Grottos: facsimile of 2 parts of Universal Architecture 1755 & 1758,* 1979.

27 For Wright's work at the house see Timothy Mowl, 'The Castle of Boncoeur and the Wizard of Durham', *Georgian Group Journal*, 1992.

28 Wright's plan for 'Mr Brags garden at Cleve Hill, near Stoke' is illustrated in Harris, *Thomas Wright*. The Ordnance Survey map of 1903 shows the layout still in existence to the north of the house.

29 See James Russell, 'The Gardens & Grounds of Cleve Hill House', *Avon Gardens Trust Newsletter*, no. 23 (Spring, 2001), pp.5-16.

30 *Ibid.*, p.13. The lodge dates from 1815 when the estate was expanded to the south by Stephen Cave.

31 Mark Laird, *The Flowering of the Landscape Garden: English Pleasure Grounds 1720-1800* (Philadelphia, 1999), pp.90-7.

32 George Mason, *An Essay on Design in Gardening*, 1795, p.117; quoted by Laird, *The Flowering*, pp.94-7.

33 Laird, *The Flowering*, p.94.

34 The Ionic rotunda is illustrated in Lambert & Harding, *Garden History*, fig. 9.

35 For a reconstruction of Bladud's Temple see Rosemary Harriott, 'Thomas Wright and Bladud's Cell at Stoke Park', *Avon Gardens Trust Newsletter*, no.23 (Spring 2001), pp.20-9; see also James Russell, 'The Archaeology of Stoke Park, Bristol', *Bristol and Avon Archaeological Society*, 8 (1989), pp.30-40.

36 The Duke's memorial is illustrated in Lambert & Harding, *Garden History*, fig.8.

37 Pococke's description is not included in the Camden Society volumes of his tours, but is quoted in full by Lambert & Harding, *Garden History*, fn.9. There were at least two other adaptations of this Roman tomb in the eighteenth-century landscape, at Werrington, Devon and at Studley Royal, Yorkshire; see David Coffin, *The English Garden: Meditation and Memorial* (Princeton, NJ, 1994), p.169.

38 Thomas's father Benjamin had improved the park with clumps of elms in the late 1720s; he also built a walled garden and an orangery (see *Victoira County History*, vol.v, pp.62-3). Thomas inherited on his father's death in 1767 and the ornamental buildings on Red Hill to the north-east of the house were added in the 1770s and illustrated by Rudder in his 1779 history of the county. The house was demolished in 1883 and the garden buildings do not survive. The park was

extensively remodelled from 1950 by Viscount Bledisloe and his successor who created an ornamental garden in a wooded valley to the north-west of the house. This is now open to the public.

39 See Harris, *Gardens of Delight*, fig.124.
40 See Harris, *Thomas Wright*.
41 W.S. Lews (ed.), *Horace Walpole's Correspondence*, vol. 10 (Montagu II 1762-1770), p.232.
42 See the plan of the complex given in *Avon Gardens Trust Newsletter* no.22 (Summer 2000), p.15.

6 Lancelot Brown and the rule of shotgun and carriage

1 For the Brown plan and his proposal for a temple on the mount see David Brown, 'Lancelot Brown and his Associates', *Garden History*, vol. 29, no. 1 (Summer, 2001), pp.5-6; colour plates 1 & 2.
2 After the 4th Duke's death in 1756 Mickle took up full time employment under Brown: see David Brown, *Garden History*, pp.5-6.
3 Maule's map is in GRO, D1610 /P18.
4 Gale's map is in GRO, D1011/P8.
5 Dorothy Stroud, *Capability Brown*, 1950, p.120: 'This bridge has hitherto been ascribed to Wyatt, but a close examination leaves no doubt that its author was Brown, and the theme of embattled towers, linked by similarly embattled walls pierced by arched windows, is closely akin to that used for the courtyard screen at Burton Constable'; plate on p.84.
6 The 1820 map is by John Dowding, GRO, D1610/P30.
7 GRO, D1610/A78, f132.
8 *Ibid.*, f.178.
9 *Ibid.*, ff.182-9.
10 *Ibid.*, f.216.
11 GRO, D1610/P21.
12 GRO, D1610/P60.
13 *Country Life*, 2 February 1924.
14 For a fuller discussion of the practical nature of Brown's schemes see Tom Williamson, *Polite Landscapes: Gardens and Society in Eighteenth-Century England* (Stroud, 1995), chapter 4.
15 Shakespeare Birthplace Trust Record Office, DR18/8/7.
16 Brown's fee was for 'Alterations about the House and Terras' and probably included the demolition of the walls enclosing the south forecourt and a simplification of the terraces. The reshaped park is recorded in Isaac Taylor's map of 1772.
17 Margaret Martyn, 'An Exile's Dream Realised: Warren Hastings at Daylesford', *Country Life*, 23 January 1975.
18 GRO, D3732/1.
19 See Andrew Ginger, 'Daylesford House and Warren Hastings', *Georgian Group Report and Journal*, 1989, pp.80-101; p.97.

20 *Ibid.*, p.96.

21 *Country Life*, 23 January 1975, plate 5.

22 The Orangery is illustrated in Ginger, *Georgian Group Report*, fig. 17.

23 *Ibid.*, p.98.

7 Humphry Repton and the winds of change

1 Edmund Burke, *A Philosophical Inquiry into the Origin of our Ideas of the Sublime and Beautiful*, 1757.

2 For the tourists see Ian Ousby, *The Englishman's England: Taste, travel and the rise of tourism* (Cambridge, 1990) and Malcolm Andrews, *The Search for the Picturesque: Landscape Aesthetics and Tourism in Britain, 1760-1800*, 1989; for the Picturesque aesthetic see David Watkin, *The English Vision: The Picturesque in Architecture, Landscape & Garden Design*, 1982.

3 For Claude Glasses see Andrews, *The Search for the Picturesque*, p.69. They were little mirrors with black painted backs.

4 Arthur Young, *A Six Weeks Tour through the Southern Counties of England and Wales* (Dublin, 1768), p.125.

5 Easily the best book on Repton, which supersedes all others, is Stephen Daniels, *Humphry Repton: Landscape Gardening and the Geography of Georgian England* (New Haven & London, 1999).

6 Repton's Red Book for Blaise is preserved at the Blaise Castle Museum; an abbreviated facsimile version of it can be bought there.

7 Blaise Castle was built in 1766 by the architect Robert Mylne for Thomas Farr. The landscape at that time is depicted in a painting now in the Blaise Castle Museum.

8 From the Blaise Red Book.

9 This is not mentioned by Repton and does not appear on his map. It has been attributed to Thomas Wright and dated to the 1760s.

10 Daniels, *Humphry Repton*, p.238, quoting from the Royal Fort Red Book.

11 Humphry Repton, *Observations on the Theory and Practice of Landscape Gardening*, 1803, p.36.

12 *Ibid.*, p.36. In the Leigh Papers at Stratford is a Repton watercolour for a canvas bath house to be sited on the lower lake (DR 18/8/8/12); it is illustrated in Kingsley, vol. 2, colour plate IV.

13 *Ibid.*, p.36.

14 *Ibid.*, pp.145-6.

15 Stewart Harding, *Repton in Avon*, Avon Gardens Trust Seminar (Bristol, 1989), no pagination.

16 Repton, *Observations*, p.10.

17 Blaise Castle Red Book.

18 Repton, *Observations*, pp.184-5.

19 For Cote Bank and Stapleton see Harding, *Repton in Avon*. Nothing of Repton's planting survives at either site.

20 Repton provided alternative designs for the Doric pavilion in Bath stone and 'wood cover'd with the Bark of trees'. It is illustrated in Gervase Jackson-Stops, *An English Arcadia, 1600-1990*, 1991, p.115.

21 From Repton's 'Designs for the Pavillion at Brighton', 1808, quoted in the Sezincote guidebook by Mr & Mrs David Peake.

22 The twentieth-century planting is well covered in a small booklet, compiled by Graham Thomas, available at the house; see also Lanning Roper, 'In the Indian Manner: The Gardens of Sezincote, Gloucestershire', *Country Life*, 2 September 1976.

23 Repton, *Observations*, p.36.

24 *Ibid.*, p.36.

25 J. & H.S. Storer & J.N. Brewer, *Delineations of Gloucestershire*, 1824, p.108; see also Nigel Temple, *John Nash & The Village Picturesque* (Gloucester, 1979).

26 J.D. Harding, *Nine Lithographic Views of the Cottages, Comprising Blaise Hamlet*, 1826.

27 Nash also worked at Barnsley Park, near Cirencester where, between 1806 and 1810, he designed an orangery and a 'pepper pot' lodge for Sir James Musgrave; see *Country Life*, 2 & 9 September 1954. G S Repton laid out the grounds in 1829 around Dumbleton Hall on the Worcestershire border, but little remains of his work there.

28 From a letter of January 1815, quoted in Daniels, *Humphry Repton*, p.101.

29 GRO, D1571 P14.

8 Gloucestershire gardenesque – the eclectic Victorians

1 John Claudius Loudon, *Gardener's Magazine*, vol. viii, p.701. Reviewing the work of William Gilpin, Loudon wrote: 'it is necessary to understand that there is such a character of art as the gardenesque, as well as the picturesque', suggesting that gardens should aim at ideal compositions immediately pleasing to the eye yet entirely contrived and artificial.

2 See Nicholas Kingsley, 'A forgotten Cotswold Elysium – Temple Guiting', *The Georgian Group in Gloucester and Avon Newsletter*, no. 3 (Autumn, 1986), pp.18-26.

3 Loudon, *Observations* (Edinburgh, 1806), p.158.

4 *Ibid.*, p.159.

5 GRO, D2318/I/16; quoted by Kingsley, 'Temple Guiting', pp.19-20.

6 The first John Jacob had left a five year old son, another John, to the care of his wife. This second John would have been only fifteen when the poem was written so his mother would have been presiding over the Picturesque landscape.

7 For Gainsborough in Bath and The Rocks connection I am indebted to Dr Susan Sloman, 'Gainsborough in Bath 1758-1774', PhD thesis for Bristol University, 2000, Bristol University library (A6120).

8 An Historic Landscape Survey prepared in 1994 by David Lambert, Mike Chapman and Alister Rankine came to the same inconclusive conclusion.

9 For Hanbury-Tracy and Toddington see *Country Life*, 30 April 1904 & 9 October 1937.

10 Quoted by Arthur Oswald in *Country Life,* 9 October 1937.

11 J C Loudon, *Treatise on the Forming, Improving & Managing Country Residences,* 1806, p.37.

12 GRO, D2426/P1: 'Plan of the Estate of William Jones & John Guise'.

13 For Pulham and Highnam see Sally Festing, 'Pulham Has Done His Work Well', *Garden History*, vol. 12, no. 2 (Autumn, 1984), pp.138-58.

14 The Restoration Plan was prepared by Jame Patton of Singleton Landscape. I am extremely grateful to Roger Head for allowing me access to this unpublished report.

15 The statue in the niche above the south doorcase is of Flora; it was originally sited in the Winter Garden Terrace and moved to its present position in 1962.

16 These Pulhamite rocks were not intended for planting with delicate flowery Alpines, but with ivy, conifers, rhododendrons, brooms and even gorse. Interest in Alpines developed in the 1860s.

17 For this creatively decadent group see Jane Abdy & Charlotte Gere, *The Souls*, 1984.

18 No precise date for the garden is recorded, but the house was built in 1811 and it is assumed that the garden was laid out soon after. A watercolour of the Temple and lake by William Crouch was painted before Crouch's death in 1840. I am indebted to Mrs Gerda Barlow for information on Stancombe.

19 The *Transactions of the Bristol & Gloucestershire Archaeological Society*, vol. 92 (1973), pp.198-201, states: 'James Hutchinson acquired the lease in 1852 and employed George Somers Clarke as architect. He also laid out the terrace and the garden with a lake, fountain and cascades and a tree lined avenue. The new building seems to have been completed by the late 1850s'; see also Kingsley, vol.3, pp.105-9.

20 GRO, D 2299/3507: Sale Particulars of 1892.

21 *Ibid.*

22 *Ibid.*

9 Gardens of stone and outdoor rooms – Cotswold Arts & Crafts

1 For the gardens of this period, including several mentioned in this chapter see David Ottewill, *Edwardian Gardens*, 1989, particularly pp.132-8.

2 The Garden Court at Lypiatt Park, laid out after 1877, could be considered a more immediate Gothic Revival garden, as Sir John Dorington connected a number of towers and tourelles, some medieval and some Victorian, by a thick wall of yew in place of stone and formalised the composition with a terrace. See *Country Life*, 1 December 1900.

3 In her brief tenure of The Mount House, Alderley (1885-90), Marianne North revised and replanted the gardens. By her painting and recording of flowers in

four continents she had done much to make the Victorians aware of the potential for enrichment of their gardens with exotic specimens. See Brenda Moon, *A Vision of Eden: The Life and Work of Marianne North* (Exeter, 1980).

4   From 'Making the Best of it', in *Hopes and Fears for Art*, 1882; quoted in Ottewill, *Edwardian Gardens*, p.29.

5   Sedding, *Garden-Craft* (1892 edition), p.28.

6   *Ibid.*, p.37.

7   See *The Architect*, 14 June 1889.

8   The entrance lodges are consciously modeled on a pair of original Elizabethan forecourt lodges at Cranborne Manor in Dorset; see Avray Tipping, *English Gardens*, 1925, plate 170.

9   For Abbotswood in its prime see Tipping, *English Gardens*, pp.1-8.

10 For The Hoo see Jane Brown, *Gardens of a Golden Afternoon*, 1985, colour plate 18.

11 The pergola is illustrated by Tipping, *English Gardens*, plate 7.

12 Another Lutyens garden in the county, since altered, is Misarden Park, Miserden where he designed a loggia and advised upon the architectural blocks of clipped yew; see *Country Life*, 5 March 1992.

13 One sad loss is a small garden laid out in 1935 by Clough Williams-Ellis at Burleigh Court, Minchinhampton, where his summerhouse has been demolished.

14 Lines 28-9; 34. See Edward Malins, 'Burnt Norton', *Garden History*, vol.7, no.1 (Spring, 1979), pp.78-85.

15 In 1896 Dawber, assisted by Alfred Parsons, designed a layout for Hartpury House, near Newent. This was superseded by a new formal design by T H Mawson in 1907; see Ottewill, *Edwardian Gardens*, pp.131-2 and plate 199.

16 The Great Rissington gazebo is illustrated in Percy Cane, *Modern Gardens British and Foreign*,1927, pp.70-1.

17 For a view of the house and gardens published in *The Architect's and Builder's Journal* of 1911 see Kingsley, vol.3, plate 136; see also *Country Life*, 21 November 1914.

18 Early photographs of the garden in about 1910 are illustrated in the National Trust guidebook (1993), written by Anna Pavord; see especially pp.14-17.

19 Anna Pavord gives an admirably frank account in the guidebook.

20 James Lees-Milne recorded on 13 August 1981: 'Hidcote looking well in spite of August season when nothing much out, but crowds so enormous that it was absolutely no pleasure pushing one's way around. Decided I don't ever wish to go there again'; see *Deep Romantic Chasm: Diaries, 1979-81*, 2000, p.165.

21 Jane Brown, *Eminent Gardeners: Some People of Influence and their Gardens 1880-1980*, 1990, p.72.

22 M H Baillie Scott, *Houses and Gardens*, 1906, p.152; quoted in Ottewill, *Edwardian Gardens,* p.137.

23 Quoted in the National Trust guidebook to Snowshill Manor, 1992, p.45; see also *Country Life*, 15 December 1988.

24 For Betjeman's illustrated account of Wade's model village, 'Wolf's Cove', see *Architectural Review*, January 1932.

25 Miss Jekyll also designed the Cliff Walk rockery below Newark Park, Ozleworth. I am indebted to Michael Claydon for this information.

26 For Pinbury see *Country Life*, 30 April 1910.

27 The revised Buildings of England volume for the Cotswolds, written by Alan Brooks (1999), has a useful, compact essay (pp.113-18) on the region's Arts and Crafts buildings

10 'When in doubt, look backwards' – the later twentieth century

1 Gordon Russell's father had founded the furniture design firm based at Broadway.

2 From his son-in-law and daughter's 1980 biography, *Gordon Russell*; quoted in Jeremy Myerson, *Gordon Russell: Designer of Furniture 1892-1992,* 1992, p.49. I am indebted to Jamie Ritblat and Trevor Chinn for information on Russell and Kingcombe.

3 Russell also commissioned lead statues from Harold Stadler, but these have since disappeared.

4 The extensions to the original garden are shown in a plan of September 1967, drawn by Russell and entitled: 'Kingcombe Garden Development Plan'. It is illustrated in *Designer's Trade, Autobiography of Gordon Russell*, 1967, endpapers.

5 There is a table commemorating the Games at the end of the Italian Garden.

6 Jane Brown, *The Modern Garden,* 2000, p.50.

7 For these garden designers see Brown, *The Modern Garden*, Chapter 2.

8 GRO, D1405/4/21.

9 *Country Life*, 14 December 1929.

10 Rosemary Verey, *Good Planting*, 1990, p.25.

11 *Ibid.*, p.16.

12 For Badminton see David Hicks, *Cotswold Gardens*, 1995, pp.32-5.

13 Most of these and other Gloucestershire gardens briefly mentioned in the text are covered in Hicks, *Cotswold Gardens*.

14 See Hicks, *Cotswold Gardens*, Introduction.

15 From the late 1970s Rosemary Verey supervised the early eighteenth century formal garden of walled enclosures and terracing at Nether Lypiatt Manor, Thrupp.

16 The exception to this is Candida Lycett Green's even handed and objective *The Garden at Highgrove*, 2000.

17 *Ibid.*, p.6.

18 The statue was presented to Sir Robert Walpole and is now in the Hall at Houghton, Norfolk.

19 The flowers were designed and forged by Simon Allison at Cropready.

Gazetteer

The following is a list of gardens of significant historic importance which are covered in this book and are open to the public.

Abbreviations

NT   National Trust
LT   Landmark Trust
P   Privately owned, but regularly open
A   Privately owned, but open only by written appointment
NGS   Privately owned, but open occasionally as part of the National Gardens Scheme
H   Hotel

Abbotswood, Stow-on-the-Wold (NGS)
Acton Court, Iron Acton (A)
Alderley Grange, Alderley (NGS)
Barnsley Park, Cirencester (A)
Barnsley House, Cirencester (P)
Batsford Arboretum, Moreton-in-Marsh (P)
Beverston Castle, Tetbury (NGS)
Blaise Castle Estate, Henbury, Bristol (P)
Blaise Hamlet, Henbury, Bristol (NT)
Bourton House, Bourton-on-the-Hill (NGS)
Campden House, Chipping Campden (LT)
Chavenage House, Tetbury (P)
Cirencester Park (P)
Cowley Manor, Seven Springs (H)
Daylesford House, Daylesford (NGS)
Dyrham Park, Dyrham (NT)
Frampton Court, Frampton-on-Severn (A)
Hardwicke Court, Gloucester (P)
Hidcote Manor, Chipping Campden (NT)
Highgrove House, Doughton (A)
Highnam Court, Gloucester (NGS)
Hodges Barn, Shipton Moyne (P)
Horton Court, Horton (NT)
Kiftsgate Court, Chipping Campden (P)

Kingcombe Court, Chipping Campden (A)
Kingsweston House, Shirehampton, Bristol (P)
Lodge Park, Sherborne (NT)
Lydney Park, Lydney (P)
Misarden Park, Miserden (P)
Newark Park, Ozleworth (NT)
Old Rectory, Quenington (NGS)
Owlpen Manor, Uley (P)
Painswick Rococo Garden (P)
Rodmarton Manor, Cirencester (P)
Sezincote, Moreton-in-Marsh (P)
Snowshill Manor, Broadway (NT)
Stancombe Park, Dursley (A)
Stanway Manor, Broadway (P)
Stowell Park, Northleach (NGS)
Sudeley Castle, Winchcombe (P)
Thornbury Castle (H)
Tortworth Court, Wotton-under-Edge (H)
Warmley, Bristol (P)
Westbury Court, Westbury-on-Severn (NT)
Westonbirt Arboretum (NT)
Westonbirt School (NGS)
Woodchester Park (NT)

Index

Page numbers in **bold** refer to illustrations and captions